# THE SOVEREIGN STREET

# THE SOVEREIGN STREET

## STREET

Making Revolution in Urban Bolivia

## CARWIL BJORK-JAMES

THE UNIVERSITY OF
ARIZONA PRESS

TUCSON

The University of Arizona Press
www.uapress.arizona.edu

ISBN-13: 978-0-8165-4015-0 (hardcover)

Cover design by Leigh McDonald
Cover photo: *Achumani Blockade in La Paz* by Carwil Bjork-James
Interior design and typesetting by Sara Thaxton
Set in 10/14 Minion Pro (text) and ITC Avant Garde Gothic Book,
Extra Light, and Bold Condensed (display)

Publication of this book is made possible in part by funding from a Vanderbilt University Research
Scholar Grant, and by the proceeds of a permanent endowment created with the assistance of a
Challenge Grant from the National Endowment for the Humanities, a federal agency.

Library of Congress Cataloging-in-Publication Data
Names: Bjork-James, Carwil, author.
Title: The sovereign street : making revolution in urban Bolivia / Carwil Bjork-James.
Description: Tucson : University of Arizona Press, 2020. | Includes bibliographical references and index.
Identifiers: LCCN 2019036800 | ISBN 9780816540150 (hardback)
Subjects: LCSH: Protest movements—Bolivia—History—21st century. | Bolivia—History—1982–
Classification: LCC F3327 .B54 2020 | DDC 984.05—dc23
LC record available at https://lccn.loc.gov/2019036800

Printed in the United States of America
♾ This paper meets the requirements of ANSI/NISO Z39.48-1992 (Permanence of Paper).

# CONTENTS

# ILLUSTRATIONS

## Figures

## Maps

## Tables

# ACKNOWLEDGMENTS

This book is about how, through acting together, people can unmake systems of power that seem permanent, how collective action changes what initially appears impossible into a collective accomplishment. So, first and above all, I am grateful to those in Bolivia who used their voices, bodies, and relationships to refuse the social order—privatized, colonized, hierarchical, and impoverished—they could no longer accepting living within. Many of you did so in spite of fear for your lives and safety; thank you for your courage. Over a hundred people died in the course of events described in this book, and thousands more buried the dead; thank you for your sacrifice. Every time an unjust order is shown to be temporary, whatever follows, the whole world becomes that much more free.

It is also about how, once that sense of possibility opens up, people offer bigger dreams and attempt to create new political possibilities. I am therefore indebted to everyone who risked believing that their present dreams could become future realities, everyone who dreamed out loud and struggled to create and defend the Bolivia they wanted to live in. Thank you for your ongoing struggles, and your ongoing work to make your dreams concrete.

This text came about through an encounter of experiences, those lived in Bolivia and in the global North. The analysis contained within it would have been impossible to perceive without the willingness of many, many people to share their experiences and perspectives freely and openly with a researcher whose appearance in their lives was quick and inquisitive. The conversations we had were made possible by affinities in our experiences, aspirations, and ways of approaching social change. In turn, innumerable teachers, thinkers, comrades, and exemplars shaped my approaches to political life, far more than I could acknowledge here.

I am grateful to all those who made the Bolivian experience part of a global conversation in the years when I was drawn to study and describe that experience, among them Indymedia Bolivia, the Notes from Nowhere collective, the Andean Information Network, and the Democracy Center. Equally, the work of those who expressed their solidarity with Bolivian movements through their on-the-ground presence and direct support made my conversations possible. Among them, I include my friends Sasha Wright and David Solnit. Fellow travelers (in the literal sense) in pursuit of such connections elsewhere also include Asha, Puck Lo, Andrea Gersh, Jeff Juris, Jennifer Whitney, Kolya Abramsky, Michal Osterweil, Sarah Shourd, Sergio Oceransky, Tristan Anderson, and the never-forgotten Marla Ruzicka; I've learned from your travels how to tell the story of my own, and the value of doing so.

Once I arrived into this transnational conversation, a variety of people provided me with connections and advice, including Carmen Medeiros, Julieta Paredes, Leny Olivera, Maria Lagos, the late Ben Kohl, Linda Farthing, Barbara Giavarini Blanco, Marxa Chávez, Jorge Derpic, and Luis Gómez. Special thanks are due to Marcela Olivera, María Eugenia Flores Castro, Marcelo Rojas, María Rita Bautista, and to all the activists who talked to an inquisitive foreigner, especially during the polarized and risky months of mid-2008. I am grateful for the stories shared by all my interviewees, and I continue to learn from them.

This work was gestated in the context of collective conversations about radical social transformation and justice in the broadest sense. My longest stint of fieldwork coincided with the remarkable 2011 revolution in Egypt, and my first extended writing took place short subway rides away from Occupy Wall Street. As a distant but attentive observer of the former, and participant in the latter, often through its offshoot the Free University of New York City, I found myself constantly drawn back to the question of how revolutionary change happens, and what people in radically different circumstances can teach one another about how to make it happen.

I thank Don Robotham, Michael Blim, Victoria Sanford, Leith Mullings, Barbara Weinstein, Ana Dopico, John Collins, Sinclair Thomson, and Marc Edelman for creating such spaces through their teaching. The Center for Place,

Culture, and Politics' seminar on transformative politics ("How to Fight") at the CUNY Graduate Center in 2011–12, led by Ruthie Gilmore and Peter Hitchcock; and the Robert Penn Warren Center's seminar on "Working for Equality and Justice," convened by Brooke Ackerly and Melissa Snarr, each provided invaluable contexts and brilliant interlocutors across a wide range of disciplines and perspectives. I am grateful for all your thoughts, and for arguments, coinciding and divergent positions, wrestling with issues, and suggestions for things to explore, both past and future. Vanderbilt professors Lesley Gill, Norbert Ross, and the extended community that animates the Political Ecology and the Contemporary in Theory seminars, as well as the faculty contingent involved in the Vanderbilt Resistance Teach-Ins, all provided further conversations and comradery when I most needed it. Vanderbilt Anthropology chair Beth Conklin provided a scholarly home, support, kindness, and continual backing for my work.

The field research for this book was supported by the City University of New York, Vanderbilt University, the Wenner-Gren Foundation for Anthropological Research, and National Science Foundation Award BCS-0962403. A Wenner-Gren Engaged Anthropology Grant and the work of Charlie Crespo at the Centro de Estudios Superiores Universitarios and Escarley Torrico and Oscar Campanini at the Centro de Documentación e Información Bolivia (CEDIB) allowed me to bring my findings back to Cochabamba and engage in a fascinating dialogue with academics and organizers. Invaluable archiving was done by Cecilia Illanes and the rest of the staff at CEDIB, and by the archivists of the National Archive and Library of Bolivia and the Library of the Plurinational Legislative Assembly.

I had the pleasure of engaging with a number of very talented social scientists and advocates, whose knowledge and perspectives contributed to my understanding of Bolivia, and whose good natures enriched my time in Bolivia, notably Anna Walnycki, Sarah Hines, Bret Gustafson, Carmen Soliz, Kathryn Ledebur, Mareike Winchell, Jeff Webber, Erin Hatheway, Emma Banks, Kylie Benton-Connell, Becky Hollender, Jason Farbman, Jeffrey Wayne, and Alder Keleman.

Portions of this text have passed through many hands and been spoken before many audiences. Even your presence as listeners and readers changed many things about it, but some of you offered so much more for me to learn from. I would like to extend particular thanks to Jeff Juris, Nick Copeland, Brooke Larson, Lesley Gill, and David Vine for thoughtful and wide-ranging feedback. My very capable research assistant, Emma Banks, reviewed, commented upon, and reformatted nearly all of the book. The example of Ahdaf Soueif's *Cairo*, her memoir of the Egyptian revolution, guided me as I worked to enliven the text. Through several brief but brilliant conversations, Silvia Rivera Cusicanqui has inspired me more than she knows.

Sinclair Thomson has been an incredibly open, supportive, and committed source of advice, context, connections, and reflection. He opened my many doors to me, but most importantly, his own. I've learned so much from talking with him. Pamela Calla has been a vital interlocutor and academic backer of my research, and a warm and generous supporter of my research path. Nicole Fabricant has been a source of guidance, connections, and good conversations about Bolivia, as well as an impressive example to follow as an ethnographer in the country. Ruthie Gilmore has offered penetrating insights and raised vital questions within an atmosphere of incredible personal and professional encouragement. Marc Edelman showed me how to bridge the ethnographic and documentary worlds through his classes, and has been exemplary in demonstrating how to maintain simultaneous commitments to relevant research, social change, intellectual honesty, and genuine curiosity about what works and what doesn't as an engaged researcher.

This book came into being alongside the precious family I share with Sophie Bjork-James, my dear partner, co-parent, and colleague. I'm grateful for her warmth and encouragement, and for our shared journeys, whether to document social movements across the hemisphere or to bask in the joys of this life. Two of those joys, Thalia and Calliope Bjork-James and all their wonder and willfulness, also animate the hope within my work.

My parents, Carolyn and Frank James, passed on their lifelong love for learning to me, and offered enduring enthusiasm and support even when my path seemed difficult to understand. My father's zest for knowledge and life is a legacy that transcends his passing shortly after my year of fieldwork. The imprint of my mom's support and capacity for both consistency and curiosity is all over this book.

Any attempt to acknowledge the personal relationships and support that made this book possible leaves me humbled by the task of acknowledgment and the scale of gratitude I feel. Naming you all would be impossible, and I hope, unnecessary. May I be blessed with the opportunities to thank you in person. In choosing to devote so much time to studying a distant process of

social transformation, I absented myself from the incredibly strong and vision-
ary communities that made me who I am, and who will make it possible to
transform our own society. Thank you for your patience with my departures.
You are my first audience for this effort, and I hope you will find that my time
on it offers enough of an expanded tool kit to you to make it worth the time
required.

# THE SOVEREIGN STREET

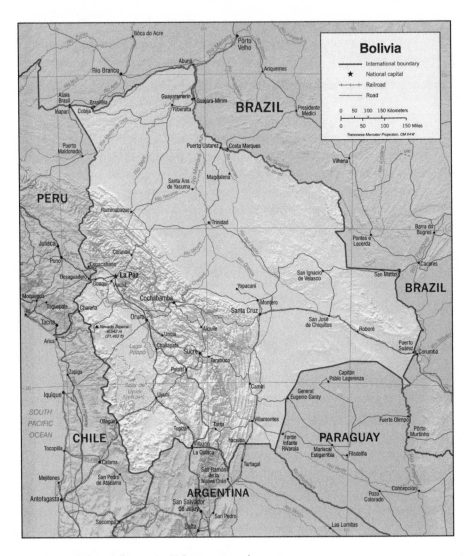

MAP 1   Bolivia (Map by the U.S. government)

# Introduction

arly on the morning of June 21, 2009, I squeeze into a crowded minivan (or *combi*) in front of a major market in La Paz, the Mercado Camacho. Behind our combi, sunlight illuminates a small east-facing spot on Mount Illimani, whose distant snowcapped slopes hang over La Paz as an ever-present reminder of the solidity of the Andes. This predawn glimmer is the first sign of the day. La Paz, a sprawling capital city set in a bowl of reddened stone, remains entirely in shadow. It is the winter solstice, Willkakuti, the day of the sun's return. This is the first time the Aymara New Year has been declared a national holiday, and the government decree means no one has to go to work.[1] Our combi is filled with people bound for the celebration, but we rise up the gently spiraling highway out of the bowl and away from the market in silence.

I should clarify that this was the *old* Mercado Camacho and that the sheer cliffside across the road would soon be filled in with concrete for the new Mercado, a modernized space with pristine new stalls built by the state for the vendor women with their blenders to serve the same *supervitamínico* juice cocktails they now were offering from makeshift wooden stalls. Soon, atop this market would rise the grand Camacho Plaza, filling what was once empty space over the newly culverted Choqueyapu River. By the time this book ends, angry crowds of workers will gather in the new plaza to demand higher wages. A new Bolivia is literally under construction, one where public funds offer spaces for Andean indigenous workers to vend their wares. And one where the same men and women who demanded that new Bolivia will fill newer and cleaner public spaces with the old sounds of street commerce and street protest.

The combi turns past a billboard reading BOLIVIA: TERRITORIO LIBRE DE ANALFABETISMO (Bolivia: Territory Free of Illiteracy), and I notice that the woman beside me is flipping through her handwritten papers, which seem to include an elementary writing assignment, though she is far beyond school age. Over four years, lessons in letters and free identity cards would expand the electorate by 40 percent, adding 1.5 million voters.

As soon as we are past the highway tollbooth that marks the entrance to El Alto, everyone gets out of the vehicle. Like my companions in the van, I spend the morning on La Ceja, the rim, the edge of the high plateau, the Altiplano, which overlooks the capital city of La Paz. El Alto, the vast city that stretches out on that plateau, has become the unofficial capital of the overwhelmingly Aymara region, which stretches north, west, and south to the Peruvian and Chilean borders. The settlement has grown rapidly since its legal incorporation in 1987, probably at the fastest pace of any Latin American city. Last night its residents poured into the streets, where they now cluster in circles of a couple dozen or in crowds numbering up to several hundred. Overnight they gathered to await the sunrise in the chilled, high-altitude air, which shortens the breath of travelers unaccustomed to it; the Alteños kept warm by drinking and dancing. Now, in the glaring morning sun, they circle around an active core of drummers and musicians, with small fires lit. Periodic shouts of "Jalalla"—an Aymara salute—honor the Aymara people, the new year, and the indigenous rebel leaders Túpaj Katari and Bartolina Sisa, in turn. Katari and Sisa's 1781–82 siege of colonial La Paz, organized on the grounds of this yet-undreamed Aymara metropolis, nearly toppled Spanish rule in the region.[2] Near the center of the circle, two people hold posters depicting the couple and inscribed with Katari's legendary dying words: "I will return, and I will be millions."

I cross a pedestrian bridge over the highway to another cluster of celebrants gathered by a bell tower. At the base of the stairs lies a llama, cut open at the back of its head—a sacrifice for the new season. Piles of burnt apples and potatoes, coca leaves, sticks, and this and that build up over time as people ignite lighter fluid squeezed out of plastic bottles; orange flames rise. An Andean flute team in handwoven ponchos provides the music for the scores of men and women drinking and dancing in this narrow space between a fenced-off park and United Nations Avenue.

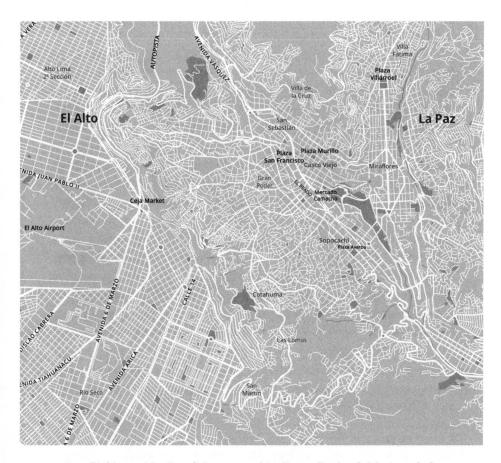

MAP 2  El Alto and La Paz. (Map prepared by Emma Banks. © Mapbox, © Open StreetMap)

I cautiously approach the group gathered there but am drawn in by a sincere, affectionate Aymara man named Andrés, who wears a black, buttonless shirt with his brown hat and jacket. He asks where I am from and talks about universal community and the continental brotherhood of the Americas. His more militant friend, Angel (pronounced the English way), approaches a bit later and stretches out a hand, but he is quick to zero in on my status as a foreigner. Angel volunteers, "If you were from Chile, I would fight you." Ever since the 1871 war, when it seized Bolivia's coastal territory, Chile has been Bolivia's greatest rival and the nearest symbol of its economic marginalization. Angel's taller and more imposing friend Andrés is quick to dispel the threat,

FIGURE 1   Alteños celebrate the Aymara New Year while overlooking La Paz in 2009.

telling him, "If you would fight someone from Chile, you would lose." "No! Why?" "They eat meat and you eat *chuño*." *Chuño* is a dark, flavorful food made by repeatedly freeze-drying potatoes in the Andean cold, but eating beef is a ready marker of economic success and is presumed to provide greater strength. The contrast between freeze-dried potatoes and meat sums up the economic gap between Bolivia—long South America's poorest country—and its wealthy neighbor (just as it would sum up the same gap between an Alteño like Angel and a resident of La Paz's posh south side).

Bolivia's great historic wound is its continual role as provider of precious resources to global powers—once the Spanish Empire, and now the United States—who inevitably make themselves wealthy in the process. Leftist nationalists in Bolivia have long mourned the loss of the country's mineral wealth, extracted laboriously but leaving few traces of opulence or industry. The historical muse of the Latin American Left, Eduardo Galeano, lamented that "the region has been condemned to sell primary products to keep foreign factories humming."[3] Galeano's polemical *Open Veins of Latin America* used the Cerro Rico silver mines in colonial Potosí and the foreign-owned tin mines of Bolivia's southwest as touchstones of extracted wealth coupled with local poverty.

In the 2003 Gas War, Bolivians did get a chance to fight that poverty and their marginalization locally and globally. Aymara campesinos marched into El Alto, where more than a thousand people began a hunger strike for greater resources and respect. Rural, urban, and indigenous movements jointly denounced President Gonzalo ("Goni") Sánchez de Lozada's proposal to export gas to California and Mexico from a Chilean port. Bolivia's resource wealth, they feared, would primarily enrich foreign corporations—British Gas, British Petroleum, and Repsol YPF—and generate industrial jobs outside the country.[4] The movements demanded that the government reverse the 1997 privatization of Bolivia's gas industry, proclaiming, "The gas is ours."[5] The uprising entailed weeks of road blockades that disrupted commerce across Bolivia, a modern echo of Katari and Sisa's siege. El Alto was ground zero: the city with the largest and longest local strike, the convergence point for regional and national mobilizations, and where at least forty-six local residents lost their lives, the vast majority shot by the military, most of them between October 11 and 13.

Undeterred, protesters rebuilt and expanded their blockades day after day, even on the day of funerals that followed that bloody weekend. Two of their most telling acts happened near where I now stood. Working together, residents pushed five train cars onto a bridge, where they had stacked stones on the tracks. With sticks and iron bars, they levered the cars off the rails and onto the streets below, transforming the vehicles into a formidable blockade. The train was the abandoned property of the publicly owned rail company Ferroviaria Andina, privatized into Chilean hands in 1995, and no longer serving La Paz or El Alto. The tollbooths, also privatized, became a target of the crowd's wrath during the Gas War. For six hours young Alteños ransacked them, dragging furniture, papers, and supplies into the streets and setting them ablaze. Like the tollbooth a generation of privatization policies would soon be reduced to ashes.

On Friday, October 17, 2003, two hundred thousand Bolivians gathered in and around La Paz's San Francisco Plaza to demand the president's resignation. Thousands of marchers had arrived from the mines of Oruro and the valleys of the Yungas and the Chapare. Meanwhile, tens of thousands marched in Cochabamba, Sucre, and Oruro, forming blockades in these cities and on rural highways.[6] In a 2004 nationwide poll, 14 percent of respondents would recall protesting against the Sánchez de Lozada government during October.[7] The protesters were backed by the hunger strikes of political elites, artists, and the middle class, united in common demands: that the gas be nationalized, that a constituent assembly be convened, and that Sánchez de Lozada resign. Matching their *chuño*-powered, unarmed bodies and an innovative set of tactics against government soldiers with guns, they prevailed.

The president fled the country on the night of that overwhelming gathering. His first destination was Miami, in the country that gave him his education, his often-ridiculed American accent, and his economic ideology. That is why, in Angel's eyes, being from the United States is nearly as bad as being Chilean. He demands to know whether I have seen Goni in my country and why the United States is protecting him. His anger fades to curiosity as I explain how I had been in Miami in 2003, not to see Goni but to protest the Summit of the Americas. Our mobilization of workers, environmentalists, and other activists had shared a demand with the leaders of the Bolivian Gas War: to stop the creation of a Free Trade Area of the Americas. And in Miami the police had clashed with us as well, unleashing tear gas, rubber bullets, and wooden projectiles as they pursued thousands of us across downtown.

As I tell him this, calm returns and many questions are posed back and forth. Andrés is pragmatic and focused on economic progress and hemispheric cooperation, whereas Angel distrusts Bolivia's richer neighbors and is ready to fight for his people's dignity. Andrés wants streets in La Paz that were like those in Chile—paved, not gravel and stones—and lined with skyscrapers. Angel is willing to defend "nuestra ciudad, nuestras calles [our city, our streets]" as they are now. It is easy to see how both perspectives had propelled Bolivia's transformation, had given people reasons to take to the streets and fight.

After walking barely five meters from Andrés and Angel, I am intercepted by an affable and gregarious man named Lucho, enveloped by the crowd of his friends, and poured the first of several cups of beer. Lucho brings my face close to his, asks just a few questions about my home and ethnic background, and welcomes me to the celebration, mentioning that earlier his crowd had seen me lingering on the edges. With these brief preliminaries complete, he raises his voice and bursts into an announcement that this group, affiliated with El Alto's Regional Labor Confederation (Confederación Obrera Regional–El Alto)—the organizers of the October 2003 urban strike is celebrating Willkakuti, reclaiming their traditional culture, and happy to welcome me, an African American who also has some European ancestry. "You are not a foreigner because in this world there are no foreigners," Lucho tells me, all of us being in our home, adding that the only true *extranjero* is someone from another planet. He proclaims, "El pueblo Afro en los Estados Unidos es también un pueblo étnico [the Afro-descendant people in the United States are also an ethnic people]" who preserve their traditions.[8]

It is a most emphatic welcome. Lucho has quickly grasped all the basics of my biography and my research ambitions and made them part of a morning-long celebration of world-spanning solidarity. Dialing his voice back down, he follows up with a fast-paced conversation, more introductions, and plenty of questions about my presence in Bolivia. When I leave, COR–El Alto calendar in hand, I walk past the newly slaughtered llama, over which women are raising a hand axe, transforming it from sacrificial offering to meat. The skin hangs over a railing, halfway to some new practical use.

Bolivia, as I encountered it in 2009, 2010, and 2011, was in the midst of a heady time, when removing the old government was a recent accomplishment and building a new society felt to many like a collective endeavor. Members of social movements who had written an ambitious new constitution marched with draft laws in hand to demand the government implement their visions. The government invited anarcha-feminists to draft a national gender policy. More than a hundred curious onlookers packed a room in the capital's public law school to hear advocates explain how to build a criminal justice system not based on imprisonment. More than ten thousand Bolivian activists slept in barracks to attend a summit enshrining the rights of Mother Earth. The government opened a vice ministry dedicated to decolonizing the state. Any redirection, no matter how fundamental, seemed possible, and the circumstances that made it possible—the upsurge of protests during the previous decade—were treated as common property, the patrimony of nearly everyone.

During that rebellion the meaning of *everyone* and the meaning of Bolivia itself had changed. The newly inaugurated president Carlos Mesa Gisbert (2003–2005) recognized those who had died in the effort to topple his predecessor. "My first obligation," the historian-turned-president told the senators and deputies, "is to render my most profoundly felt and admired homage to the women and men of Bolivia who in these days offered up their lives for the homeland, for democracy, for the future, and for life."[9] At his invitation the National Congress stood in silent homage to those who had died protesting the old system.

The next day Mesa joined a gathering of about eight thousand people in El Alto in memory of the fallen. Alteños replaced much of the president's traditional escort when he left his presidential car at the ransacked tollbooth that marked entrance to the city. Standing atop the first pedestrian overpass on Avenida 6 de Marzo, Mesa read the names of each of those killed, with his voice joining "in a duet with one of the family members," stirring the emotions of those gathered. The city's Catholic bishop led a prayer "for the heroes of the Gas War." In La Paz's Plaza San Francisco, Bolivia's national union confederation (the Central Obrera Boliviana) hosted a massive celebration of President Sánchez de Lozada's fall. Many organizations present were unwilling to simply accept a new face in the presidential palace as a victory. Rather, they said, it was time for what they termed a truce, to allow Mesa the time to meet their demands. The Alteño labor leader Roberto de la Cruz ended his speech by asking "the workers to make the sign of the cross and solemnly swear to not betray the Bolivian social movement and to fight tirelessly until the poor accede to power."[10]

These were extraordinary moves, public demonstrations that the president needed the forbearance of the protesters more than they needed his leadership. Mesa's acts in those days, his honoring of the dead and symbolic deference to the crowd, were the first official recognition that the authority and legitimacy of the Bolivian street now exceeded that of the lawfully chosen head of state. If, as Benedict Anderson proposes in *Imagined Communities*, the modern nation-state strives for the eternal by memorializing its fallen soldiers, the consecration of participants in an uprising marked the decisive reimagining of the Bolivian political community.[11]

Two years later, in 2005, Evo Morales, a leader of Aymara coca growers, scored Bolivia's most convincing electoral victory in four decades when he was elected president of Bolivia. Hundreds of campesinos in red ponchos, traditional leaders (*mallkus* and *jilacatas*) from indigenous communities, and helmeted cooperative miners escorted him from his presidential inauguration to a massive crowd in the Plaza San Francisco.[12] Before him stood all the movements that had collaborated for five years in an extraordinary series of protests. Addressing them, Morales declared, "Now we have the responsibility to govern. Together, we will govern, brothers and sisters."[13] His vice president, Álvaro García Linera, promised to return to the square and provide an account of what the new government would accomplish in the coming years.

In the early twenty-first century, streets and plazas became the decisively important spaces for acting politically in Bolivia, rivaling and at times exceeding voting booths and halls of government. Drawing on twelve months of ethnographic fieldwork, interviews with protest participants, and documentary research, this book provides an up-close history of the protests that changed Bolivia. The point is not only to encounter these extraordinary events from the inside but also to explain how these events affected the existing balance of power, reshaping relations of class, race, and authority. At the heart of the study is a new approach to the interaction of protest actions and the urban landscape. Such "space-claiming protests" both communicate a message and exercise practical control through the combination of what they do and where they are. To unpack that meaning, this book examines both protest tactics (as experiences and as tools) and meaning-laden spaces (whose meaning is part of the racial and political geography of the city), offering a new way of understanding how protests transform politics. Taking the streets of Cochabamba, Sucre, and La Paz as its vantage point, *The Sovereign Street* investigates the material, emotional, and symbolic processes through which grassroots activists claimed to represent the people at large and pressed that claim on the government.

## From Seattle to Bolivia: Affinity and Solidarity Against Corporate Globalization

I first encountered Bolivia's remarkable political upheaval as part of the movement against corporate globalization. The nongovernmental organization that had just hired me, Project Underground, was one of dozens of international solidarity groups weaving bonds among community leaders from the global South, American union workers, environmental activists, and direct-action protesters, in preparation for the Ministerial Meeting of the World Trade Organization in Seattle. My first day on the job, I boarded a bus in Oakland, California, to bring about eighty environmental rights activists directly to the protest against the WTO.

Just before 7:00 a.m. on November 30, 1999, the N30 Global Day of Action, about two dozen of us formed three circles where Pike Street and Boren Avenue cross. In each circle we linked arms through long tubular "lockboxes."[14] Sliding our arms into the tubes, and clipping our wrists to a concealed pin, we made the circle a unit, breakable only at the risk of serious harm to the limbs concealed within. I got to know my coworkers while helping to occupy this intersection and thereby block the delegates from reaching the meeting. We shared the crossing with dozens of other protesters ready to link arms at a moment's notice. Any delegates looking for a way into the Ministerial Meeting would have to push their way through us or another group of protesters ringing the Seattle Convention Center. By nightfall the first day of talks had been canceled, and Seattle's mayor had declared a state of emergency. Surrounded by this display of North American resistance, long-skeptical delegates from the global South saw that U.S. and European negotiators lacked the support of their own people. Many African, Latin American, and Asian delegations then emerged as critics of the WTO's plans for the seamless flow of capital and commodities, and the talks collapsed. The Direct Action Network, the coordinating body that orchestrated the blockades, mushroomed into a movement of tens of thousands of activists eager to converge upon summits of the powerful, including the World Petroleum Congress, Democratic and Republican political conventions, and the World Economic Forum.[15] Seemingly overnight, challenges to the power and global reach of corporate capitalism became front-page news.

The collapse of the Ministerial Meeting led to cancellation of the Millennium Round of free-trade negotiations just as Bolivians were facing the real effects of corporate-designed trade and investment policies. The government had been aggressively seeking foreign buyers for public enterprises and utilities since 1993 and had found one for the municipal water company of Cochabamba in September 1999. The privatized company's first water bills—some of them double or triple the previous rate—came out on December 1, 1999. Protests in downtown Cochabamba on that day coincided with the arrest of more than five hundred protesters—including me—in Seattle. By April three waves of mass protests had rocked Cochabamba and thrown out the foreign owners of Aguas del Tunari, restoring public ownership of the city's water utility.

News of Cochabamba's Water War rippled into the San Francisco Bay Area because one of the main foreign owners of Aguas del Tunari was the San Francisco–based private construction firm Bechtel. The story of Cochabamba's victory was shared by guests at the glittering awards ceremony for the prestigious Goldman Environmental Prize, held in San Francisco's imposing War Memorial Opera House, and by protesters assembled on Market Street for the rally against the World Bank on April 23, 2001.[16] I attended both, slipping out of the opulent Goldman reception to join the drumming and marching three blocks away beneath handcrafted cardboard puppets.

In 2001 the Goldman Prize committee made Oscar Olivera, the Water War spokesperson, the first trade unionist to receive the $150,000 award. In his prepared remarks Olivera proclaimed, "During the last fifteen years, we have been told that the market will resolve everything. But we can see that isn't true." In

Bolivia, like much of Latin America, what American protesters called corporate globalization was known as neoliberalism, the ideology that guided what Olivera termed "the impositions of the international financial institutions."[17] Together with their U.S.-trained advisers, a generation of Bolivian politicians had embraced an experiment in undiluted neoliberal economic policies. They had sold off the electrical grid, urban water systems, the airports, even the toll roads.

Cochabamba's victory was the harbinger of a dramatic, and continent-wide, turnaround. As the new century began, turbulent protests and new political actors arose across Latin America to question a generation of globalization-oriented economic policies. Peasant, labor, indigenous, Black, and environmental movements—many of whose members had been networking across borders for years—joined together through the annual "World Social Forum" gatherings. In Bolivia large but regional mobilizations challenged the government's coca, taxes, water, gas, land, and rural policies. Civil unrest brought down governments in Ecuador and Argentina, two countries gripped by financial crises. Ecuador's January 2000 protests began with indigenous protesters occupying the National Congress, leading to an improbable and fleeting military-indigenous alliance that governed the country for a day.[18] In Argentina overwhelming protests forced two presidents from power on December 19 and 20, 2001, while crowds chanted that "All of them must go"—presidents, members of Congress, and the whole political class.[19]

In late 2003 tens of thousands of global justice activists from across the United States converged on Miami outside a summit to discuss the proposed hemispheric Free Trade Area of the Americas. Some of us had followed the dramatic news of Bolivia's Gas War as we prepared for Miami, largely through the Independent Media Center (an electronic network that was itself a product of the global justice movement).[20] We knew that Bolivia's exiled president Sánchez de Lozada had arrived in Miami before us. Presumably he had found a comfortable temporary residence by the time police unleashed tear gas, smoke grenades, and rubber bullets on the summit protesters downtown. The Miami mobilization was the last of a series of summit protests against corporate globalization to achieve critical mass in the United States (even as protests continued against the Iraq War). Many attributed the failure of mass protests to the "Miami model" of aggressive policing.[21]

Just as U.S.-based protests against corporate globalization were losing momentum, our South American allies were moving from protests to political power. Between 2002 and 2010, eleven presidents in ten Latin American countries were voted into office on the promise of rolling back neoliberal economic policies.[22] This so-called pink tide portended a regional revival of the Left and renewed hopes for an organized anticapitalist politics. In 2005 fifty thousand protesters surrounded the next Summit of the Americas in Mar de la Plata, Argentina, as President Néstor Kirchner, who had been swept into office by the pink tide, delivered the fatal blow to the proposed free trade area.[23] Those who followed events on both continents wondered: How could a small and poor country like Bolivia strike such a frontal blow to neoliberalism? How might we understand and learn from the alliances, strategic choices, and tactics that had upended a political consensus among all major political parties? What allowed their protests to cohere, endure, and reshape the political landscape in the face of much greater repression? Asking and answering these questions drove many participants in the global justice movement into graduate studies and intercontinental travel or, as in my case, both.

My travels brought me face-to-face with scores of Bolivian activists with their own memories and strategic reflections. Many were propelled into activism by the mobilizations of the early 2000s, from the Water War to the fall of Carlos Mesa in June 2005. Others were longtime organizers who had impatiently endured fifteen years of neoliberal rule. They found reason for hope and new possibilities in the mass protests. The conversations that this book draws upon are thus the words of Bolivians immersed in struggle and addressed to North Americans seeking to learn from their experience.

My political background, identity, and experience made these conversations possible. As in my first conversation with Angel, I often found myself being questioned about my intentions and political orientation by the Bolivians with whom I spoke. While there were many elements of my past to draw on, I repeatedly saw a click of recognition (one I didn't expect) when I mentioned Seattle and the fight against the free trade area. And another click when I shared knowledge of occupying intersections and facing down riot police. At those moments I watched my interviewees' skepticism dissolve and curiosity arise in its place, or I listened as their narratives shifted from putting forward a political claim (why we deserve what we struggle for) to remembering the process of struggle itself (how we work to get it). When the Cochabamba Water War participant Marcelo Rojas and I started talking about how to handle being teargassed, that very conversation made us comrades in struggle. Both political and tactical affinities opened the door to deeper conversations that considered the lessons of the first decade of the twenty-first century.

## Seeing with Both Eyes: Witnessing Race in Bolivia

The grassroots upsurge, while led by Bolivia's indigenous majority, foregrounded the economic struggle against neoliberalism. However, once the neoliberal government fell, the focus turned to race: indigenous political forces and social movements sought to claim a space for themselves within the Constituent Assembly and the state apparatus itself. This proved deeply unsettling to many white and mestizo Bolivians, and their fears converged with the Bolivian right wing's attempts to regroup and stall the Morales government's agenda. My fieldwork began during this later period, when narratives of race and racism were at the forefront.

On a June night in 2008, darkness has fallen over the colonial-style town center of Sucre, Bolivia. I stand at the threshold of a three-story building, asking to enter by mentioning the name of an activist I had interviewed and detailing my political background, both in an effort to demonstrate my good intentions. (This was one of the times when *Seattle* was the right word to say.) Admitted by those guarding the door, I enter an unmarked wooden doorway and ascend the stairs to the main room of the downtown district office of Walther Valda's campaign for election as prefect of the Department of Chuquisaca. (Bolivia has nine departments, which are comparable to states in the United States.) It looks like any other campaign office the night before election day: volunteers, giant banners, posters of the candidate, a calendar, and an office phone with a clearly posted phone number. But to the public it doesn't exist. Valda is the candidate of President Morales's party, but in Sucre his party is limited to word-of-mouth campaigning and going door to door. Some backers of Valda's opponent, Savina Cuellar, have placed stickers on their front doors declaring, "This is a dignified house and will vote for the ACI [Inter-Institutional Committee Alliance]. ¡Don't insist [on knocking]!" Walking around one sees posters and graffiti pasted up on behalf of both candidates, but only the ACI has flags flying from windows. Residents who are flying the flags of the MAS-IPSP, I am told at the campaign office, have faced attacks on their property and their persons.

Two acts from the previous month had heightened the climate of fear. On the night of May 21, right-wing civic movement protesters tossed tear gas canisters into Valda's original campaign headquarters as he spoke at its grand opening. During a daylong spectacle on May 24, civic movement protesters who "swore not to let the President set foot in Sucre" deterred Morales by initiating a chaotic confrontation with the police and military. Members of

## Box 1. Bolivia's Turbulent Recent History

The events described in this book stretch from 1999 to 2012. This extremely complex and turbulent period in Bolivia's history can be divided into three phases.

The 1999–2005 **grassroots upsurge** has been cast as a third Bolivian revolution by Adolfo Gilly, Sinclair Thomson and Forest Hylton, and James Dunkerley.[24] These years had a decisive historical impact that continues to be felt in Bolivian politics. They began with the Cochabamba Water War, which gave lie to the inevitability of neoliberal economic policies, and the April 2000 peasant mobilization across the high altitude plain, or Altiplano. More "wars" like this—outbreaks of sustained disruptive protest—challenged the government in regard to coca, taxes, water, gas, land, and rural policy. The ousting of two presidents, Gonzalo Sánchez de Lozada (October 2003) and Carlos Mesa Gisbert (June 2005), fit the classic structure of a political revolution, but all sides found a constitutional and democratic exit. In the end the caretaker government of Eduardo Rodríguez Veltzé oversaw new elections, permitting Evo Morales's party (the Movement Toward Socialism—Political Instrument for the Sovereignty of the Peoples, known as MAS-IPSP) to become the vehicle of state transformation.[25] These events laid a lasting foundation for the Bolivian political agenda. On a typical day in 2010 or 2011, any one of these three legacies—countering neoliberalism, the October agenda, and the construction of the plurinational state—might be used to orient a policy debate, explain a government decision, or justify a new protest.

The MAS-IPSP promised to function as a "government of social movements" and suggested a simple transformation from protest to politics. The process of redefining the country was carried forward through the Constituent Assembly from August 2006 to December 2007; the MAS-IPSP held a simple majority in the assembly. However, the first four years of the MAS-IPSP government were complicated by intransigent right-wing opposition and became known as the catastrophic stalemate (*empate catastrófico*). Neoliberal and right-wing politicians still had considerable institutional resources: control of the Senate, a significant minority within the Constituent Assembly, and the leadership of departmental governments in Santa Cruz, Beni, Pando, Tarija, and Cochabamba. So-called civic movements organized these forces into a backlash that counterposed regional autonomy to the proposed plurinational order. The Constituent Assembly spent months in deadlock, while mobilizations by the Left and Right competed for urban space and public backing. The government usually relied on its grassroots base rather than the police to respond to protest. Finally, it turned the tide against this challenge during the August–October 2008 political crisis, as described in chapter 6. In this period politics continued to depend on protest, and the leftist grassroots movement and right-wing civic movement used overlapping repertoires of tactics, as well as contests at the ballot box, including the final approval of the new constitution by a 61 percent vote in January 2009.

Recent years have been a period **of mobilization and countermobilization within the Plurinational State**, as the government was renamed on January 22, 2010, during Evo Morales's second inauguration. In national and regional elections, in December 2009 and April 2010, respectively, the MAS-IPSP secured its place as the premier political force in the country, but it was joined by a growing ecosystem of grassroots, leftist, and indigenous forces that held municipal and departmental offices. Sectors that had stood with the Morales government during the catastrophic stalemate now voiced their demands by taking to the streets. Their demands for regional development, higher wages, indigenous rights, disability pensions, and environmental protection became challenges to the government they had helped install. In response the government denounced these actions by its erstwhile allies as a continuation of the right-wing campaign to destabilize the national government. While the government's legitimacy rests upon the voices of social movements, it seeks to mobilize its allies to defeat its critics. The house of the grassroots Left has become a divided one.

the Inter-Institutional Committee Alliance, including Cuellar, negotiated the withdrawal of the security forces, though the protesters continued to pelt them with rocks as they left. The urban protesters then attacked the rural leaders with whom Morales was scheduled to meet and took more than fifty indigenous men and women captive. After releasing the women, the right-wing protesters publicly humiliated the men in the city's central square. Eighty people were injured; they were overwhelmingly campesinos but included a soldier who suffered a severe spinal injury during the morning confrontation with civic movement protesters.[26]

Amid the scenes of public humiliation, one moment stands out for me. The captives have already been stripped of their clothes and paraded half-naked around the square. Then a lone shout, "De rodillas" (On your knees), escalates into a crowd chant, "¡De rodillas, carajo!" (On your knees, damn it!). With a new wave of blank stares, the wary captive men fall to their knees in a tight group. As they crouch on their knees in the plaza, the crowd chants, "Sucre de pie, Evo derrotado" (Sucre on its feet, Evo defeated). Meanwhile civic movement protesters set fire to an indigenous wiphala flag (a flag formed of a seven-by-seven-square checkerboard in a rainbow pattern that has long been a symbol of Andean indigenous identity), a multicolored poncho, and a pro-MAS-IPSP banner. "The hostages," the Defensoría del Pueblo (the Bolivian ombudsman office) later reports, "were mistreated, insulted, and forced to repeat chants, to kneel, to beg for forgiveness, to kiss the ground, to burn their own symbols, to take off their clothes, and to carry banners" of the right wing of Chuquisaca.[27]

I had first seen the shocking scenes from Sucre's plaza—contextualized by Cesar Brie's hastily produced video documentary *Humiliados y Ofendidos* (The Humiliated and Offended)—on my fifth night in Bolivia. Three days later I was marching into Sucre with attendees of the National Women's Social Summit, which chose to bring thousands of mostly rural and indigenous women into that same plaza as an act of *desagravio* (redress for aggression). An organizer who saw my camera, and no doubt my foreign appearance, urged me to stay toward the back of the march—"They always attack from the back," she told me (the assumption was that having a foreigner with a camera would protect the march from attack). And so it was that my observing became a form of solidarity.

But there was another component of that night at the election office. As I took in the situation of an election campaign driven underground, of head-on violence directed at a racialized minority when they dared to represent themselves politically, of the reenactment of colonial-era violence as a form of voter intimidation, I became aware of the relevance of my Blackness to my ethnographic work. I could not fail to see the parallels between the backlash against Bolivia's indigenous-led political movements and the repeated attempts to violently silence African Americans in moments of struggle. Firebombing and voter suppression, secret meetings and public punishment all cut too close to our own history to ignore. My racial identity, embodied experience, and knowledge of the historical legacy of the African American struggle made me attentive to a racial dimension of the power struggle in Bolivia that outsiders are too willing to look past.

There has been a tendency among anthropologists to differently characterize the nature of indigenous and Afro-descendant peoples of the Americas and therefore the nature of their subordination.[28] Under this approach indigenous peoples are said to "have" culture, while their bodies have the potential to be biologically assimilated, become mestizos, and be whitened through intermarriage or education. On the other hand peoples of African descent are said to "lack" meaningful culture but have a more troublesome and obdurate biological

FIGURE 2  Rural women attending the Nation Women's Social Summit march in Sucre in June 2008 in a public repudiation of the events of May 24. Graffiti on the wall behind them reads, "MASistas out!"

race that contaminates all their descendants. Because of this split perspective, it's possible to approach indigenous inclusion in multicultural or even plurinational societies without mentioning race or racism. It is something of a norm (for outside writers) to leave the vast repertoire of knowledge about race and racism behind when addressing indigenous subordination in Latin America. Bolivian social scientists' discussion of transformations of racial power, however, is rich and varied. Ever in dialogue with social movements, they have taken on the Katarista invocation to "see with two eyes" and recognize race and class in every situation.[29]

"Cochabamba changed," the Cochabamba grassroots activist María Eugenia Flores Castro tells me, recalling the worst days of confrontation during the catastrophic stalemate, "in the sense that racism has been made more visible, much more visible than before." But that racism was not new, she says, correcting herself: "I think it's not that it changed. . . . The colonial and racist Cochabamba became visible."[30] Attentiveness to race in Bolivia led me to

## Box 2. Race in Bolivia

Racial identity in Bolivia is complex and layered with history, multiple meanings, and contradictions. Throughout Latin America race is a product of colonial rule, built around the privileging of people of European origins. In the colonial period the highest status was accorded to *peninsular* (born in the Iberian peninsula) and *criollo* individuals (creoles, born in the Americas but of entirely European origins). After independence the strata shifted to include mestizos (people of European but also indigenous origins) at the top of the social ladder. Throughout this time the keys to public life—property ownership, higher education, professional training, and public service—were restricted by race. Most Indians gained the vote only with the introduction of universal, gender-neutral suffrage in 1952.[31]

Beyond the cities European-descended elites exercised control over indigenous labor and land. These people, primarily speakers of Quechua and Aymara, experienced class subordination in the mines, large agrarian estates, and cities that coincided with their racial positioning. In rural areas they were racialized as *indios*, while in cities they were termed *cholos* and *cholas*, once disparaging terms for so-called acculturated Indians. The Nationalist Revolutionary Movement, which carried out the 1952 Revolution, envisioned integrating them into a homogeneous mestizo nation, but its designation of peasants as "campesinos, not indios," only made *campesinos* into a new label for the same quasi-racial category. Since the 1970s Bolivian peasant movements have grown increasingly vocal about defending their indigenous identities, connecting present struggles to anticolonial resistance.

*Indigenous* is no one's sole identification in Bolivia but a way of grouping together multiple identities, experiences, and political projects. As elsewhere, *indigenous* is a word used by and about people "who are engaged in an often desperate struggle for political rights, for land, for a place and space within a modern nation's economy and society."[32] Lowland communities organized within the Confederation of Indigenous Peoples of Bolivia use *indígena*; in this text I call them "lowland indigenous." Highland communities that seek to reconstitute their *ayllu* structures as a basis for territorial governance are organized through the National Council of Ayllus and Markas of Qullasuyu (Consejo Nacional de Ayllus y Markas del Qullasuyu) and use the term *indígena originario*.[33] Peasant communities, including members of the Unified Union Confederation of Rural Bolivian Workers (Confederación Sindical Única de Trabajadores Campesinos de Bolivia), use *indígena, originario,* and *campesino.* The

Union Confederation of Colonists of Bolivia, made up primarily of Aymara and Quechua migrants, renamed itself the Union Confederation of Intercultural Communities of Bolivia (Confederación Sindical de Comunidades Interculturales de Bolivia), and its members self-identify as *interculturales*. Theoretically a part of this federation, the Six Federations of the Tropic of Cochabamba identify primarily as *cocaleros*, or coca growers.[34] Where relevant I refer to the last two groups as agricultural colonists or as indigenous migrants. Collectively these groups have articulated the term *indígena originaria campesino*, which covers all these identities. Felix Ticona Quispe, then a senior official in the rural Bolivian workers union, described the differences in terms as "only in organizational matters. . . . The name is from the mode of representation that we have," while "in the end, we are the same, we eat the same things, we feel the same things."[35] I use *indigenous* in place of this overarching identity and to identify members of any of its subgroupings in their relations with groups outside this broad category.

Alicia Ortiz, a midcentury visitor from Argentina who "at first could not distinguish the *india* from the *chola*" during her 1952–53 trip, was surprised to have a Bolivian man inform her that the difference was "their dress."[36] The man proceeded to briefly list distinguishing garments for Indian and cholo men and women.[37] In twenty-first-century Bolivia, both dress and place of residence continue to be crucial markers of racial identity. Rubber sandals (*ojotas*), for instance, mark a man as indigenous. Racial differentiation by dress applies more strongly to women, however. Dressing *de pollera*, with a pleated skirt and characteristic hat (black bowler hats in the Altiplano, straw hats in the valleys), marks a woman as a chola. Conversely, wearing a modern dress—dressing *de vestido*—defines the same woman as mestiza. This distinction is so attached to identity that it can be used as a demographic category, notably in accounts of the first women *de pollera* to serve in various national offices.

Self-identification is both complex and shifting in Bolivia. When confronted with a series of racial categories (white, mestizo, black, indigenous, and other), *mestizo* was the preferred choice of three out of four Bolivians (76 percent) in 2012.[38] The mestizo category has grown at the expense of white and (to a lesser extent) indigenous self-identification. At the same time 72 percent declared they belong to a specific indigenous people, including two-thirds of the mestizos.[39] This category, too, continues to grow.[40] Social scientists and many political advocates use the last categorization, included in the 2001 and 2012 Census, to term Bolivia a majority-indigenous country.[41]

recognize the ways that race structures the city and the spaces that have been critical for protest and governance during the past two decades of upheaval and change. It led me to consider Bolivia's vibrant mass protests not just in terms of their paralyzing capacity to interrupt commerce and their daring claims to popular sovereignty but also the way they overturn the long-standing exclusion of indigenous peoples from political participation. Later they led me to also reconsider the ways that plurinational statecraft deliberately inserts symbols and practices of indigenous self-rule into creole/mestizo spaces that had long negated them.

## Broader Trends at Work in Bolivia

The surge of Bolivian grassroots movements described in this book is part of a continent-wide story. As the new century began, turbulent protests and new political actors arose across Latin America to question a generation of globalization-oriented economic policies. Members of peasant, labor, indigenous, Afro-descendant, and environmental movements—many of whom had been networking across borders for years—came together through the World Social Forum. The slogan of this multivocal counterweight to capitalist economics insisted, "Another World Is Possible", through mass mobilization and radical social change. This continental rethinking of economic direction and race relations was propelled from below: people in the hundreds or thousands marched, blockaded roads and erected barricades, and thronged city streets to demand change. These methods emerged in Venezuela during the 1989 Caracazo protests against the end of fuel subsidies; in the Argentinazo, regional and national mobilizations in Argentina that began in 1993 and made global headlines in December 2001; and in the 2006 uprising led by the Popular Assembly of the Peoples of Oaxaca. That these complex political events require new names—sometimes ending in *-azo* to denote a blow or shock struck in (or by) a particular place—is symptomatic of their novelty, impact, and local specificity. Their very names claim that all residents have spoken decisively as one. The Bolivian events detailed in this book also became defining moments in local history and required scholars and strategists to rethink our categories to understand them. (The 2000 Water War in Cochabamba was also first known as the *tarifazo*, although that name is attached more to the water rate hike itself;

the December 2010 Gasolinazo refers to both a price increase and the protests that reversed it.)

These means of collective action, deployed across Latin America around the turn of the millennium, have become part of a global language of protest. Road blockades have been important features of Chinese labor protests, Thai political conflicts, urban and rural conflicts in the Andean region, the Canadian indigenous movement, North American environmental and antiwar movements, and European opposition to austerity measures. Plaza occupations, long a key feature of national political action, acquired worldwide visibility in 2011. Mass occupations of Tahrir Square and the Pearl River Roundabout during the Arab Spring, of Zuccotti Park by the Occupy Wall Street movement, and of Syntagma Square and Puerta del Sol in European anti-austerity protests all have demonstrated the pivotal role that takeovers of public space can play in national and transnational politics.

Many analyses of the 2011 movements have emphasized their space-claiming nature. "The fundamental social form of the movement was the occupation of public space," writes Manuel Castells. They opened up "a public space where the movement could openly exist in its diverse reality," and they were "charged with the symbolic power of invading sites of state power, or financial institutions."[42] In all these ways the dynamics of these movements echo those in this book. Where they diverge most clearly is in the digital form of networking that so many have described as central to the 2011 uprisings. Bolivia's protests were not coordinated online, but mass media (mostly radio and newspapers), in-person assemblies, telephones, and person-to-person networks of connection were more than adequate to accomplish many of the tasks later done over the Internet. "It was like this, face-to-face," the water rights activist Marcela Olivera told me. "I remember that the comrades would distribute themselves among the neighborhoods, with each person taking one neighborhood, right?, to go and meet."[43] (They did benefit from "the ability to cheaply and easily connect on global scale," for example, through the networks that brought Bolivia's movements to my awareness.[44]) Like smartphone-based tools, offline media and community connections have their own affordances for facilitating social movements, as Zeynep Tufekci explores in her work on digitally networked protests.[45] Finally, direct means of applying economic and political pressure—principally strikes and blockades—as well as tactical contests for control of urban streets were vital to the success or failure of the 2011 movements. In the conclusion I will return to how these tactical elements, which are the core topic of this book, impacted the trajectories of 2011 movements.

These two waves of revolt had an unmistakably urban face. Globalization policies had propelled urbanization in the global South by squeezing rural areas, through lower prices for crops and reduced demand for agricultural workers. This drove a worldwide "exodus of surplus rural labor to urban slums," even when there weren't enough jobs there to employ these new arrivals.[46] Anthropologists and political observers have increasingly turned their eyes toward the self-organized neighborhoods on the edges of exploding cities as sites of grassroots political power. Locally these so-called slums function as "places in which residents use their ingenuity to create a world of adaptations, connections, and strategies with which to inhabit modern metropolises on better terms."[47] Unemployed or underemployed, but educated and organized, these new urbanites are increasingly seen as protagonists of political change.

As South America's poorest and most indigenous country, Bolivia's protest dynamics seem to distill these larger trends. The self-organized urban peripheries of La Paz, El Alto, and Cochabamba—described ethnographically by Sian Lazar, Robert Albro, Daniel Goldstein, and Amonah Achi Chritèle and Marcelo Delgado—all played pivotal roles in the early twenty-first-century political upsurge.[48] If revolution is understood as the intervention of mass participation in politics to alter the established order, nowhere in South America has that intervention been more direct, turbulent, or sustained than Bolivia. Further, that intervention, powered by overlapping urban and indigenous majorities, and guided by long-standing traditions of anticolonial and working-class revolt, promised fundamental shifts in Bolivia's political and economic direction and its racial order.

Bolivian social movements have some of the most effective and interesting practices of political action in the world. Their reach across the population is extraordinary: Bolivia consistently ranks as the Latin American country with the highest level of protest participation (see table 1), and few countries globally have wider participation in protest.[49] Through a variety of tactics, its urban residents and indigenous-identified population have reclaimed urban spaces, asserted and taken the right to speak for Bolivia, and redirected its political life. This book explores the innovations of their political practice, its effectiveness and limitations, alongside the extraordinarily complex political landscape they inhabit.

TABLE 1   Protest participation in Bolivia

| Have you participated in protest in the last twelve months? | | | | | |
| --- | --- | --- | --- | --- | --- |
| 2004 | 2006 | 2008 | 2010 | 2012 | 2014 |
| Sometimes 20.70% | | Sometimes 21.97% | | | |
| Almost never 15.16% | | Almost never 7.59% | | | |
| Total 35.86% | 11.08% | 29.57% | 11.37% | 16.94% | 14.14% |

*Note*: LAPOP asked the same question in each of these years but varied the choices it gave respondents for their answers: "Sometimes," "Almost never," and "No" in some years and simply yes or no in others.

*Source*: The AmericasBarometer by the Latin American Public Opinion Project, www .LapopSurveys.org. For more about using LAPOP's System for Online Data Analysis (SODA), go to http://lapop.ccp.ucr.ac.cr/Lapop_English.html.

## Methods

When trying to understand Bolivia, I learned to see with two eyes: race and class but also the global agenda and the local struggles, the revolution against neoliberalism and the parallel one against centuries-old social exclusion, and ultimately the struggle through the government to remake Bolivia alongside the struggle against the government because of its direction. These indigenous and leftist revolutions of twenty-first-century Bolivia have been justifiably explored in great depth through reporting, political theorizing, narrative history, and social science. What this investigation addresses, however, is not the change in who engages in politics nor in the overall political direction of Bolivian society but a shift in how politics is carried out. It especially looks at how Bolivians reclaimed, contested, and fought over streets, public buildings, downtowns, and practical and symbolic centers of power in the course of the country's unprecedented twenty-first-century upheaval. Recent changes in political practices—particularly the much greater importance of space-claiming mass mobilization and collective decision making within social movement structures—are part of a region-wide pattern. Domestically they are at least as fundamental to understanding Bolivia's new political configuration as are the plurinational ideal, "twenty-first century socialism," Vivir Bien/Living Well, and the workings of the Movement Toward Socialism–Political Instrument for the Sovereignty of the Peoples.

At the time of my fieldwork for this book there was only one direct flight from the United States to Bolivia, a late-night departure from Miami. The singular timing of that American Airlines flight provided a kind of rhythm that makes memories echo across trips. The late evening in a departure lounge populated by young North Americans (adventurous tourists in pairs or clusters, and inevitably a few dozen wearing the freshly silk-screened T-shirts of one or another missionary service trip) and generally older Bolivians, the pitch-black view of the Caribbean Sea en route, the 5:00 a.m. wake-up onboard the plane to the scent of commercial breakfast, and then the high-speed landing on the darkened tarmac of El Alto. There is what you see when you are tired, who you hear when falling asleep in a slightly creaky aircraft seat, what voices you hear waking you after just six hours of sleep, how you walk out of the plane in a space that is still dark but no longer night, and how you stand unsteadily and exhausted, staring at the geometric pattern of the floor tiles while waiting to have your visa inspected. You've taken off from the Atlantic shore and landed 4,061 meters above sea level, but the effects of the altitude come gradually. First, the cold, hypoxic air infiltrates your lungs, and then the low air pressure gradually induces an ache in your skull from the forehead out. Only later will your calves and hamstrings burn with that strange heat that comes with your first days at high altitude, warmed inside by the extra blood you must circulate to keep climbing La Paz's vertiginous hills but chilled by the air that lacks the thickness to keep your skin warm.

All this now appears to me like clockwork, tied to the same circadian rhythms of the earth and our own bodies. Catching that paired sequence—like a gear and a chain on a bicycle you ride again and again—I remember my first arrival in Bolivia.

My passport bore a visa that seemed improvised at best. I had watched the Bolivian consular officials in New York print it out on an inkjet printer. They had been dignified and serious as they questioned me about my research plans but were still adjusting to the administrative formalities of issuing visas to U.S. citizens. The requirement was imposed to put Americans on the same level as Bolivians entering the United States. "Bolivia, even as a small country called underdeveloped, has as much dignity as any other country," President Morales had said in announcing the policy in 2007.[50] But in early 2008 it still was necessary to take the visa fee in cash to a bank near the consulate and return with a slip showing you had made a deposit. In later years the whole transaction would seem more official, down to the preprinted and numbered visa forms issued by the new Plurinational State of Bolivia. Either way, a bit of fluent Spanish and simple, serious answers ensured that crisp entry stamps rapidly ended up on my passport.

Having passed through immigration, I was standing near the baggage carousels in the secure zone of the airport as I watched Bolivian television news for the first time. Video segments were short, presented repeatedly, choppily edited, and captioned on-screen—a pattern that would soon become familiar. A turbulent scene led the headlines that day in June 2008: a crowd marching in protest, then confronting and tussling with the police. Outside the U.S. Embassy, the protesters were denouncing what was, in effect, a grant of political asylum to the former defense minister Carlos Sánchez de Berzaín—Goni's enforcer. The marchers had descended from El Alto to demand accountability for the deaths of scores of protesters killed in the 2003 Gas War. The scenes were chaotic and a bit threatening. My first thought, though, was: Why hadn't I chosen to fly in a day sooner?

For me as an ethnographer, the clashes on the streets of La Paz were one perfect opportunity to see how political conflicts are enacted physically. This was a one-day civic strike, intended by its organizers to bring the city to a halt.[51] Had I been there, I might have documented how multiple columns of marchers made their way through La Paz, the way their presence tied up downtown traffic, and how they shouted demands to vendors to close their shops or risk being looted: "One, two, three, close your doors!"[52] I could have seen the vendors on Calle Tumusla (where I would later rent an apartment) comply with this request or the broken windows at a watch vendor that did not. I could have seen how one march of Altiplano peasants outflanked the police cordon behind the embassy and how another police contingent formed a line across Avenue Arce, only to have their metal crowd barriers taken by the angry crowd. I would have seen how this crowd gathered before the looming gates of the towering building, burning photos of the exiled minister and shouting for the head of the ambassador. Finally, I would have seen how riot police gathered in front of the embassy and eventually fired tear gas to disperse this crowd and retake the streets.

Instead I was first observing this on an early morning news report above my baggage, reading about it through the multiple newspaper accounts I collected on that first morning, and scanning the façade of the imposing American embassy for signs of damage. Later, other elements of that day would become clearer through their similarities to events I did witness and actions that interviewees described to me. The crowd's enforcing of the closure of business along its route—as if the march itself were a general strike—turned out to be a commonly accepted tactic, one that I later observed directly.[53] The government's dismissal of the commanding officer at the scene turned out to be part of a general expectation (with important exceptions) that police should use methods of crowd control that de-escalate, rather than escalate, confrontational situations.

Metaphorically my late arrival that day (and not the day before) reflects essential and inescapable challenges of doing fieldwork in the service of historical anthropology. Events with vital importance often precede the ethnographer's arrival; they can arise unexpectedly outside a prepared gaze and stretch across cities, regions, or the whole country; and the events one does witness are inevitably charged with meanings that refer to actions, traditions, or patterns of culture that the researcher becomes familiar with only in the process of untangling their importance. Fortunately Bolivia's remarkable political trajectory accommodated these concerns. While the central events that are the subject of my project—large-scale space-claiming protests that address issues of national significance—are not daily occurrences, in recent years no more than a few months have passed without such protests. Keeping a fairly open definition of which new events might qualify allowed me to encounter smaller-scale protests before they became national flashpoints and to see some commonalities between transformational and everyday methods of protest. This project's orientation around public spaces and the mass political actions that take place in them allowed me to look across different movements as they came into that same space.

Even with new conflicts arising in the streets, though, I needed to understand some of the central events in the first years of the upheaval, before I arrived to Bolivia. To do so, I used a variety of forms of enduring evidence: documents and media recording the events as they happened; the patterns and spatial locations of smaller-scale protests, which often echo those of high-intensity periods; the memories, identities, and oral history narratives of protest participants and observers; the continuing use of previous moments of protest in present political discourse; and monuments and other physical markers erected in recognition of protest events. The public nature of these protests, the wide variety of media that documented them, the willingness of people to share their experiences (and the pride, sincerity, and clarity with which they did so), and the active efforts of memoirists, biographers, archivists, and social scientists in Bolivia all made this task easier.

To unearth and chart the upheaval of 1999 to 2005, I had to begin in Cochabamba, the city where it originated. Recent history also led me to Sucre, where

June 2005 blockades ushered Carlos Mesa from the presidency and host of the Constituent Assembly in 2006 and 2007. The departments of Cochabamba and Chuquisaca (of which Sucre is the capital) lie between a secure base for the MAS-IPSP in the western highlands and the right-leaning eastern lowlands whose prefects led opposition to the Morales government. In the years of regional polarization, leftist grassroots movements squared off against urban right-wing politicians in battles about the direction of both these pivotal departments.

Most accounts of the Bolivian upheaval center on El Alto and La Paz Department, which suffered the greatest human toll from state repression.[54] Research focused on these cities foregrounds the commonalities of the two main mobilizing forces in La Paz Department, the Aymara Altiplano, and the urban neighborhoods of El Alto.[55] This led to narratives of an Aymara revolution, grounded in the tight cultural continuity between new urbanites and the combative rural Altiplano, and an overwhelming demographic advantage vis-à-vis nonindigenous Bolivians. In contrast Cochabamba and Sucre were less densely organized and less ethnically homogeneous yet played their own crucial roles in the decade of revolt. Shifting the geographic focus eastward allowed me to probe the roles of mestizo, middle-class, and lifelong urban dwellers in grassroots mobilizations. The uprisings in Cochabamba and Sucre were necessarily plural and multiracial events and thereby offer greater insight into the possibilities for revolutionary action—and backlash against it—in the heterogeneous settings typical of Latin American cities.

My research combined documentary sources, oral histories, ethnographic participant observation, and interviews to examine the pivotal role of Cochabamba and Sucre in the last decade's political upheaval. I amassed this data during twelve months of fieldwork (March–April 2010; July 2010–April 2011), as well as ten weeks of visits in 2008, 2009, 2013, and 2015. I observed at least fifty-two space-claiming protests and fifteen public forums or social movement summits. I followed three movement campaigns: the urban opposition to a new highway to be routed through the Isiboro-Sécure National Park and Indigenous Territory, a labor movement seeking to organize subcontracted workers, and a wave of multisector labor strikes. I conducted semistructured interviews with approximately thirty movement leaders, organizers, and participants in space-claiming protests, and I took extended life histories from eight longtime movement participants. Documentary sources included newspaper and other print accounts; documentary films and other media that recorded the events as they happened; and photos, notes, audio recordings, leaflets, posters, and other ephemera solicited from protest participants. I also collected information about the spaces these movements contested—from interviewees and regular ethnographic observation of the main sites—including the presence and spatial form of significant cultural and political events that occur in these spaces and the racialized geography of these two cities.

Using a mix of methods to analyze, contextualize, and directly and indirectly observe dramatic events has precedents in the extended-case method advocated by Max Gluckman and others at the Rhodes-Livingstone Institute.[56] I modeled my research on this method, seeking the larger social meanings that are present in events and analyzing moments of crisis for insights into how political life functions.[57] The most straightforward ethnographic approach—tracking a small community or movement organization through the upheaval—risks leaving out the larger-scale shifts that constitute transformative political change.[58] Instead I situated myself in the downtown meeting grounds of protest movements and sought out the experiences of diverse participants in pivotal events. Rather than presenting a comprehensive view of the interior of each of those movements, this approach illuminates the common spaces and practices they created through joint action.

Several generations of studies of revolution—globally and in Bolivia—have sought out a single revolutionary subject behind whom others should coalesce. These studies look at the period described in this book and see one or another vanguard group: peripheral urban neighborhoods, ethnically conscious indigenous militants, or a novel political party. But no single sector of society, acting alone, has replicated the political impact of the plural episodes of collaboration that remade Bolivia. No single ideology, constitutional principle, or political party monopolized power in the wake of the past decade's turmoil.

This study asks instead about how revolution is carried out and what its acts mean, rather than which actors are best suited to initiate revolution. To understand Bolivia's present and future, we must examine the turbulent forms of political contestation, the new principles of democratic legitimacy, and the new forms of representation of grassroots actors in public life that make up a new way of doing politics. This book describes the tactics movements use to win political change in the "repertoire of contention," the current tool kit for protest in a given society.[59] Even when protest is highly spontaneous, participants often choose among long-established forms of political action. During periods of heightened political mobilization, the repertoire of contention can expand to include new forms of action, new symbols, and new ideologies that make sense of them.[60] Throughout this book I describe the Bolivian protest tool kit and how and why these tools work.

Changes in Bolivia's repertoire of contention show up in data from long-term protest monitoring, like those compiled by the Centro de Estudios de la Realidad Económica y Social (Center for Studies of Economic and Social Reality).[61] (See figures 3 and 4.) The data show two major waves of mass action: a significant protest boom after the restoration of democracy (from 1982 to 1985), and a larger, ongoing tide of protest from the end of the 1990s to the present. Expressive protest, like marches and demonstrations, never stopped during the post-1982 democratic era. Direct-action protest (represented by "confrontations, takeovers, and riots," urban blockades, and rural blockades), however, nearly disappeared after neoliberal shock therapy was imposed in 1985 and then began to proliferate again in 1997. Over the years active and confrontational forms of protest have become the most common acts by social movements in Bolivia.[62] The increased pace and intensity of protest did not end with the election of Evo

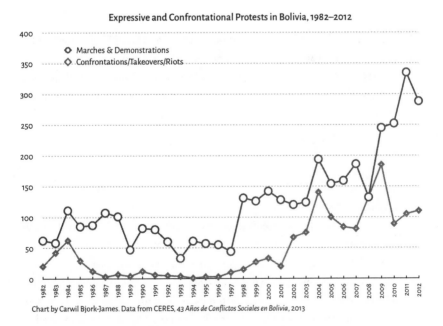

Chart by Carwil Bjork-James. Data from CERES, *43 Años de Conflictos Sociales en Bolivia*, 2013

FIGURE 3 Expressive and confrontational protests in Bolivia, 1982–2012.

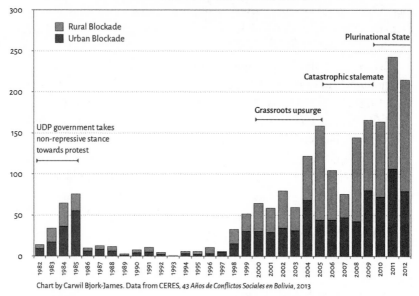

FIGURE 4 Urban and rural blockades in Bolivia, 1982–2012.

Morales in 2005. Instead it continued on an upswing through the catastrophic stalemate—when protests were deployed by both the right-wing civic movements and the leftist grassroots movement—and remained a part of political life once the Plurinational State was established. This book charts not just the (re-)emergence of disruptive protest but its incorporation in the ongoing political life of Bolivia.[63]

## Moments of Sovereignty

Revolutionary events are moments of contact between on-the-street disruption, the ideals of democratic rule, and the ceremonies of statecraft. Street protests aspire to embody national popular sovereignty and can claim it through surprisingly ceremonial action. A crowd moves from fighting with police to intoning the national anthem. A plaza filled with people declares itself a popular assembly representing the city or the country. In turn a suddenly elevated head of state honors the personal sacrifices made by street protesters, memorializing

## Box 3. Organic Grassroots Organizations and Civic Movements

At the heart of the leftist grassroots coalition are dense sector-by-sector organizations designed to build political power from the bottom up. This kind of organization seeks to comprehensively, or at least densely, involve all people who share a particular class or identity position (such as all peasant women or itinerant street vendors) in a single organization. Participation in the organization and its collective actions is treated as a social obligation, while leadership is concentrated in a small number of positions arranged in a vertical hierarchy. However, leaders are in turn constrained by a set of ethical precepts I have described elsewhere as "organic grassroots ethics," requiring accountability to the membership, selfless service, and disdaining corruption and individualistic behavior.[64] (In this book I refer to these organizations as "the grassroots Left" or "organic grassroots organizations.")

On the other hand, right-wing politics in twenty-first-century Bolivia is centered in establishment institutions, including businesses, political parties, elite cultural institutions, and sometimes universities. The term *civic movements* reflects self-identification and the institutional role of civic committees (something like an expanded chamber of commerce that includes nonbusiness elites) in these right-wing mobilizations. The right-wing movements also identified with regional identities like Cruceñidad (Santa Cruz-ness). The term *civic* stems from the notion of an urban citizenry that has the right to govern. In Bolivia this notion has long been racialized to white and mestizo urbanites and enforced by violent exclusion. Given the uncivil nature of many so-called civic movements, this term has prompted many questions. I invite readers to live with that discomfort and consider how urban notions of dignity and propriety may rest upon violence and exclusion.

Throughout this book *grassroots Left* and *civic movements* are terms of art for these two political coalitions, including both their movement and government components, even when they act in ways that are uncivil or unaccountable to the grassroots.

their deaths with a moment of silence in the halls of government. How do movements build up a claim to sovereignty? What can compel a government to recognize this claim? How can their actions build up to become a claim about who constitutes the nation, about who has the right to direct it? This book examines and unpacks the events in which protesters' use of urban space became a claim to sovereignty. It is at once an "eventful history" of recent Bolivian revolution, an insider's how-to guide for the ways those events came together, and an analytical exploration of why these kinds of actions had the political impact they did.[65]

The book is arranged to provide a roughly chronological account of mass mobilization in the twenty-first century, centered on the politically pivotal cities of Cochabamba and Sucre, where I did the majority of my ethnographic field-work. Each chapter centers on one or two different forms of space claiming and their efficacy, but the overall sequence is designed to provide people unfamiliar with Bolivia's recent history with a complete story of the dozen years from 2000 to 2011. In some cases, notably the political crises of 2005 and 2008 and the protest waves of 2010 and 2011, this book provides one of the first English-language accounts, and, accordingly, I switch to providing a more detailed his-torical narrative than elsewhere in the text.

Chapter 1 summarizes scholarly and activist understandings of what revolu-tion is, a master template for radical change that combines disruptive action and sociopolitical transformation. Revolution, in the view of contentious politics scholars, is a highly contagious idea, a process that emerged several centuries ago and became the origin story and justification for later governments: some past revolution justifies nearly every present-day state. Yet the process of revo-lution has changed, from Minutemen and revolutionary wars to workers' parties and urban insurrections and again to people power and sovereign crowds. The enigma that this book seeks to solve is exactly how these contemporary upris-ings produce political change. To address that question I introduce the theoret-ical framework of space-claiming protest, which proposes that the significance and impact of protest results from the interaction between protest tactics and the political, racial, and logistical geography of the city.

A reading note: I use scholarly language from multiple disciplines, as well as more commonsense tools, to tell this story and describe my theoretical tool kit in detail in chapter 1. If you're wondering what good anthropology is for study-ing revolution, and what this book will contribute to that study, this chapter is essential. Similarly, the chapter is designed to serve as an orientation briefing where anthropological, sociological, political scientific, and activist practitioners' ideas of revolution are sketched out. If you'd rather just dive into Bolivia's radical transformations, feel free to skip ahead to chapter 2, perhaps after reading its opening section and the section called "Revolutionary Identities and Ideologies in Bolivia."

Chapter 2 begins this story with Cochabamba's 1999–2000 Water War. Even as it centered on a local issue, participants used this mobilization to raise fundamental questions about who rules Cochabamba and to what end. Pressing their claims required both innovating means of collective pressure and articulating a new form of organization, the Coordinadora, which claimed it was better able to represent the public will than either the government or establishment civil society organizations. I argue that the Water War, and subsequent mobilizations, function by alternating demonstrations of paralyzing pressure and broad public backing.

I analyze these two aspects of successful mobilization—the moment of mass pressure and the moment of popular legitimacy—though a step-by-step description of how movements enact them through actions on the street. In chapter 3, I trace the role of the individual road blockade and show the various ways it can be scaled up to a paralyzing metropolis-wide civic strike. The chapter explores how blockades are organized, how and why people participate in them, and the impact that coordinated blockades have on the economy and daily life. I show how both aggressive strike tactics and public solidarity amplify that impact and why political decision makers might feel forced to give in to public demands expressed through a civic strike.

In chapter 4, I show how several tactics contribute to creating a feeling of broad political unity in mobilization and the ways that central plazas are taken over to give this unified political subject a sovereign voice. I propose that effective mobilizations create the feeling that everyone—the public at large, or at least an unexpectedly broad segment of it—is working together. Doing so requires demonstrating that participation is diverse and widespread, as well as numerous. Marches that converge and the deployment of numerous blockades or confrontational crowds across a large landscape can create this sense for both protesters and the government. Significantly (and contrary to most prevailing theories of revolution) these movements are more cross-class and cross-race than generally acknowledged.

The central institution for representing these mobilizations, for allowing them to speak, is the *cabildo abierto*, or mass public meeting, typically held in central plazas. Cabildos can be a further way of representing the popular legitimacy of a movement, but they also are the focal points for coordinating mass pressure campaigns. By embodying the mobilization's ability to control the urban landscape, they become nuclei of popular sovereignty. When the government attempts to repress or disperse these mobilizations, it begins a physical contest about who rules urban space. When a government tries and fails to repress a movement claiming to embody "the people," it finds its authority under fundamental question. I trace how sustained confrontations of this form led two presidents to resign in 2003 and 2005, effectively accepting that the streets were more sovereign than they were.

Chapters 5 and 6 concern acts of space claiming that question and transform the racial geography of the city. As they demand that grassroots decisions should be respected by the state, twenty-first-century mass protests deploy indigenous symbols and bring their visibly indigenous bodies into spaces where they were once treated as servants, outsiders, or intruders. To explain in chapter 5 why this arrival is so significant, I look at the emotional impact of laws, rules, and customs that once excluded indigenous people from central plazas, required them to yield the sidewalk to whiter residents, and made them ineligible to vote or hold professional and public offices. Rural movements defied these customs by boldly claiming central spaces in Cochabamba following the 1952 Revolution as they pushed for land reform. This electrifying reversal was experienced again in contemporary protests, including the marches by lowland indigenous people who have trekked to La Paz, often through Cochabamba, since 1990. Through ethnographic description of one such march and a pro-coca protest, I show how the very act of being visibly indigenous in public spaces can be a political weapon, grounding movement demands.

In chapter 6, I turn to the confrontations involving race, space, and governance that marked the politically polarized years of the catastrophic stalemate. The Morales government and its grassroots allies used the Constituent Assembly in Sucre's historic downtown as a stage for symbolically refounding the country. Within the assembly indigenous people made up a majority of legislators, and their presence upended long-standing cultural assumptions of creole/mestizo rule. However, the assembly and the constitution it was drafting also became the center of gravity for a nationwide confrontation between right- and left-wing forces. In Cochabamba and Sucre this confrontation led to major racialized and violent confrontations between civic movement protesters and leftist grassroots protesters. I examine these events as efforts to reassert a notion of creole/mestizo ownership of the city and governing spaces. The years-long conflict finally came to a close during the August–October 2008 political crisis, with crucial roles played by mass blockades, a cross-country march, and the crowd that surrounded the National Congress.

In chapter 7, "A House Divided," I focus on the emerging tensions between parts of the grassroots Left and the Morales government in regard to environment, indigenous rights, prices, and wages. In four separate mobilizations longtime allies of the government advanced demands that challenged it, while the government tried to rally its own supporters in the street. From a four-day national backlash that paralyzed fuel price increases to a countrywide wave of labor strikes to the indigenous mobilization in defense of the Isiboro-Sécure territory, these efforts directly contested the Morales government's practical and moral authority. These actions paralleled some of the more globally visible revolutions of 2011. The chapter also examines the increasingly fractured relationship between mass movements and the MAS-IPSP government, and it listens to the voices of grassroots critics of the government.

In the conclusion I bring together the multiple forms of space claiming discussed in the study. As the turbulent years of 2010 and 2011 show, each of these tactics continues to be an active part of Bolivian politics. Rather than merely a means to obtain desired political changes, space claiming has become part of a new, more dynamic political culture. While the transformation demanded by the grassroots remains incomplete, I argue that the process of upheaval has rendered Bolivia a country more open to further change from below. Moreover the Bolivian experience should encourage us to reconsider how we think about revolutions more generally.

Whenever I make presentations about revolution, I encounter people who want to engage in a conversation about which factors that contributed to revolutionary change in Bolivia (for example) are unavailable in the United States (or wherever we sit at the moment). I have come to call this conversation "the amateur sociology of revolutionary impossibility." People want to know why it *couldn't* happen here, often in spite of their own self-professed political desire for radical change. It's easy enough to find a list of unique factors that make Bolivia uniquely hospitable to revolutionary change—for example, dense involvement in grassroots organizations founded by leftist revolutionaries, tight connections to close-knit indigenous communities, and an infrastructure vulnerable to direct-action blockades. But to do so is to forget that all these assets were present during the years of frustration under neoliberal rule. These factors did not suddenly appear in Bolivia at the turn of the century. Instead a replicable form of mass mobilization did. Nor did the absence of all these factors prevent massive participation in, say, the 2011 Egyptian revolution. Powerful, successful examples—the Water War in 2000 and the Tunisian uprising, in these two cases—create their own sense of possibility.

At a deeper level I think this game of finding the necessary but absent conditions for revolution is—at least for those people who believe radical change is desirable—a way of justifying our own inaction. It's not our fault that our society is too racially divided (or is it that discrimination isn't blatant enough?), that people are too disengaged from the democratic system (or too seduced by its possibilities), or that people are too complacent (or perhaps too cynical). Knowing that revolution can happen—but not here or not now—spares us a great deal of responsibility for changing our political future. There's another way to read about revolutions: eagerly seek out parallels, find new solutions to common problems, and become aware of the tremendous diversity of courageous acts in circumstances both alike and radically different from our own. I invite you to read this book with this alternative approach in mind, to benefit from the experiences of people who radically remade their society, in spite of many conditions that suggested they could not do so.

## CHAPTER 1

# Urban Space Claiming and Revolutionary Events

*When you look into history and you look at what revolution is, you have an idea that is quite vague and distant from what it actually is. But when you are in the middle of something, it's completely different. . . . It made [me] understand that there are things that can be done, however difficult they might seem. For me, the notion that "Damn, that can't be done" is gone, because, look, it already has been done.*

—MARCELA OLIVERA

Cochabamba, Bolivia's fourth-largest city, lies on the infrastructural corridor between La Paz and El Alto and the lowland agricultural center in Santa Cruz. This corridor (the so-called *eje troncal*, or trunk axis) is the economic heart of Bolivia, home to nearly half its population and most of its economic activity. The highway south from El Alto emerges from an urban avenue and extends, straight as an arrow, over the dry Altiplano. Mountains loom in the distance but seem never to approach until the road divides into separate routes to Cochabamba and Oruro. That junction, and the nearby town of Caracollo or the village of Caihausi, is where protest campaigns gather their members for six- to eight-day "national marches" on La Paz. Taking the left turn east to Cochabamba, you find your vehicle suddenly submerged within the topography as the dry, chilly, and nearly vegetationless plain gives way to curves descending among the rock-strewn mountains. You have crossed into the fertile and temperate middle-altitude region of Bolivia, known as the Valleys. Tuck through a few curves and you encounter the valley—relatively flat, vast, and finally green—where the city of Cochabamba lies, warmed in the eternal spring of the tropics at 2,558 meters (8,392 feet) above sea level. To the north (on your left) is the verdant escarpment of the Tunari National Park, within which lurks the snowcapped peak of Mount Tunari. Straight ahead sits a ridge topped by a thirty-four-meter statue of Jesus, his arms open wide to form a cross. And to the right several hilly promontories jut inward from the south.

The region of Cochabamba, fed by rain and meltwater from these mountains, has provided food and grain since its colonization by the Inca Empire in the early sixteenth century. Under Spanish rule, plantations based on coerced and/or dependent labor took deep root here. Most of the land-owning agrarian elite lived on their haciendas during the colonial period, but they eventually took up residence in the eponymous capital city. Boundaries sometimes blurred socially, but occupational status and landownership remained highly stratified between elites and the indigenous majority.[1] As of 1950, three-quarters of the department's residents saw themselves as indigenous and slightly more spoke Quechua.[2] Peasants in Cochabamba's valleys and trade unionists in the metropolis have played leading roles in their respective national movements.[3]

A long ride down Avenida Blanco Galindo awaits the visitor arriving in Cochabamba by bus from La Paz. Both the Manaco shoe factory (the flagship worksite for the Cochabamban labor movement) and the Coca-Cola bottling plant (a sign of globalization's reach) lie within a couple blocks of the roadway, while a civil engineer's dream showcase of bridges cross over it. This broad-shouldered thoroughfare finally shrinks to human scale when it crosses the Río Rocha, whose riverbed is flanked by roadways and political, artistic, and commercial murals. Once at the edge of the city, the river now marks the entrance to its downtown. Avenida Heroínas (the continuation of Blanco Galindo) and Avenida Ayacucho, which run perpendicular to each other, are wide and cut through the narrow, square street grid of the old colonial city. Tucked one city block away from their modernized crossroad is the Plaza 14 de Septiembre, the city's original center and the focal point of Cochabamba's street democracy at the turn of the twenty-first century.

On my first visit to the city I sit at the plaza's northeast corner. During the Water War in 2000, the Gas War in 2003, and the campaign to repudiate departmental prefect Manfred Reyes Villa in January 2007, dense throngs of people gathered here in cabildos abiertos, or mass public assemblies. These organized crowds represented an alternative to the form of government practiced inside city hall, the *alcaldía*, which takes up the north face of the square. Looking to the right of the alcaldía on the same corner, you first find the Club Social, a high-society organization whose affiliates, landlords, and members of the commercial elite largely filled the offices of mayor and prefect from its founding

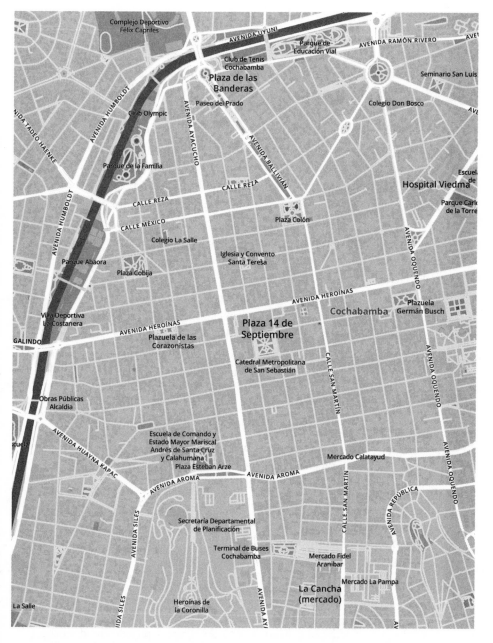

MAP 3 Central Cochabamba. (Map prepared by Carwil Bjork-James. © Mapbox, © OpenStreetMap)

in 1890 until the 1952 Revolution.[4] Turn further to the right, and you find the headquarters building of the Cochabamba Departmental Federation of Factory Workers (Federación Departamental de Trabajadores Fabriles de Cochabamba).

It was from the third-floor balcony of this building that protesters laid out their demands and promised to disrupt the daily life of the city until they were met. The headquarters of the Fabriles (factory workers; locals typically use the term to mean the union itself) takes up the third floor of the building it shares with the Cochabamba Federation of Neighborhood Councils (Federación de Juntas Vecinales), and the Cochabamba Forum on the Environment and Development (Foro Cochabambino sobre Medio Ambiente y Desarrollo). Two loudspeakers and a microphone are sufficient to turn the entire Fabriles building into a stage for rallies and a speaking platform for dozens of allied organizations. From the balcony, speakers with megaphones address crowds of hundreds, thousands, or tens of thousands, whose approval and commitment to participate in further actions can make or break the campaign of the moment. None of the other buildings on the square—not the city hall or the Departmental Palace (home to Cochabamba's regional government, then called the Prefectura and since renamed the Gobernación) or even the Catholic cathedral—are designed for mass crowds. Like the Club Social they look inward with a self-confidence born of privilege: anyone deserving a say already has a seat at the table. The Fabriles' balcony, the hive of activity that is able to crowd within it, and the crowds that can surge before it propose a different form of democracy, grounded in mass participation and a cacophony of voices.

But on July 4, 2008, I am not hearing the voice of thousands but of just one, an artist of the Arte Willka collective. "We were propelled," Roger tells me, "to contribute, as people who make art, to a political process, to a struggle of the people that is historic." Members of the group produce documentary films chronicling each wave of protest and confrontation. Their murals celebrate contemporary grassroots struggles of Bolivia and place them within a longer history of indigenous resistance. "Due to our origins, and due to our roots, we believe that art has to respond to its time," he says. "And our time is not of flowers and of roses; rather it is a time of war, a time of confrontation."[5] Arte Willka's mural celebrating the Water War is striking: a masked figure aiming a slingshot stands in for the entire mobilization, with the figure depicted behind a brick wall painted with the demand that activists hung on the façade of the Fabriles building: ¡EL AGUA ES NUESTRA, CARAJO! (The Water Is Ours, Damn It!). It is dusk, my voice is failing a bit after a week when I seem to be constantly asking

FIGURE 5  Arte Willka mural celebrating the tenth anniversary of the Water War.

questions, and my first visit to Cochabamba will end when I get on an over-night bus. Yet his explanation plants the seed of an inquiry: How does a protest become a historic process? How does a demand become a popular mandate? What makes a slingshot speak for a city?

When I lived in Cochabamba in 2010 and 2011, I spent my days in and around the old downtown. Leafy plazas are scattered across the area, providing open spaces near the university, the prison, the cocaleros' union, and the nearby residential area where I made my home. Beyond the central area lie, to the south, the sprawling working-class market known as the Cancha; to the east, the Hospital Clínico Viedma and San Simón University; and to the north, the Recoleta and Cala Cala, the nearest zones of middle- and upper-class apartments. A modest high-rise midtown has grown up along the linear garden of the Prado, a park lined with banks, corporate offices, and luxury hotels.

These spaces are icons of the Garden City model for Cochabamba, which emphasizes public spaces—plazas in each residential neighborhood, tree-lined boulevards, and linear parks flanking irrigation canals—across the metropolis.[6] However, these plans were executed only in the center and north of the city, where, writes Carmen Ledo García, residents "have all the services and are provided with green and open spaces," housing is optimal, and the well-off population lives in "areas that have the most benevolent living and working conditions."[7] Daniel Goldstein highlights a sharp class division between residents of the actually existing Garden City and poorer neighborhoods of the urban periphery, where canals and urban greenery (along with public utilities of all kinds) are sparse at best. Seen from the elite's perspective, the problem is the poorer residents themselves: "The migrant settlers of the periphery are a threat and an affront, intruders on Cochabamba's urban landscape, thieves of public land and destroyers of urban rationality."[8] It was these outsiders, of course, who were at the forefront of a new era of political mobilization in the twenty-first century.

During those ten months I observed thirty marches, nearly all of which began or ended here at the central square. Protests about wages, gasoline subsidies, transit fares, retirement protections, a polluting dump, and a highway threatening deforestation rose and fell in waves. Behind the walls of the Fabriles' headquarters, or in a dozen other meeting sites across town, organizers and representatives met to plan these mobilizations. Their supporters converged here, made their demands, gauged their strength, and pledged new means of pressure. When they swelled in number, their leaders climbed the stairs inside the Fabriles' headquarters, took megaphone in hand, and asked the crowd to escalate their protest actions. When their adversaries in government could not accept either their demands or their interruptions, they sent the police to clear the protesters from the spaces they had claimed. Sometimes, unable to win this contest, these official adversaries gave in, conceded to the protesters' demands, and recognized their legitimacy. On rare occasions officials have conceded their offices as well.

When he was Bolivia's newly elected president, Carlos Mesa Gisbert came to one such cabildo abierto, gathered in La Paz's Plaza San Francisco, to plead with largely Aymara protesters who were celebrating Goni's recent downfall. Mesa told them: "I know that if you think that I am a bad president, I will not be able to continue. . . . I do not cling to the office of president, because I can only be president so long as I truly serve you. If I serve myself at your expense, you are going to throw me out with one kick . . . so that I am well and truly thrown out. I hope that I may serve you. I hope that I can be the Number One servant of Bolivia and of you."[9] This statement alone is shocking, nearly as shocking as the events that led Mesa's predecessor to resign. What might constitute the kick that Mesa spoke of? If a government falls to an invasion or a coup d'état, the logic is clear enough. It is a kick from the military. Or if a government falls by failing to win reelection, the logic is electoral, the calculus of coalitions and charisma, a kick from the voters. Had the walls of Jericho fallen to a catapult, no rethinking would have been needed, but trumpets prompt deeper reflection. When the form of change is unusual, unexpected, novel, we have to question what the walls are made of and how the trumpets have an impact. Neither ballistics nor political science is enough. These are questions of meaning, of practice, of experience. We have to ask what sovereignty is, what political legitimacy is, and how protests can undermine or create these things. These are anthropological questions, questions of political culture.

This chapter sets the scene and lays the theoretical groundwork for analyzing how mass mobilization can induce revolutionary shifts in politics and race. It first describes how revolution functions as a cultural phenomenon that passes from one society to another and how Bolivians have cultivated particular ways of understanding and strategizing for revolution. The power of efforts to make radical political change is amplified in a country with a history of organizing for revolution, and the meaning of taking over spaces depends greatly on those spaces' role in society. With that foundation laid, we can think about how brief events in which people take over public space have a political impact. At the core of my approach is analyzing how protest tactics interact with the meanings that are already present in urban spaces. Protests use these tactics not just to seize urban spaces but to advance far-reaching claims about democracy, collective ownership, racial equality, and the right to choose their political destiny.

## Revolution as a Cultural Phenomenon

A revolution is a momentous period in which people make history by purposefully changing the political balance of power. Acting as both strategist and historian, Leon Trotsky defined revolutions as "the direct intervention of the masses in historical events. . . . those crucial moments when the old order becomes no longer endurable . . . [and] they break over the barriers excluding them from the political arena, sweep aside their traditional representatives, and create by their own interference the initial groundwork for a new régime."[10]

Scholarly definitions of revolution emphasize the power shifts that accompany these regimes, asking whether a given disruption genuinely changed the balance of power, either by displacing a regime from power while altering the basis for participating in politics (a political revolution) or by altering economic relations—ownership of land and resources, the organization of workplaces, and the distribution of wealth—so as to change the relationship among classes or other major social divisions (a social revolution).[11] Since parties carrying out political revolutions often do so while identifying with a subordinated group, they do so with a promise (implicit or explicit) of also delivering a social revolution. Taken together, these concepts supply a definition of revolution that combines grassroots action, ideological vision, new political actors, and changes in the social order.

At the heart of revolution stand events: people act in ways that are outside normal channels, and the organization of society changes. Both are surprising: rules of action are broken, and so too are the expectations of how society functions. And yet this is not so surprising as it once was. The word *revolution* names this pattern of change, makes it an element of our political vocabulary, and gives us familiarity with the unexpected. Douglas McAdam and William Sewell argue that, beginning in the late eighteenth century, the concept of revolution has served as a "master template" for social transformations. In conceptual terms revolution was a novel "and potent category . . . for political action . . . that governments all over the world have had to worry about ever since." While a source of fear for established powers, the concept inspired "a new category of political actors— . . . 'revolutionaries'—who dedicated their lives to the making of revolutions."[12] The revolution as template has a viral existence, replicating because one revolution demonstrates another is possible, spreading through imitation, and changing forms through multiple mutations.[13]

To say that revolution is a template for action is another way of saying that revolution is a cultural phenomenon, one that owes its existence to the same kinds of societal agreements that make other social constructions into social facts. The template of revolution is a collective understanding that elevates certain conflictive events—armed rebellions, urban insurrections, peasant wars, and, more recently, prolonged mass protests—to lasting historical significance, and through that collective understanding particular collective actions stand in for the sovereign populace.

Bolivia's long history of revolutions means that an unusual amount of the country's political life is understood in revolutionary terms. Whether they summon the heritage of indigenous uprisings or the anticolonial independence struggle, the 1952 Revolution, or radical class struggle, politicians and grassroots political actors often ground their claims on revolutionary foundations. These struggles are part of a local and transnational political conversation in which revolutionaries self-consciously strategize which path that the next revolution will take. Before explaining the way this study looks at events, I need to consider the major frameworks put forward by Bolivia's revolutionaries themselves.

## Revolutionary Identities and Ideologies in Bolivia

Nearly every weekday during my time in Cochabamba, activists gathered around a four-sided information panel near the center of the Plaza 14 de Septiembre. The sides of the panel are covered with paper, most of it fresh newspaper articles from the previous week, selectively clipped and then heavily commented upon. Annotations and highlights, celebrations and mocking jeers claim much of the white space on the newsprint and crowd out the photographs. A leader in the on-paper discussion writes in thick marker, inevitably skewering the wealthy and right-wing and celebrating local traditions as anticolonial victories. Quechua mixes into the Spanish, and written laughter (*JAJAJAJA*) intrudes on multisyllabic polemic. Layers of newsprint build up, taped or tacked over by event announcements and the ephemera of rising social movements. Around this metal V of grassroots political commentary and organizing aspirations,

## Box 4: Was There a Revolution in Bolivia in the Early Twenty-First Century?

Ever since the dramatic events of early twenty-first-century Bolivia began, people have debated whether those events really were really revolutionary. Numerous early descriptions of the Bolivian upheaval said yes (from *The Economist* to the radical historian of Bolivia James Dunkerley), while several more recent accounts emphasize the limited, illusory, even fraudulent nature of the political changes wrought in the first fifteen years of the twenty-first century. Six years passed between President Gonzalo Sánchez de Lozada's sudden flight from the country and the formal installation of the Plurinational State under a new constitution on February 7, 2009. If the ouster of two presidents by waves of blockades, marches, and hunger strikes put the word *revolution* into conversation, the peaceful election of Evo Morales in 2005 and the legalistic maneuvering of the Constituent Assembly of 2006 and 2007 made Bolivia's process of change seem less fundamentally disruptive. Analysts of the period and of the Morales administration have questioned whether the new government ushered in a fundamental, and therefore revolutionary, change in economic life or the inclusion of Bolivia's indigenous plurality. Again, enthusiasm tended to precede disappointment in these analyses. In 2017 Pablo Mamani Ramírez wrote, "Only in its discourse is [Bolivia] a country in transformation." Rather, "the project of the plurinational State has become a reality of a neocolonial State, given that the transformations [proposed] by the Indian or indigenous movements did not take place."[14]

The three aspects of revolution laid out here—extraparliamentary intervention of the excluded masses, transformation of the political system, and reordering of economic relations—allow us to get a handle on these divergent views. The intervention of the public in political life was extraordinary and massive. On the other hand, political and economic transformations have been significant but well below those imagined in 2006.[15] Social movements demanded radical change along three fundamental axes: a leftist challenge to capitalism, a plurinationalist challenge to colonial hierarchies of culture and race, and an ethnoecological critique of a distanced and destructive relationship with nature. During its early years the Morales government was able to openly embrace the more radical versions of these visions, particularly in the lengthy constitutional text, presidential discourse, and international diplomacy. (And many social scientists took these official words for reality. It was, after all, shocking to hear such words from heads of state or to find them embodied in new government institutions.) The government's practice, however, has been to limit these aspirations, offering indigenous participation but limited territorial rights, social democratic redistribution tempered by macroeconomic stability, and embracing both nationalized resource revenues and large-scale capitalism.[16] With each passing year, it becomes more difficult to call this combination either socialist or plurinational. Instead it increasingly resembles the populist and nationalist agenda of the mid-twentieth-century Revolutionary Nationalist Movement (Movimiento Nacionalista Revolucionario).[17]

This book emphasizes the first aspect of revolution: a process rather than a product. Revolution is not simply the transformation of the state but an interruption of the conventional ways people act politically. Unofficial and unauthorized assemblies displace formal representative institutions. Without disregarding presidents, legislatures, and policy, this book tells the story of how political change is demanded, insisted upon, and enacted from the streets. It also narrates the tensions that emerged between parts of the Bolivian grassroots Left and the Evo Morales government as their visions diverged. As those tensions accumulated, mass participation in disruptive protest remained the mechanism through which the government and its critics battled about the direction of the country. That contest has been far from one-sided: protests have forced the Morales government to reverse course on significant issues, as I discuss in chapter 7. One lasting change in Bolivian political culture is the normalization of disruptive protest as a critical means of political participation.

For what it's worth, this kind of debate is not new. In fact, nearly every revolution has been subjected to it, starting with the three revolutions—French, American, and Haitian—at the birth of the modern concept of revolution. The most seemingly transformative revolutions have been plagued by crackdowns on revolutionary comrades, installation of new dictatorships, continuities in inequitable institutions, and even restorations of earlier systems of rule. The very same revolutions have also seeded new principles of legitimacy, elevated new political actors to the political stage, and propelled ideologies never before associated with governmental office into global conversations. Their long-term impact depends less on the first set of leaders they installed than on the traditions they instilled and the generations of subsequent revolutionaries they inspire. In a half century will we remember Bolivia's upheaval as a revolution and, more so, as one that changed Latin American politics? As Chinese premier Zhou Enlai infamously said of the French Revolution, it's still too soon to tell.[18]

pockets of people gather to read and debate. Alone or in pairs, vendors sit, selling political literature and striking up conversations.

"The Water War was like a political school for many youth of my age," María Eugenia ("Mauge") Flores Castro told me. "My activism was born in 2000." Together with four other youths, she formed Red Tinku, the collective that ten years later still erects the bulletin board in the same plaza (*tinku* is Quechua for encounter or a ritual fight; the Spanish word *red* means network). Red Tinku also continued its monthly *k'oa*, an evening of traditional festivities—burning coca-leaf offerings and sharing the fermented corn beverage chicha—that build activists' camaraderie. By 2016 Flores Castro had become an active force on her neighborhood's council. Among the youth of this generation was Marcelo ("Banderas") Rojas, whose life was changed by his first major protest during the Water War and who would become the president of the workers' union at the municipal water company. At time of the Water War, Eliana Quiñones Guzmán had been working with multiple political collectives, including those of students at the public university, punk-loving youth, and factory workers. A decade later both Quiñones Guzmán and Flores Castro had become significant voices within the anarchist-feminist collective Las Imillas (Aymara for girls but reclaimed by the group because it is used as a condescending slur against visibly indigenous adult women). Marcela Olivera, who took on a key role in communicating the Water War's progress to the outside world, dedicated the next decade to connecting antiprivatization struggles, in part as coordinator of the Red VIDA, the Inter-American Network for the Defense and Right to Water.

For Quiñones Guzmán, like many Bolivians, indigeneity is not separate from politics. It describes a kind of culture, connected to ancestral traditions, dissidence from present power structures, and in an intimate relation with the land.[19] "I identify as a daughter of this land," she tells me. "I have the inheritance of a wise people, an ancestral people, of a millennium-spanning people, a harmonious people. . . . Through these inheritances come my principles, including recovering this identity."[20] Many of the urban grassroots activists I encountered are inspired by indigenous movements and actively translate the visions of indigenous movements to urban contexts. Ángel Hurtado, a former miner who was displaced to Cochabamba's Zona Sur at the height of privatization of the mines, is one such champion of indigenous political and cultural revival. He sees the collective work that built his neighborhood, Barrio Primero de Mayo, from the ground up as rooted in the decision-making structures and values of Quechua-Aymara communal life. Once a devout Marxist-Leninist, he now speaks of restoring indigenous values as the paramount political act: recovering, recuperating, and "returning to practice" the values that constitute a way of life. Remembering his father's stories of nineteenth-century indigenous resistance, he said, "I came to recall that solidarity, for example, is called *ayni* here, right? It's called *ayni* in our culture and in the Aymara culture as well."[21] The collective work that built his communities' roads, water system, and political organizations embodied for Hurtado a cultural logic more powerful than his previous political orientation because "everyday we practice it in our lives, we Quechuas and Aymaras." "We have discovered this," he said, "in everyday struggles, in living, in the assemblies."[22]

Bolivian activists draw on a rich revolutionary tradition arising from seeds planted by generations of struggle and passed on through both families and movements. Rojas, who accompanied his uncles to his first protest, knew to bring a bandana (as protection and disguise) and ended up throwing himself into the fray as soon as tear gas fell on the crowd. Quiñones Guzmán grew up politicized, following in the footsteps of her grandfather, who was part of the Popular Assembly that interrupted the rightward trend of military dictatorships during the 1969–71 political opening. "Within my family, they always inculcated the struggle for justice within me," she said.[23]

Revolution has become a Bolivian tradition. Newly successful disruptive protest both prompted and justified no fewer than four regimes in Bolivia: military socialism (in 1936), the Nationalist Revolution (in 1952), the restoration of representative democracy (in 1979 and 1982); and the Plurinational State (in 2003–2009).[24] These governments have orchestrated dramatic public moments, replete with crowds and ceremony, to acknowledge the movements that intervened in politics and to connect new state officials or policies to those movements (see table A1 in the appendix). In these handoffs from street to state each side recognizes and reinforces the other's legitimacy. For eight decades this history of legitimate revolution has created precedents for the right of grassroots actors to disrupt the established order.

The tradition of revolutionary struggle helps many Bolivians define who they are, shaping worldviews and guiding political aspirations. Politically active Bolivians claim with pride adjectives like *combativa* and *luchadora* (literally fighting, brave, tenacious) and situate themselves strategically through imported and homegrown political ideologies. More often than not, these claims are made collectively: an individual proclaims him- or herself *de origen humilde* (of humble origin) but also part of *un sector combativa* (a combative sector of workers) or *un pueblo luchadora* (a fighting people).[25] Asked to name her class identity, Quiñones Guzmán paused, then said, *"La clase luchadora."* Laughing, she continued, "The class that works, the class that proposes, the humble class. I feel myself a part of the working people. And I am of this class, of the people."[26] More than sociological categories, class and racial identities undergird and represent many Bolivians' conscious involvement in political action.

Grassroots leftists build their politics on comprehensive organization in dense sectoral organizations as well as traditional rural community structures. The union structure is widely replicated, federating school and neighborhood councils and rural community unions into city and nationwide networks. Sian Lazar describes a central role for both union and communal systems of organization, which merge in "a kind of political syncretism" in Katarismo, El Alto urban movements, and the Movement Toward Socialism—Political Instrument for the Sovereignty of the Peoples (MAS–IPSP).[27] All these forces can be mobilized into collective actions, principally strikes—the suspension of work—but also in joint labor directed toward social conflict, from blockading urban space to supplying basic needs. All their disruptive actions create a break from normal arrangements of economic life that can be resolved only when the state, employers, or other powerful entities agree to concessions. Conventional understandings allow *sindicatos* (unions) to sanction their members for nonparticipation and provide exemption from criminal laws for certain actions during collective conflict. That is, sindicatos are treated as part of the political mechanism of collective representation. While they organize conflict, union and civic associations are also a conduit for resources and projects from the state and for demands from constituents.[28]

Historically the Bolivian grassroots Left has embraced three broad visions for how grassroots organizations can alter the direction of the state: rural indigenous uprisings, labor syndicalism, and a revolutionary political party that leads an armed uprising. The current generation of activists is working toward a fourth model built around the coordinated application of strikes and blockades in both rural and urban spaces as a tool for exercising power from below.

Rural indigenous visions of rebellion comprise the oldest tradition of revolt in Bolivia. Through the crucible of conflict, campesinos developed ethical positions grounded in both native peoples' original sovereignty and in the legal system of the state.[29] In the long history of rural revolt in Bolivia, campesinos repeatedly took up arms in pursuit of legal claims to rights and property.[30] Indigenous uprisings were also linked to a deeper historical memory of colonialism and violent resistance to it. On occasion these revolts dared to herald the restoration of an indigenous political order, but even when they did not go so far, they authorized autonomous violence by Indian communities against the state and local elites.[31] Ethnic militancy lives on in celebrations of Túpaj Katari, Bartolina Sisa, Zarate Willka, and the language of siege and rebellion, all of which urban as well as rural indigenous movements embrace.[32]

The Bolivian labor movement, a product of rigorous organizing in the first half of the twentieth century, joined with the Revolutionary Nationalist Movement (Movimiento Nacionalista Revolucionario, or MNR) during the 1952 Revolution. Labor's participation was led by the highly active and politically radical Union Federation of Mining Workers of Bolivia (Federación Sindical de Trabajadores Mineros de Bolivia, or FSTMB), which embraced the need for the working class to back a national revolution in its 1946 Thesis of Pulacayo. In Trotskyist terms this was a "bourgeois democratic" revolution in which a cross-class alliance seized state power, destroyed feudalism in the fields and oligarchical control of the mines, expanded the rights of the majority, and redirected the economy. To complete the vision, workers alone would then have to lead a socialist revolution. The miners saw themselves as providers of political orientation to the working class, making the revolution possible.[33] The mining leader Juan Lechín headed the new overarching labor confederation, the Bolivian Workers' Central union confederation (Central Obrera Boliviana, or COB) after the 1952 Revolution, and the first chair in its leadership has been reserved for a miner ever since.

Just six years after the revolution, the miners found themselves disillusioned by the MNR's many rightward shifts. Adopting the text proposed by Guillermo Lora, another Trotskyist, the FSTMB put forward an independent political position under which "unions ought not to make themselves the agents of any party, even if that party is in power and calls itself revolutionary." Within the unions "the most diverse tendencies" could coexist "with the sole condition that they are inspired by revolutionary principles."[34] These ideals, labeled classist (*clasista*), kept the COB firmly committed to independent action, even during sympathetic administrations in 1969–71 and 1982–85, and continued to guide the organization's position up to the current period (see chapter 7).

One can understand the long history of Bolivian social movements as a story of the repeated alliances and falling outs of indigenous rebellion and oppositional political projects within urban and mestizo/creole society. (Forrest Hylton and Sinclair Thomson offer just such a narrative in their book

*Revolutionary Horizons*, while Brooke Larson and Laura Gotkowitz offer histories of indigenous engagement with liberal and military socialist projects.)[35] Leftist and campesino movements came together practically and theoretically in the first decades of the twentieth century, combining a strong leftist opposition to the servitude of indigenous peasants and the recasting of rural revolts in the language of syndicalism. In the late 1960s a new generation—primarily the urban-educated children of Aymara campesinos—formulated the position of Katarismo. Katarismo placed rural organizers in a tradition of anticolonial resistance that reached back beyond the colonial era to an Inca social order understood as free and autonomous. A prophecy of this repetition of history was seen in the legendary dying words of Katari (ca. 1750–81): "I die, but I will come back as millions." Kataristas proposed syndicalist and communal self-organization of rural indigenous peoples, independent of the existing political parties and based on their own political traditions.[36] In the 1973 Tiwanaku Manifesto, Kataristas declared independence from the MNR, which it blamed for co-opting the struggle of indigenous peoples. Like workers' classism, Katarismo emphasized autonomy, although with an on indigenous culture: "It would be best for us campesinos if governments and political parties were to leave us to elect our own leaders freely and democratically so that we could formulate our own socioeconomic policy inspired by our own cultural roots." In parallel to the workers' movement, Kataristas saw the indigenous campesinos as a focal point for the coming together of many social groups: "Miners, factory workers, building workers, transport workers, the impoverished middle classes, all are our brothers, victims in different ways of the same exploitation."[37] In their rhetoric and outlook the Kataristas envisioned a pluralistic grassroots Left that was conscious of both race and class.[38]

These positions dovetailed with a rise in autonomist Marxism and, later, popular anarchism across Latin America.[39] Propelled by pessimistic reflections on the Soviet Union and Sendero Luminoso in Peru, and optimistic inspiration from the Zapatistas in Mexico and the Movimento Sem Terra in Brazil, many leftists in Bolivia engaged in a general rethinking of the primacy of state power, the centrality of formal wage labor to the working class, and the interaction of class and racial oppression.[40] Raquel Gutiérrez Aguilar—who lamented the Soviet experience as "a work of ordering [society] apparently distinct [from capitalism] but at the same time, in reality, scandalously similar"—is representative of this rethinking.[41] A Mexican national inspired by the insurgencies of Central America, Gutiérrez Aguilar threw herself into Bolivian struggles, eventually taking part in the Altiplano-based Túpaj Katari Guerrilla Army alongside Álvaro García Linera, who became Morales's vice president.[42] Gutiérrez Aguilar's militancy evolved through a stint in a Bolivian jail, participation in the Cochabamba Water War, and writing a chronicle of recent Bolivian history. She interprets Marx's call for the destruction of the state "as its real abolition [*anulación*], its nonutilization, which is only possible through the energy deployed by communities exercising self-determination."[43] Filemón Escóbar, once a communist activist in the mines and co-founder of the MAS–IPSP, recentered his perspective from class to colonial suppression of Andean lifeways.[44]

The Comuna group of intellectuals in La Paz brought together public intellectuals, including Raúl Prada Alcoreza, Luis Tapia, García Linera, and Gutiérrez Aguilar, all of whom sought to understand the independent power of grassroots forces. They made themselves researchers of the self-determination of which Gutiérrez Aguilar spoke, although they regarded the path to its realization in different ways. Across Latin America, social movement practices of assemblies and the rejection of formal hierarchies within grassroots movements have become a hallmark of antineoliberal organizing. The organizational structure pioneered in Cochabamba's Water War reflects these horizontal relations, and its activists took part in continent-wide conversations that made this way of organizing into a model.

Running somewhat counter to these state-skeptical lines of thought was the articulation of a "political instrument" for social movements to intervene in politics. Rural and campesino grassroots confederations used this term to mark as different from a political party the organization they were building, even as it was capable of assuming a representative role in state institutions.[45] The instrument was established in 1995, and the faction led by Evo Morales became the MAS-IPSP in January 1999. Alongside the remnant Assembly for the Sovereignty of the Peoples and Felipe Quispe Huanca's Pachakuti Indigenous Movement, the MAS–IPSP represented an extraordinary indigenous intervention in conventional politics. Since its 2005 electoral victory, it has worked to gain electoral dominance by rapidly expanding into every Bolivian municipality. This makes for a patchwork organization within which the ideal of the party's subordination to social movements competes with local political celebrity and loyalty to the national leadership as organizing principles. García Linera took the office of vice president with a promise of keeping the national party accountable to grassroots movements, but he has left autonomism behind to become an advocate of a strong Jacobin, or Leninist, national leadership and the formation of party cadre. When movement-state fractures arise—as I explore in chapter 7—critics from a variety of revolutionary traditions trade polemics with progovernment forces urging a strong state and a unified party.

## Revolution and the Ethnography of Events

If revolution is a cultural phenomenon, anthropologists—specialists in studying culture—have something unique to contribute to understanding how revolutions operate. And yet, as Bjørn Thomassen observed in 2012, "Anthropologists have, with a very few exceptions . . . generally refrained from studying actual political revolutionary events as ethnographic cases, and consequently they have also left comparison of the processes involved to political scientists."[46] June Nash's work on Bolivia's militant mine workers exemplifies how ethnographers instead offered insights into the daily lives and political perspectives of actors on their way to (rather than in the midst of) revolutionary upheavals.[47] Perhaps the highest-profile anthropological text on revolution, Eric Wolf's *Peasant Wars of the Twentieth Century*, deployed knowledge of the social position and community life of peasants to explain how they had become leading actors in six twentieth-century revolutions. The late twentieth-century fracturing of the international Left and postmodern criticism of grand narratives pushed attention away from revolution as an object of anthropological study. In the decades since, anthropologists have paid more attention to local resistance than to society-wide transformations. Nonetheless, serious examination of resistance, autonomy, the subaltern, and the domains and "weapons of the weak" offer a valuable new perspective. Where structural theories of revolution have often marginalized the rural and indigenous, anthropologists have cultivated an expertise in their life and politics.

Anthropology offers several angles of insight into contemporary political revolution. Anthropologists can contribute knowledge about the cultural construction of politics, the ritualistic nature of revolutionary actions, and the lived experience of revolutionary events. Some early anthropological attempts to theorize revolution saw heady moments of political transformation as akin to ritual or even sociality itself. Émile Durkheim addressed "revolutionary or creative epochs," with the French Revolution as a prime example, as moments of collective effervescence that enable bold action: "Within a crowd moved by a common passion, we become susceptible to feelings and actions of which we are incapable on our own."[48] Victor Turner's exploration of communitas and liminality—during historical social change as well as in socially prescribed rituals—argues that these states constitute "anti-structures" that are dangerous to existing social orders and that have the potential to facilitate their transformation.[49] Edith Turner surveys the history of emotionally intense experiences in violent revolution and nonviolent protest in her elaboration of the concept of communitas.[50] In short, these anthropologists theorized an emotional flexibility, born of common action, as a vital ingredient in revolutionary transformations.

Secrecy, long duration, and danger have historically made revolutions poor sites for ethnography. Recent years, however, have seen numerous major political upheavals that expand quickly, involve enormous numbers of people, and experience relatively limited amounts of armed violence. These characteristics have allowed ethnographers to experience revolutionary changes as they occur and to document dramatic events at a closer distance. Two decades after her work in Bolivian mining communities, June Nash was able to describe the revolutionary visions and activities of Zapatista communities from a closer vantage point.[51] In the twenty-first century, anthropologists have increasingly been at the scene of major upheavals, including Latin American revolts against neoliberalism and regime-unseating protest movements from Argentina to Egypt to Thailand to Ukraine.

A generation ago the political scientist Aristide Zolberg urged his colleagues to pay more serious attention to revolutionary upheavals. He argues that a different logic governs these events than the "'normal' political events" that occupy the discipline's attention but that these events have "lasting political accomplishments that are perhaps made possible only by the suspension of disbelief in the impossible which is characteristic of [these] moments of madness."[52] As in the 1980 strike wave that initiated Poland's Solidarity trade union, the 1955 Montgomery bus boycott, or the 1789 storming of the Bastille, such events can herald the arrival of new political actors, new principles of legitimacy, and new practices of participation. As Doug McAdam and William Sewell observe, "Anyone who has actively participated in a social movement has surely experienced at least one of these moments of concentrated transformation, when dramatic confrontations and feverish activity definitively change the course of the movement's history."[53]

This work on transformative events intersects with the longer tradition of historical anthropology and its limited forays into exploring political revolutions. The historical approach within anthropology has a long lineage but is necessarily in tension with much of cultural anthropology's focus on enduring cultural patterns, roles, rituals, and traditions. When ethnographers began to situate events in political context and trace their impact, they could no longer describe traditional societies as living in a timeless "ethnographic present" in which "the Zulu" of today are the same as they had always been.[54] On the other hand, historically informed ethnography has an advantage over episodic history in that it can draw in longer-term cultural features to understand the significance of historical events.

While events can reveal structures, a more difficult challenge—but one essential to studying revolutionary events—is to understand how they transform these structures. Marshall Sahlins proposed a theory in which surprising events force alterations in the meaning of cultural categories. Even so, Sahlins (structuralist that he is) insists that the overall cultural schema endures, orienting how people understand the changed world.[55] The historian William Sewell takes up and adapts this framework to describe the genuine ideological and material transformations that constitute revolutionary change. He uses the example of the French Revolution to articulate a model of how brief events relate to large-scale political transformations.[56] I draw upon this model to interpret revolutionary events in Bolivia in recent decades.

In the tangible events that make these revolutions possible, many other human-scale, experiential, and cultural features beyond emotion and communitas are extremely consequential. As Thomassen argues, "Anthropologists might have quite a lot to say about exactly those 'big events,' those extraordinary moments or situations where existing power configurations crumble and collapse in brief and drastic events."[57] In this investigation, as I study the takeover and use of public space, I devote close attention to anthropological elements of life: embodied experience, the significance of place, everyday urban stratification, and practices used by social movements.

## Space Claiming as a Theoretical Construct

On April 5, 2000, an idea took shape in the crowd gathered in Cochabamba's main square. Worried that attendance was flagging, the leading organizers, affiliated with the Coordinadora in Defense of Water and Life, had proposed giving the government a deadline of twenty-four hours to restore municipal ownership of the local water company. "It was to gain another day to see what we could do the next day," recalled Marcela Olivera, who was on the Fabriles' balcony with her brother, spokesman Oscar Olivera, and other organizers. But people below, among the campesinos, had another idea: "If the government doesn't throw out the transnational [corporation], we will go and take over the water company." That idea caught the imagination of the five thousand Cochabambinos assembled there. "And the people said, no, let's go and take over the water company *right now*," Marcela Olivera continued. "And so it was that, shouting, the people left to take it over. . . . Everyone who had been on the balcony had to go down running, and going along behind the people."[58]

When they finally got to the main headquarters—a walled-off block encompassing a small office building, treatment plants, pumping equipment, utility trucks, and a house-sized union office situated above Circumvalación Avenue and overlooking the city from the north—everyone had gone. The police presence, which was minimal throughout Cochabamba on those first two days of mobilization (in an attempt to avoid energizing the movement with scenes of confrontation), was nil. The crowd pulled open the doors to the head office, flooded in, and then "the same people said, 'No. Come out, come out!' And they shut the door. They said," Marcela Olivera remembered, "'We aren't going to break anything because this is ours. This doesn't belong to that foreign company; it is ours.'" Balanced precariously atop a chain-link fence, a young man spray-painted AGUAS DEL PUEBLO (The people's water) on the treatment plant sign. Through these acts members of the Cochabamban public asserted a daring claim about public ownership of the utility. Through further actions that same week, they would compel the government to recognize that claim and offer the Coordinadora a role in managing the water company.

This ephemeral but iconic action is one example of what I call "space-claiming protest." Through occupations of plazas and roads, sit-ins, road blockades, public assemblies, and other measures, space-claiming protesters physically control or symbolically claim urban space. A related form of space claiming, also analyzed in this book, is the legally authorized use, reappropriation, and redesigning of spaces belonging to the state.

As a theoretical construct, space claiming brings together two parts—tactics of collective action and meanings of public spaces—and looks at the consequences of their interaction. The argument I develop in this book responds to Charles Tilly's call for research on how and why spaces and places matter to the meaning and efficacy of collective political struggle.[59] By taking over the streets of urban centers, blockading interprovincial roadways, and occupying symbolically important spaces, indigenous and grassroots protesters have disrupted economic flows, seized the political stage, and transgressed the racial norms that informally regulate urban space. Simultaneously hundreds of thousands of Bolivians engaged in collective experiences of organization, disruptive action, demand making, talking politics, and meeting their daily needs while sharing physical space. Their space-claiming actions communicate meaning and exercise practical control.

Space-claiming protests are political tools with real consequences. Just as the takeover of Aguas del Tunari presaged its return to public ownership, a 2005 blockade in Sucre physically, then politically, prevented the hardline, right-wing Senate president from succeeding to the presidency (see chapter 4, "2005: Intervening in Succession"). Three years later a vigil surrounding the National Congress was the final stage in a campaign to demand a referendum on Bolivia's plurinational constitution (see page 187). How are we to understand these events and their remarkable efficacy?

These acts of space claiming are at once communicative, symbolic, and tactical. They put forward a claim to sovereign power while physically taking over spaces associated with governing (but not the apparatus of government).[60] Their means, while often combative, cannot be reduced to the mere seizure and retention of desired spaces; rather, they claim space to express meaning. They use forceful means but rely on political legitimacy rather than superiority in violence to make their adversaries retreat. As such, these space-claiming protests are conceptually adjacent to protest spectacles and street theater, to armed insurrection, and to long-term occupations that take over factories or occupy land for use. I describe these actions as adjacent, rather than contrasting, to emphasize that my project is not about creating categorical divisions. Indeed recent extensions of these concepts—insurrections "of a new type," direct-action protest—offer reasonable ways to think about the same events.[61] However, I advance the concept of space claiming because only by looking at the relation between protest tactics and meaning-laden spaces can we understand the extraordinary political impact of recent Bolivian protest.

## Spaces That Are Meaningful: Power, Race, Commerce

Space claiming can transform society because the social order is enacted through the spaces of public life, and it must be continually reenacted in order to remain the same. Both political life and everyday inequalities are organized and enacted through particular spaces, the uses that are made of them, and the expectations that are imposed upon the people who enter them. The feminist geographer Doreen Massey insists on the socially constructed nature of space, describing it as a repository of cultural meaning rather than a passive arena for frictionless movement. "Space," she writes, "is by its very nature full of power and symbolism, a complex web of relations of domination and subordination, of solidarity and co-operation."[62] Equally, Massey calls for exploring and documenting the "spatial construction of society," the ways in which interactions in space define social roles and positions.[63]

In this study I consider spaces as full of meaning and analyze how social movements use those meanings in efforts to remake their society. Social movements that act spatially can use the power and symbolism that has accumulated in certain spaces or they can interrupt the reproduction of social inequalities by enacting different social relations in space. I look for these meanings and interruptions of space in three domains of life: governance, race, and commerce. Urban spaces are marked by the roles, routines, and meanings of both the government and the prevailing racial hierarchy. I call these separate relationships between space and state politics and between space and racial difference the "political geography" of the city and the "racial geography" of the city, respectively. (Chapters 3 and 4 focus on political power and authority, while chapters 5 and 6 center on racial power and marginalization.) In addition, I consider the streets and infrastructural corridors that run within and between cities as logistical spaces that are vital to commerce.

Governance takes place in particular spaces. Those used most frequently, that are most connected to other sites, become central nodes in political life. Bruno Latour's work reminds us that every space, even a president's office or the New York Stock Exchange, is local.[64] Yet, as nodes, some spaces are layered with multiple connections that allow actions in these politically significant localities to have real and profound consequences in many other localities. Certain spaces "can become at once local and national spaces for the construction, mediation, and regulation of social identities."[65] In normal times a state draws up its own rules for participation in political life—from voting eligibility to parliamentary rules of order—and designs spaces around these routines. In that context the physical spaces of government can seem like passive arenas in which the political system just happens to take place. However, when a parliament building is surrounded until a bill is passed or when a vote for the expulsion of a corporation takes place on a public square, the relations among political participation, social decision making, and tangible spaces are thrown off their usual path. To understand these unauthorized interventions into politics, we have to rethink how politically important spaces can be claimed and used by means that go beyond the established channels.

Public spaces accommodate the circulation and presence of people crossing all lines of identity in society. Theorists of the public sphere have portrayed public spaces as arenas of civic equality, grounding this idea in the presence of diverse individuals and presumed freedom of movement. However, just as liberal accounts of universal citizenship have been called into question for their various exclusions, numerous studies of public spaces show how interactions within them are raced, gendered, and classed. As Susan Ruddick observes, these "interactions in and through public space are crucial to the formation and maintenance of social identities."[66]

Across Spanish America, Spain ruled its territories through institutions that Angel Rama called the "lettered city": "A convergence of different forms of written administration: lawmaking, religious doctrine, missionization, land demarcation, and education." Members of the lettered city were trained in universities, schools, and monasteries; performed their organizing labor in courts and archives; and displayed their wealth in ostentatious public and private buildings in and around the plaza.[67] In urban public spaces the rules of labor service, obligations of employees, and conventions of decorum conspired to require deference from racial subordinates. Governing spaces allowed indigenous people to enter as builders, servants, and attendants but excluded them from self-representation, much less defining the rules of the political game.

The racially exclusive tradition of governance in the lettered city suggests an equivalence of power geography and racial geography. Such an equivalence can be found in the colonial cityscape as envisioned by Fanon in *The Wretched of the Earth*, "a world divided in two" and characterized by "mutual exclusion," "a world compartmentalized, Manichaean, and petrified," where colonist and powerful, and native and powerless appear as synonyms.[68] In Bolivia, too, ownership of urban space has long been attached to creole (and, later, mestizo) identity, while indigenous peoples have been associated with rural areas. This stark vision echoes in the daily lives of contemporary Bolivians who feel excluded from the city and the state, in the rhetoric of ethnically militant activists, and in significant scholarly treatments of recent conflicts.[69]

Yet when we treat state power, class, and race as interchangeable, we lose the ability to perceive transformations in their relationship, even as we gain insight about the emotional impact of a world so divided. Even where geographies of power and race are identical, separating them conceptually can aid our understanding. It explains, for example, how participation in governance requires miming or performing the dominant racial identity, a world in which indigenous entrants wear white masks. Dividing politics from race also allows us to reconsider how spaces of governance are racialized and how the meanings of spaces shift as people act to claim them. The political and racial geography of Bolivia continues to shift under the influence of numerous factors, including governance, political stratification, labor, and commercial life.

This book explores deliberate attempts to use the meanings embodied in urban spaces to redefine who has access to power. Charles Tilly draws attention to "established and meaningful itineraries for public displays of force"—that is, sites and routes of protest that use the meanings embedded in public space as amplifiers of the power of mass movements.[70] Protesters return again and again to spaces that symbolize established power—London's Whitehall, New York's Wall Street, La Paz's Plaza Murillo. The memory of past protest, too, becomes layered into the meaning of spaces, making certain streets—Cairo's Tahrir, Washington's Reflecting Pool, and La Paz's Plaza San Francisco—emblematic of grassroots power. In their collective movement protesters also establish regular pathways—Tilly's itineraries of protest—to convey their power inward, like a tide that surges upon the metaphorical and literal defenses of established power.

Finally, many public spaces are logistical spaces: streets and highways, bus terminals and airports, pipelines and waterworks all contain commercially vital flows. Alongside its political role as part of the public sphere, the street is fundamentally an arena for movement. Work depends on the arrival of workers, while commerce depends on circulation of goods. In Bolivia the mechanics of the general strike has shifted from the mass withdrawal of organized labor to the interruption of these flows. When this happens, the tactical actions of strikers—who are actually marchers, blockaders, parkers of buses, and, yes, striking teachers, transit drivers, and factory workers—encounter the physical spaces of the roadways and interrupt logistical flows. Through these interruptions the vital importance of the street for the commerce of city, the economic health of the nation, and the course of politics suddenly comes into focus. The continuation of normal economic life, of complete school years, and of daily meals is shown to depend on making these flows—particularly of fuel, food, and laborers—resume. Commercial trade and global investment flows—which advocates of globalization tell us are boundless forces of connection—actually require control and operation of very specific spaces and technologies. As Neil

Smith argues, the most global of systems all have local vulnerabilities.[71] At those sites the seemingly larger scales of regional economies, national governance (or ungovernability), and international trade and investment are made and unmade.

## Street Sovereignty: From Disruption to Revolution

Power and authority over a given domain—such as the government's power over the economy—imply the ability to maintain its normal operations. When Bolivians began to make practical decisions on the streets about whether cities would be allowed to function, they shifted the place where decision making happens. When protests brought tens of thousands of working, indigenous, and poor people into central urban spaces to talk about their future, they broke old patterns of exclusion. Through many such actions the grassroots Left began to redefine "the people" to whom the country's democracy belongs and created new spaces for collectively deliberating and exercising power. They turned city streets into spaces of sovereignty.

If a movement has demonstrated a broad popular mandate and practical sovereignty, but the government is unwilling to yield to the movement's demands, we have a situation of fundamental uncertainty about who is in charge, about whose is the truly sovereign voice. Revolutionary change becomes possible when there is a crisis of authority and a viable alternative claims practical control and political legitimacy. To understand this we must look at these actions both in tactical and experiential terms (How do they displace the state from exercising control?) and in terms of their social significance (How do they come to represent the popular will?).

William Sewell considers this process at length in his study of the French Revolution. He argues that "remarkable collective creativity" deployed in "a time when political structures were massively dislocated" allowed a relatively small set of actions—like the storming of the Bastille—to politically redefine national life.[72] Three elements of his analysis are relevant to contemporary Bolivian politics as well as to the country's longer tradition of revolution. First, cultural transformation both creates and depends upon practical possibilities for political change. The introduction of new tactics is one form of this transformation. Another is the breakthrough ability of social actors to evade controls on their political action or to exert new control over space. In either case the preexisting street-level routine is interrupted in a way that shifts the balance from established power to those who defy it. In contemporary Bolivia the central (but not only) tactical breakthrough is the ability of rural and periurban residents, and of metropolitan coalitions, to paralyze economic life through civic strikes, which I describe in chapter 3.

Second, protests become revolutions only when the society at large accepts that local, short-term, embodied events genuinely represent wider social forces. As the taking of the Bastille began to have its historic impact, protagonists of the French Revolution described "an episode of urban popular violence as an act of the sovereign will, and hence a legitimate basis for a new form of government."[73] Of course, equating street actors with state sovereignty violates the traditional distinction between the "disorder" of subordinate masses and the "politics" of established actors. Yet the more that revolutions happen, the easier it becomes for movements, their state adversaries, and the public to interpret disruptive actions as legitimate. Revolution is the everyday name for outsiders claiming the state's right to rule. Mass participation in these events is laden with significance, involves innovation and flux, and elicits heightened emotion. The sense of remaking history comes at the intersection of uncertainty in the structures of power and powerful feelings of creativity, communitas, risk, and overcoming boundaries that I will explore in detail in chapters 4 and 5.

Between disruptive moments of protest and major political changes, then, lies a process of practical action and meaning making. This book argues that movements gain their political traction through the way their actions interact with spaces. For those making revolution, space-claiming protest is where the rubber meets the road. By locating their mass assemblies in the central space of governance, Bolivian protest participants have modeled a realignment of the political system that places social movements, community organizations, and politically and racially excluded groups at the center of civic and political life. At their height mass protests have an ability to affect daily life and to claim political legitimacy for their choices that rivals the state, unbalancing the existing political order. Beyond these brief enactments of self-rule lie "political horizons" of autonomy, variously envisioned around the working class, Qullasuyu, indigenous villages and cities, and regional formations.[74] New governments secure their legitimacy by claiming to represent these new movements and to continue this revolutionary legacy.

## CHAPTER 2

# "This, This Is How We Have to All Fight Together"

*The Water War as Precedent and Prototype*

> *We came out of our homes and our communities to speak among ourselves, to get to know one another, to learn anew how to trust one another. We have occupied the streets because we are their true owners. . . . For us, the working people of the city and the country-side, this is the authentic meaning of democracy: We risk our lives to carry out what we ourselves proposed, what we consider just. Democracy is the sovereignty of the people, and that is what we have done.*
>
> —COMMUNIQUÉ FROM THE COORDINADORA
> IN DEFENSE OF WATER AND LIFE

Before he became a neighborhood leader in Cochabamba's Zona Sur, Ángel Hurtado was once a "relocated miner"—that is, he had been laid off from the state mining company COMIBOL as a result of neoliberal shock therapy policies. The Siglo XX mine in Llallagua Municipality, Potosí, where Hurtado worked, was the stronghold of Bolivia's highly politicized mine workers described by June Nash in *We Eat the Mines and the Mines Eat Us*. And in turn, the Union Federation of Mining Workers of Bolivia was the vanguard of Bolivia's labor movement. Mine workers endured government massacres from the 1920s to the 1970s and were the anchor of the Bolivian Workers Central in the early 1980s. The dictatorship finally fell in 1982 after an avalanche of strikes that included a thirty-four-day strike by miners. In the class-conscious and radical mining towns various leftist factions competed for adherents while cooperating in strikes and labor organizing. As a young man Hurtado had affiliated with a Maoist communist party and aspired to take part in a revolution through armed struggle.

Supreme Decree 21060 of August 1985 changed all that. President Víctor Paz Estenssoro had tapped then-senator Gonzalo Sánchez de Lozada to draft an emergency economic program. The Harvard economist Jeffrey Sachs accepted an invitation from Hugo Banzer Suarez, a former dictator and the frontrunner in the 1985 presidential election, to come to La Paz and draft a plan to reverse hyperinflation. Sánchez de Lozada had a bigger vision: "'It's one thing to stop hyperinflation, but this country needs a complete overhaul,'" Sachs remembered he had said.[1] The president had urged that multiple measures be implemented right away and quoted Machiavelli when he spoke to the task force that was drafting the decree: "Do bad things all at once, and do good things little by little."[2] Jeffrey Sachs and other neoliberal economists called this approach shock therapy—"a rapid, comprehensive, and far-reaching set of reforms to implement 'normal' capitalism"—and offered it as medicine to state-centered economies for the next quarter century.[3]

Sánchez de Lozada's "complete overhaul" went far beyond ending hyperinflation. The decree sharply devalued the currency, raised commodity prices, and froze public sector wages. It also shuttered government-owned smelting and transport businesses and began massive layoffs across the state sector.[4] While wages were frozen, the government slashed subsidized pricing of fuel and food; real wages dipped by over 30 percent and would remain stagnant for the next eight years.[5] Twenty-three thousand of COMIBOL's thirty thousand miners lost their jobs. Looking back, Hurtado recalls, "The Miners' Federation had been the strongest organization in Bolivia, which could change and propose policies. [But] beginning with [Supreme Decree] 21060, we, the miners, disappeared as an organization in Bolivia. All of us went away in all directions, to La Paz, to Santa Cruz, to Cochabamba, to everywhere in the end."[6] The displacements of Hurtado's generation remade Cochabamba, which exploded with migrants from Potosí, Oruro, and La Paz. New neighborhoods, partially constructed by their residents, fanned across former farmland and climbed the dusty hills of the Zona Sur.[7] They steadily rose up the slopes into the Tunari National Park to the north. The industrial center of Quillacollo (to the west), town of Sacaba, and green and idyllic Tiquipaya all swelled until their urban streets intertwined. The seven-municipality metropolitan region counted 1,141,094 residents in 2012. On the Avenida Blanco Galindo, the Avenida Petrolera, and the highway through Sacaba to the Chapare, the spines that connect the metropolis no longer have breaks between the cities but flow through a seamless corridor of neighborhoods, roadside restaurants, fuel stations, factories, and miscellaneous enterprises.

Hurtado and some other highly politicized miners ended up in a part of Zona Sur's District 8. The neighborhood was then called Eduardo Avaroa, after the home province of its first residents, campesino migrants from Potosí. The influx of relocated miners was so influential, however, that the neighborhood was renamed in honor of the martyrs of International Workers' Day, May 1.

In 1989 eighty families living in Barrio Primero de Mayo formed a water committee, a local collective that built and owned a well, to supply water to affiliated families. As in most neighborhoods in the Zona Sur, municipal water service was absent. Such water committees are made up of everyone who has a faucet and a meter, and all have "the right to speak and to vote, and the right to take on leadership positions."[8] The water committee met in assemblies, organized collective labor, assessed dues, and built its collective infrastructure. But it wasn't a union and it didn't go on strike—yet.

"There was no strong organization," Hurtado recalled. "From 1985 to 1995, more or less, there was no organization on the political scene that could face

FIGURE 6   Brick and cement homes extend up a hillside in Barrio Primero de Mayo, in District 9 of the Zona Sur, Cochabamba.

down neoliberalism, understand? There was none." Still, he saw a role for relocated revolutionaries like himself. "We, the miners, distributed in different places, we were able to reorient [the people] in a revolutionary process in Bolivia."[9] Another famous union, Cochabamba's Departmental Federation of Factory Workers, the Fabriles, had also lost much of its mobilizing power. Workers without contracts or salaries outnumbered those with centralized worksites and union cards. General strikes were unable to turn back the tide. But prompted in part by their own identity as the vanguard of the working class, the Fabriles became ardent networkers and eventually co-founded the Coordinadora [Coordinator] in Defense of Water and Life.

From October 1999 to April 2000, the Coordinadora led an urban uprising in Cochabamba against the privatization of water provision by the foreign-owned Aguas del Tunari corporation. "It was such a mobilization," the Zona Sur community leader Christian Mamani told me as we sat outside during the tenth anniversary commemoration of the Water War, "[one] of nearly six months of preparation, march after march, blockade, and in the end a war was unleashed."[10] What began with small demonstrations on the plaza escalated to "one hundred thousand people who were in streets and ready to do anything."[11]

When organizing for the Water War began, the neighborhoods of the Zona Sur (many of them beyond the water grid) unexpectedly became a core force in the citywide struggle. Large-scale assemblies at the district level backed the campaign against water privatization. Long-used organizational forms like neighborhood and district assemblies became rallying places for participation. Water committees reoriented themselves to all-out pressure campaigns, blockading outlying roads and traveling daily into the city center to join in street battles in the central blocks of downtown. Hurtado spoke of Primero de Mayo's mobilization for the Water War with pride, like a father might speak of a long-awaited child:

> We [in our neighborhood] have such a quantity of vehicles, of microbuses, around forty. And from here the neighbors went down [to the city center to fight in the Water War] in one line. They were setting off dynamite, it was fearsome. And the people watched—because those from this sector, those born here, the Cochabambans, had never seen this class of mobilization. And since we, the miners, are of a revolutionary character and have always been fighters. That is what we have induced here in Cochabamba.

In downtown Cochabamba the demonstrators from Primero de Mayo mingled and collaborated with factory workers, teachers, middle-class residents, cocaleros, and campesinos. They sent delegates to assemblies at the Fabriles Federation on the central square and debated their next moves in cabildos (mass meetings) below its balcony.[12] Activists hung a giant red banner on the front of the building, declaring, EL AGUA ES NUESTRA, ¡¡CARAJO!! (The Water Is Ours, Damn It!). Their protests became street battles and then, finally, a different kind of strike, one that put the city as whole on strike against the state. In April marches, a civic strike, the symbolic taking of key locations, and street barricades paralyzed the city. The government tried and failed to bring the city under control by deploying riot police and imposing a state of emergency. In the end the government sat down with representatives of the Coordinadora and agreed to expel Aguas del Tunari from Bolivia altogether.

Cochabamba's Water War was the first major event in Bolivia's early twenty-first-century grassroots upsurge. Ten years later Mamani recalled the city government's capitulation as a point of "rejoicing, because in some way we had established a precedent that all of us united together could mark out our own

FIGURE 7 Speakers address a cabildo from the balcony of the Fabriles building in the Plaza 14 de Septiembre during the Water War. (Photo by Thomas Kruse from the collection of the Coordinadora)

destiny, we could decide."[13] Overlapping with mobilizations in Seattle against the World Trade Organization, and in Washington, D.C., against the World Bank, the Water War was also one of the most direct and successful confrontations in an emerging worldwide challenge to the power of transnational corporations.[14] It set a number of strategic precedents for future mobilizations: the vulnerability of neoliberal policies to grassroots opposition, the power of urban-rural alliances, and a new collective attitude in its signature slogan: "The Water Is Ours." The tactics activists used in Cochabamba would quickly become the tool kit for mobilization nationwide.

## The Privatization and the Resistance

While named after the imposing local mountain that looms north of Cochabamba, Aguas del Tunari's ownership of the municipal water supplier had put the region's water into foreign hands. It was a custom-crafted corporate entity, the majority (55 percent) owned by International Water Ltd., a subsidiary of the privately owned U.S. construction firm Bechtel, with the remainder held by the Spanish corporation Abengoa and politically well-connected Bolivian investors.[15] The corporation, which was formally established on August 28, signed a forty-year contract to take over and operate Cochabamba's municipal water system (Servicio Municipal de Agua Potable y Alcantarillado de Cochabamba, or SEMAPA) on September 3, 1999. Under the terms of the deal Aguas del Tunari was guaranteed a sizable return on its investment and was obliged to invest in long-sought-after improvements to the city's water infrastructure, including the signature Misicuni dam project.[16] On October 29 Hugo Banzer promulgated the Potable Water and Sewage Service Law, which permitted the privatization of water provision and sanitation. The corporation, privatization contract, and law fit together hand in glove. Within the neoliberal policy vision, this fit was intended: the state was turning assets over to the private sector in exchange for new foreign dollars. Foreign investment, Cochabambans were promised, would remedy the utility's inability to provide water to half the city's population. However, the investors did not have to provide the money for improvements themselves. The law permitted them to raise this investment capital directly from their customers by freely raising water prices. The law also stipulated that any privately constructed well in the concession area—including those built by the water committees—could be privatized and metered.

The privatization aroused opposition from several quarters. Traditional rural users of irrigation water—organized as the Cochabamba Departmental Federation of Irrigation Users (Federación Departamental Cochabambina de Regantes, hereafter, the Regantes)—feared losing their informally recognized rights or having to pay fees that might drive them into bankruptcy. Engineers, lawyers, and economists raised concerns about rising water prices through the recently formed Defense Committee of Water and the Family Economy (Comité para la Defensa del Agua y la Economía Familiar).[17] Protesters demanded both the cancellation of Aguas del Tunari's contract and the repeal of Law 2029. The law had put years of work by both the neighborhood water committees of the urban outskirts and the Regantes at risk. Then Aguas del Tunari slapped higher charges on ratepayers, setting off price increases that quickly became known as the *tarifazo*. This rate hike generated broad-based opposition in the urban core and even in the wealthier districts on the north side of the city.

At the September signing ceremony for the Aguas del Tunari water concession contract, Banzer dismissed the noisy protests outside, declaring, "I am accustomed to that background music."[18] (Banzer, elected in 1997, had been military dictator from 1971 to 1978.) From that day's demonstration to the April denouement, the campaigners behind the Water War gradually found ways to make their voices and actions impossible for the national government to ignore. Through four waves of actions, when protest overshadowed all other daily activities in the city, opponents built to a crescendo of mobilization that paralyzed the city and forced the government's hand. At the heart of this process were two organizational forms: the metropolitan-scale strike, carried out through large numbers of road blockades, and the Coordinadora, which was a novel form of organization. In different ways, each became the embodiment of popular rejection of privatization.

The Coordinadora for the Defense of Water and Life was founded at a November 12 assembly, initially convened by the Regantes, the Fabriles, and the Defense Committee of Water and the Family Economy. At its formation a steering committee representing the most influential sectors was chosen: Oscar Olivera, executive of the Fabriles and longtime Manaco shoe factory worker, became president of the Coordinadora; Omar Fernández, the Regantes leader, was named vice president; and Gabriel Herbas became general secretary.[19] These titles quickly became somewhat honorary, and the trio presented themselves more as spokesmen than leaders. The Coordinadora initially comprised some twenty associations but grew to forty-five by December 18, including unions of peasants and of urban workers, the Chapare coca growers, provincial civic committees, water committees, and irrigation associations.[20]

Together these organized forces formed the skeleton of a larger mass mobilization involving thousands who participated as outraged individuals or who made connections and took on regular roles only once they were in the streets. Activists made the Plaza 14 de Septiembre into a new space for public discussion. Ratepayers concerned about the size of their bills simply came to the Fabriles office to connect with the Coordinadora. The office became "a privileged space for meeting and taking decisions" and "a space where the people could go to converse with people from other sectors and, above all, where everyone did so in a totally informal manner during moments of intense social confrontation," wrote Raquel Gutiérrez Aguilar.[21]

Gutiérrez Aguilar, who was a member of the Coordinadora's technical team, described it as a hybrid organization that "oscillates among" different levels of coordination. Mass meetings, or cabildos abiertos, held in the plaza were both the movement's highest decision-making body and the gauge of its popular support. These coexisted with assemblies of affiliated organizations and "the more or less permanent meeting of several representatives who are in charge of carrying on daily activities and maintaining the Coordinadora's function of facilitating popular unity and mobilization."[22] Marcela Olivera, a researcher on labor conditions who volunteered in the Coordinadora's outreach and communications efforts, remembers this fluidity as essential to the movement's success: "There were various levels of organization, but it was a mix of all of them. And at times the Coordinadora was—like in April, you see—a hundred thousand people in the plaza, and at times it was Oscar Olivera [her brother] sending faxes from his office, right? . . . And I believe that this breadth, and this flexibility of the organization, was also what made it so what could be done was done, and what was achieved came to pass."

The Coordinadora's most powerful weapon was a civic strike: simultaneous rural and urban blockades, as well as battles for control of the city center that brought daily life to a halt. The form of the strike itself and the open structure of Coordinadora meetings effectively bound everyone together in a single effort. To win, the Coordinadora had to wield mass pressure, establish its legitimacy, gain a seat at the bargaining table, and convince the government to completely reverse the privatization. The moment of mass pressure involved blockades and other disruptive actions to win the annulling of the contract.[23] The moment of legitimacy consisted of convening assemblies, cabildos, and holding an unofficial referendum, or *consulta popular*, to register public opposition to water policies. Like Oaxaca's 2006 Popular Assembly movement, the neighborhood assemblies of Argentina after 2001, and other open assembly-based forms of protest, the Coordinadora raised basic questions about what democracy truly is. While pressure and legitimacy represent two distinct moments of the mobilization, they worked in tandem, like two legs walking: road blockades organized across the city and the surrounding region built up into an overwhelming civic strike, while marches flowed together into the large-scale meetings (cabildos) often held in the central plaza. The civic strike was the cabildo's operative arm, its means of exerting pressure, and the cabildo was the strike's brains and voice, its place of decision and its source of legitimacy. Without either, the Coordinadora and the Water War it fought would have come to naught. In chapters 3 and 4, I analyze how each of these capacities function, whereas this chapter explains how they worked in tandem.

## Concerted Pressure Through Blockades

The Water War featured three major battles—that is, episodes of concentrated activity designed to interrupt daily life in the city and secure the movement's demands. Like more conventional strikes, these civic strikes deployed economic pressure to initiate and win negotiations. The mobilizations of January 11–13, 2000, convinced the government to join the Civic Committee and the Coordinadora at the bargaining table to negotiate each clause of the Aguas del Tunari contract and Law 2029 as well as on the fee schedule. The government also conceded that water committees and the Regantes would maintain control of their water facilities and the water apportioned to them by *usos y costumbres* (traditional rights to resources and forms of self-governance), respectively. However, the privatization itself and the rate increase remained in effect.

The February 4–5 mobilization was promoted well in advance by the Coordinadora as the "takeover of Cochabamba." The organization's spokesmen were at pains to describe their plans as peaceful, reading the very word as a metaphor for democratic power.[24] Recounting their rhetoric in writing, Coordinadora spokesman Oscar Olivera recalled: "We said we were coming to take what is ours—the main plaza—to take it over physically and in a peaceful way. We were coming to take each other by the hand—workers in the city and in the countryside—and we were coming to take our own decisions. That is why we called it *la toma* (the takeover)."[25] However, even a symbolic takeover aroused fears of racial insubordination and rebellion. The government sent seven hundred troops and threatened a state of siege, while Civic Committee urged the Coordinadora to call off its mobilization.[26]

On the morning of Friday, February 4, hundreds of Cochabamba-based police and the Special Security Group, a riot squad, from La Paz (Grupo Especial de Seguridad, popularly known as the *dálmatas,* Dalmatians, for their black-and-white camouflage) attempted to stop the takeover. Thousands of rural protesters advanced toward the main square from the four corners of the city, fanning out to directly confront police at hastily built barricades across downtown. Protesters clashed throughout downtown with police forces using tear gas and rubber bullets. A few protesters paused to spray-paint NO MORE GASSING. BLOOD FLOWS. 4 FEBRUARY 2000 (*No más gasificación. Sangre corre. 4-II-00*) on a wall three blocks west of the plaza. (A variety of these spray-painted memoranda of defiance remained visible in downtown Cochabamba a decade later.) The daylong street battles lasted through Friday and Saturday. At the end of the first day Coordinadora representatives met in the Plaza Colón and issued demands for an end to repression. After spending a day on the sidelines both the Civic Committee and the Departmental Federation of Neighborhood Councils closed ranks with the Coordinadora and joined the pressure campaign in the streets.[27] The state's defense of the plaza ended at 11:30 p.m. on the second day.[28] Following a substantial expenditure on crowd-control munitions, and facing dissent over tactics from the police, the government agreed to a stopgap measure: the rate hike would be suspended pending negotiations on both the privatization contract and Law 2029 among the government, the Civic Committee, and the Coordinadora.

In mid-March, acting alone, the Civic Committee reached a preliminary deal with the government to suspend the tarifazo, which would instead be phased in gradually beginning in December. Coordinadora activists refused to accept this framework and organized a novel response to show the public was on their side. They prepared a grassroots referendum (consulta popular) so Cochabambans could vote on the Coordinadora's principal demands.[29] Coordinadora activists set up about 150 voting precincts on Sunday, March 26, and collected the votes of 48,276 people. This "represented 10 percent of the population of Cochabamba and was equivalent to 31 percent of the votes in the December 1999 municipal election."[30] More than 46,000 voters repudiated Law 2029, the privatization contract, and the rate increase.

With these votes as justification, the Coordinadora pushed for making the water utility public property once again. On March 30, 2000, the Coordinadora's general assembly passed a resolution calling for an all-out pressure campaign:

1. To decree an INDEFINITE GENERAL BLOCKADE of the department and of the city, beginning 6:00 a.m. on Tuesday, April 4, 2000.
2. This gigantic mobilization of Cochabambans will be named THE FINAL BATTLE BECAUSE WATER AND LIFE CONTINUE TO BE OURS.
3. This blockade will be realized in the provinces with road blockades and in the city with the blockading of streets, avenues, and bridges, in each neighborhood and in each house.[31]

The April mobilization started out with fewer than five thousand participants, but gradually gained adherents and density throughout the city. Blockades became ubiquitous, while protesters mobilized to sites of negotiation and properties of the water utility. In a counterproductive move the government arrested the Coordinadora's negotiating team late on April 6 and declared a state of emergency (*estado de sitio*) on April 7. On April 8 a new wave of protesters defied a new ban on demonstrations, seized the central plaza, and began to establish barricades to keep it. Street battles raged even after the military fired live ammunition at protesters, wounding at least seventeen civilians, one of them fatally.[32] The next day the Bolivian government revoked the contract with Aguas del Tunari. The crowds gathered in a cabildo in the square were not easily convinced of this concession and waited until April 10 to lift citywide blockades. In the end the Coordinadora was able to press not only its overarching demands but also for a role in redesigning SEMAPA's directorate in ways it hoped would be more responsive to community representation.

Two parts of the story of the Water War deserve separate attention: the tactics protesters used and the way the Coordinadora edged its way into the role of speaking for the city and the region. I turn to these now.

## Street Battles, Property Destruction, and Symbolic Attacks

In the course of the mobilization, many Cochabambans engaged in what I call unarmed militancy: the use of forceful, combative tactics—such as barricades, property destruction, hands-on pushes, and thrown projectiles—to serve symbolic, tactical, and strategic goals.[33] On many days of the Water War physical confrontations occurred nearly everywhere, with thousands of stones, fireworks, and other objects thrown at the police in street battles. Thousands more stones, boulders, sections of rebar, tree limbs, and tires (sometimes set alight) were brought into the streets to make them impassible or to serve as protective barricades for protests. When the confrontations reached a feverish pace on February 4 and 5, war was the obvious metaphor. The mainstream daily newspaper, *Los Tiempos*, described the city as "an immense battlefield in which police repression had no limits."[34] The Coordinadora was quick to claim these battles as its own. After taking the plaza on the night of February 5, activists wrote a communiqué that merged tactical and political elements in a single thread of action: "Stones have defeated the gases and the rubber bullets! The dignity of the citizens has defeated the cowardice of the mediocre and corrupt government functionaries! . . . Cochabambans, the blood that has been shed, the efforts that have been carried out, the gases and rubber bullets that have been endured and resisted have been worth the effort. We have won another battle, and there is hope, there is a future, there is life."[35] While some of these words are militaristic, the Coordinadora also maintained a qualitative distinction between its force and that used by the government. The same communiqué denounced the state's threatened massacre and celebrated the people who "have managed to stop it."

Not infrequently protesters also directed their stones against the façades of hated institutions. However, taking over those buildings—which began to occur on April 5—represented an escalation. On that day enthusiastic militants led the charge and assaulted the doors of the Civic Committee on the Plaza Colón as well as the entryway and sign at Aguas del Tunari headquarters and purification plant in the El Temporal neighborhood. The physical actions at the water company's headquarters—a half-dozen protesters hanging on and ripping down the sign, scores pulling open the gate, and hundreds rushing in, with one masked protester repainting a wooden AGUAS DEL TUNARI sign with AGUAS DEL PUEBLO—became some of the most resonant images of the conflict. Yet these were neither attempts at general destruction nor efforts to hold an ongoing occupation.

In the days that followed, government moves—the arrest of the Coordinadora's leadership, attempts to seize the plaza, announcement of a curfew, and a state of siege—drove escalating confrontations. Protesters dragged construction equipment, doors, and tiles into the street to reinforce their barricades and protect themselves from police bullets. According to the Permanent Assembly of Human Rights, a teenage bystander was shot dead by a sharpshooter, and twenty-one protesters suffered bullet wounds.[36] The same day protesters attacked and burned parts of the Corporación de Desarrollo de Cochabamba as well as buildings belonging to police and military units, destroying large parts of the Grupo Especial de Seguridad's riot squad building, and windows and office equipment at the Departmental Police Command. A crowd even took over the ground floor of the army's Seventh Brigade headquarters. These combative actions served two ends, demonstrating the incapacity of police to control the situation and inflicting symbolic harm on hated institutions.

## Who Speaks for Cochabamba?

Interwoven with these moments of mobilization was the Coordinadora's campaign to be recognized as the voice of Cochabambans in the water dispute. More established voices—the Civic Committee of Cochabamba and Mayor Manfred Reyes Villa—already claimed that right. They had institutional clout and legality on their side, whereas the Coordinadora was a new actor on the political stage. Still, the Coordinadora did have some advantages in this, namely, that its radical demands could resolve the many problems caused by the difficult-to-alter water concession contract and the political harm suffered by the mayor and the Civic Committee after the Coordinadora exposed their involvement in approving that contract. The critical factor, however, was street mobilization. What made the Coordinadora a force to be reckoned with was its power to convene mass resistance in the streets.

Each of the major cities in Bolivia has a civic committee, composed of prominent figures from commercial interests and civic organizations.[37] Edgar Montaño, president of the Civic Committee in Cochabamba until the late 1999 municipal elections, followed a conventional path from heading the organization to serving as a member of the city council and later as mayor. Manfred Reyes Villa, founder of the New Republican Force Party (Nueva Fuerza Republicana), was in his third term as mayor and had built an impressive political machine. Some of the neighborhood councils were among the local organizations involved in the mayor's political patronage network. Reyes Villa was fond of grandiose public works—from the branching ramps and bridges that systematize road traffic into central Cochabamba to the Cristo de la Concordia statue that overlooks the city—and embraced the construction of a water and electric power-supplying dam on the Misicuni River as a priority. The dam project, and the unmet water needs it promised to fulfill, became the raison d'être for water privatization in Cochabamba.

From its formation in November, the Coordinadora disputed the authority of the Civic Committee to represent Cochabambans. On January 10, for example, the Coordinadora called for a cabildo that would declare both Reyes Villa and Montaño "enemies of Cochabamba" and "derecognize [desconocer] the Civic Committee as a representative body."[38] This challenge pushed the Civic Committee toward stronger protests against the rate hike and to insist that it was the voice of Cochabambans. Popular revulsion at the tarifazo repeatedly drew the Civic Committee into cosponsoring Coordinadora-initiated mobilizations even as the committee sought to distance itself from the grassroots organization. In November and December the Civic Committee shifted to a public stance in opposition to the severe rate hikes for water imposed by Aguas del Tunari and sought to work out a softer or slower adjustment. On January 11 the Committee and Reyes Villa put themselves at the front of the parade and endorsed the first day of the three-day strike called by the Coordinadora. This made the forty-eight hours following midnight on January 12 into a critical test of the Coordinadora's relative mobilizing capacity. With the help of the Regantes and the water committees the strike held, winning the Coordinadora a seat at the bargaining table. Transportation unions, whose loyalties were divided, brought Coordinadora and Civic Committee representatives together and helped foster an accord in which the dueling "representatives of Cochabamba" agreed not to negotiate without one another.

From then on the accumulating weight of mobilization brought an exceptionally broad coalition behind the Coordinadora's negotiating position. On January 23 the centrist daily *Los Tiempos* reported that Reyes Villa and Montaño were among the authorities who had signed the Aguas del Tunari contract, which specifically authorized a rate hike.[39] In rapid succession condominium owners announced the formation of an association and their refusal "to pay even one cent" of the increase; the Chamber of Industry declared itself on alert; and Archbishop Tito Solari attacked the tarifazo as an "anti-popular" measure. The archbishop urged government authorities to put their "eyes, ears, and hearts on the side of the people" and reverse it.[40] These uncharacteristically bold actions by establishment actors were another side of the snowballing tendency to identify Cochabamba, the water conflict, and to some extent the Coordinadora as a single cause.[41] Without this broadly held sense of the situation, the grassroots victory in the conflict would surely have been impossible.

## A Citizens' Union?

The Water War showed that a new kind of metropolitan strike was possible. But what was the nature of this power? If this was a strike, was the Coordinadora its strike committee, its union, or a political subject like the working class itself? Oscar Olivera, coming from a long history of formal unionism, termed the Coordinadora "a kind of citizen union which brings together different social sectors, from the city as well as the countryside," and said it was "like a traditional union . . . but broadened to the whole society."[42] During and after the Water War, it was tempting for participants to understand the mobilization as embodying the city itself. After all, backed by tens of thousands of demonstrators, the Coordinadora had in fact been negotiating on behalf of the metropolis as a whole. Yet this enthusiastic perspective was not a clear-eyed analysis. The Coordinadora's central demand was a simple nullification of the laws enabling water privatization. Opposing these laws united the different sectors whose demands were variously around rate hikes, the lack of universal provision of water service, property ownership in collectively built infrastructure, and continued access to water for rural irrigation. Once the contract was broken, the disparate forces—each with its particular element in this set of demands—no longer necessarily gelled as a political alliance.

For proof that the Coordinadora only episodically represented all Cochabambans, one need look no further than the issue that led to its founding. While inspirational, its organization of the days of the Water War and the substitution of its power for governmental control did not last beyond the agreement that made its principal demands into law. The still-dismal state of water provision in periurban Cochabamba has not generated a citywide mobilization since the Water War. Middle-class and wealthy neighborhoods get water from SEMAPA without the threat of a sudden price hike, while poorer citizens across town pay five times as much to have their communal cisterns filled. The public is well aware of the failures of SEMAPA's water provision, the need for resources to improve water committees' infrastructure, and environmental threats to Cochabamba's water supplies, but they are no longer equally affected by these problems. The most dramatic activism has come from residents who live near the K'ara K'ara municipal dump, which contaminates their communal water sources. An alliance called Yaku Pacha, which includes organizations led by Christian Mamani and Maria Rita Bautista, organized scores of actions in an attempt to enforce judicial rulings that the dump be closed to further waste and rehabilitated to prevent pollution. While the alliance has blockaded the dump (creating citywide garbage crises) and even built a ring of garbage-laden blockades around downtown, it has not been able to draw the rest of the city into a new civic strike. While the moment of the strike may be illuminating as to preexisting capacities for organization, it is also a moment of choosing sides that may or may not reflect moderates' level of commitment to transformative politics.[43] Coordinated mobilization and felt solidarity on this scale are the exception, not the rule.

## Lasting Memories of the Water War

The Water War assumed an international profile when it was still in motion, and the spotlight it cast upon Cochabamba still connects the town with many people far beyond Bolivia's borders. The privatization contract seemed to connect all the concerns of neoliberalism's critics: corporate control, the commercialization of an essential common resource, and disadvantaging the poor. Coming just months after the Seattle protests against the World Trade Organization and days before similar protests against the World Bank in Washington, D.C., the Cochabamba victory over privatization became an overnight cause célèbre of the global justice movement.

The experience of the Water War generated a variety of collectives and spurred many of its participants to lasting participation in grassroots politics. The activists who maintained a bulletin board on panels in the plaza became Red Tinku, a cultural-political collective that regularly hosts activist events and still forms a nucleus for public political conversations around its panels in the plaza. The anarcha-feminist collective Las Imillas gained much of its membership from Water War veterans. The Coordinadora continued to meet in spaces offered by the Fabriles, and its structure was emulated in national efforts. It spun off the Fundación Abril (the April Foundation), dedicated to stopping and rolling back water privatization around the world.

Protagonists of the Water War held two separate gatherings to commemorate its tenth anniversary. On a Sunday afternoon—April 11, 2010, ten years to

FIGURE 8 Dozens of water committees march to celebrate the tenth anniversary of victory in the Cochabamba Water War.

the day from the government's capitulation to grassroots demands—President Evo Morales presided over a lengthy ceremony at the Federation of Campesinos of Cochabamba, heavily attended by cocaleros, campesinos, and Regantes. In his speech Morales argued that the events of 1999 and 2000 were just the beginning of a "permanent uprising" to "do away with a pro-imperialist, pro-capitalist state."[44] "The struggle was not in vain," he declared, because the human right to water is now guaranteed by the constitution. It is not only on anniversaries that MAS-IPSP luminaries celebrate the Water War; it has a prominent place in the party's narrative of recent history and is mentioned in the preamble to the 2009 constitution. Vice President Álvaro García Linera termed it the beginning of "the first phase of the revolutionary epoch."[45] The Morales administration fashions itself the torchbearer of the grassroots movement for common resources and against privatization.

Four days after that ceremony water activists within the city organized a less-celebratory and more critical commemoration. As if to signify that the time for protest had not yet passed, they marched through the streets of Cochabamba, beginning at the Plaza 14 de Septiembre. Thousands of Cochabambans and about two hundred international visitors paraded from downtown to the Fabriles' sporting complex, 2.5 kilometers west of downtown. Most marched behind the banners of dozens of water committees and associations that provide water service to about one fifth of Cochabambans, organized on a neighborhood-by-neighborhood basis.[46] They were joined by the Bolivian Forum on Environment and Development (Foro Boliviano sobre Medio Ambiente y Desarrollo), a delegation of Fabriles, and organizers for public water ownership and environmental causes from across the Americas. The march, led by a re-created EL AGUA ES NUESTRA ¡¡CARAJO!! banner, was peppered with flags celebrating 10 YEARS OF STRUGGLE and cardboard spigots demanding WATER TO THE ZONA SUR.

Speakers from four continents talked about the inspiration that the Cochabamba Water War provided for their movements. In a ceremony opening the event, each poured a small vial of water from their homeland into a common vessel. So began the inauguration of the Third International Water Fair, an alternately practical and political teach-in on how to operate a local water system and how to organize communities and cities against privatization and environmental threats. Three sides of a soccer field were surrounded by tents showcasing the work of water committees, complete with handmade scale models of their neighborhoods and the self-financed and often improvised machinery they use to supply water. Nowadays, when the water committee members dream of the future, they do so outside of SEMAPA. An association of the committees called ASICA-SUR is engaged in running trucks with water to supply committees that have no water source, maintaining water quality standards, facilitating new committees, and planning for universal access. For Water Fair organizers like Oscar Olivera, self-reliant community organizations are the only real alternative to privatization, and the democratic promise of multitudes in Cochabamba's streets a decade ago cannot be realized through political parties like the MAS–IPSP.

*También la Lluvia*, a feature film set during the Water War, premiered in Bolivian theaters in mid-March 2011, a late but glittering entry to the parade of tenth anniversary remembrances. It introduces the Water War through the eyes of Spanish filmmakers who enlist indigenous Bolivian extras (residents of the Zona Sur of Cochabamba and Yuracaré people to the northeast) to film the story of Columbus's landing in the Caribbean. Seeking a low-cost production setting for an anticolonial feature film, they are drawn into a colonial story of the present, where Bolivian politicians and police defend the corporation that has privatized "even the rain" of a largely Indian city. The filmmakers, played by Gael García Bernal and Luis Tosar, watch with a combination of paternalistic frustration, horror, and (belatedly) respect and admiration as their local star (played by the Aymara actor Juan Carlos Aduviri) takes time away from performing as Taino leader Hatuey to rally his community against privatization. *También la Lluvia* premiered twice in Cochabamba, once at an outdoor projection in the Zona Sur and once with a commercial screening at the upscale CineCenter on the Rocha River. In a cab from that theater to my apartment in central Cochabamba, I chatted with my driver about the film and the Water War that had inspired it. In 1999 he had been a shop vendor on the plaza that had been thronged with protesters and clouded with tear gas. "It was a lovely beginning," he said of the upheaval, "but now it is having the worst conclusion." At the time he spoke the Morales government was at the nadir of its popularity in the wake of the December 2010 Gasolinazo (its decision to eliminate fuel price subsidies) and the brief but costly inflationary spiral that followed.

My driver's was not the only melancholy memory of the Water War. Ángel Hurtado also speaks of disillusionment and frustration when his community's sacrifice is remembered: "These days we see with much disappointment that we have not achieved anything. We don't have water. Neither the national government nor the departmental government, much less the mayor's office, can solve our problem; no one."[47] The public utility SEMAPA, on whose board Hurtado briefly served as a public representative, has been plagued by mismanagement, failure to invest in major expansion, and internal corruption.[48] The municipal water service provides water to only about half the city's burgeoning population. Instead of the renewed public investment his neighbors had hoped for, Hurtado's neighborhood was forced to manage an increasingly scarce resource, cutting back from continuous water provision to a few hours each week when residents can fill their household tanks. Still, this seasoned activist sees the Water War as the beginning of a transformative political struggle for "an indigenous government that we have put in power." This new political order and the continuing tangible reality remain poles apart, he says: "The fighting has served to change the political system, but there are still no concrete solutions to the matter of water."[49]

Nonetheless, the Water War became the paradigmatic example a new kind of metropolitan protest that secured grassroots demands. As the Zona Sur organizer Christian Mamani recalled, "I personally had said: 'This, this is how we have to all fight together.'" With an enthusiasm that would become familiar to me, he began to speak of the effort as an example for the future: "This is the way we must forge links, must defend our interests as a society."[50] To understand the paradigm, however, it is necessary to once again look into its component parts: mass pressure and public legitimacy. In the years that followed, the tactical challenge for participants in major upheavals was to replicate and extend the success of the Water War, but their political challenge was to transform conflicts like the one about water privatization into a fundamental rethinking of democracy in Bolivia. In this the Water War offered a seed for the future but not a blueprint for success. In chapter 3, I take up the functioning of the central tools of the Water War, the tactic of blockading roads and its extension to an urban scale through the civic strike. That chapter examines how blockades are organized and why their interruption of flows, commerce, and normal daily activity proves so persuasive to adversaries in government. At the same time its mass assemblies and popular referendum raised the possibility of an alternative grassroots sovereignty over resources and government decisions. In chapter 4, I consider the process by which disruptive grassroots mobilization interacts with the spatiality of the city to constitute a collective subject capable and worthy of demanding new ways of being represented politically.

## CHAPTER 3

# The Power of Interruption

*From Blockades to Civic Strikes*

> *The worker, contrary to what the government proclaims, never loses with the strike or blockade.*
>
> —ESCUELA DEL PUEBLO PRIMERO DE MAYO, MÉTODOS DE LUCHA

> *The only way that we are heard is this, because we have no other way to speak. . . . If we don't use a coercive method, we achieve nothing.*
>
> —LUBIA VARGAS PADILLA

**N**estled among the other tables at the 2010 Water Fair in Cochabamba sit two young representatives of May 1 People's School (Escuela del Pueblo Primero de Mayo). While members of neighborhood water committees at the other tables explain the pumps, wells, and cisterns that supply water to their communities, these activists are interested in a different kind of mechanics: the organization and exercising of collective pressure like that which won the Water War a decade earlier. One hands me a tiny handbook: *Métodos de Lucha* (Methods of Struggle).[1] In its thirty-two pages I find a palm-sized compendium of the Bolivian repertoire of contention. The various measures described form a toolbox of protest strategies, each of which amplifies the first and most basic: the strike. The manual's fundamental point is that "strikes, work stoppages, meetings, marches, blockades, voluntary fasts and other forms of pressure put the government in check and allow the working sector to secure economic and political victories that would not be reached with mere dialogue." Like any good do-it-yourself guide, it is also filled with cautionary phrases about the misapplication of pressure. Mostly, though, the booklet is stocked with examples showing that when pressure succeeds, "Bolivian history is written on the basis of these measures, some of them heroic."[2]

In the same white-tiled room as the Water Fair, on the ground floor of the Fabriles' sports complex, organizers of the May 1 People's School have gathered a small crowd for a film screening in late April 2010. The People's School is a workers' education collective associated with the Cochabamba Factory Workers' union (the Fabriles). The evening's focus is the 1886 general strike for an eight-hour working day in the United States. Union members, young activists, and workers who are involved in a precarious workers' assembly have come at dusk to watch the story of the May Day mobilization, when 300,000 to 500,000 U.S. workers went on strike. Famously, at least six workers died in clashes during the strike, while four more were sent to the gallows as punishment for a bomb that killed seven police officers.[3] Three years later the American Federation of Labor and the Second International collaborated to hold the first International Workers' Day on May 1, 1890, with the eight-hour day as the principal global demand. The names of both the Fabriles' school and Ángel Hurtado's neighborhood in the Zona Sur recall these general strikes.

In Cochabamba factory workers have historically taken part in many city-wide and nationwide general strikes. Backed by Marxist ideas about the industrial workers as the vanguard of the working class, the Cochabamba Fabriles took a leading role in the 1974 mobilization to protest food prices, the pro-democracy mobilizations of 1978–82, and the 1985 effort to turn back Supreme Decree 21060, the neoliberal economic policy promulgated by President Víctor Paz Estenssoro to combat the country's runaway inflation. Because of their militant history, factory workers expected to literally be at the head of the parade during citywide work stoppages.[4] But the neoliberal era undercut the power of traditional unions.

The first round of neoliberal shock therapy in Bolivia froze factory workers' salaries and introduced "free contracting," or at-will employment, in the sector. Over the years thousands of employees were transferred to subcontractors, increasing wage insecurity and making it harder to hold employers accountable for working conditions. While the number of manufacturing workers in Bolivia climbed from 83,000 in 1986 to 390,000 in 1997, fewer than half worked in shops with more than thirty employees. A third were in small workshops of fewer than five workers.[5] Even though economic growth returned in 1987, wages did not rise. The vast majority of workers, who do not receive formal salaries, saw their median income sink from four times the poverty level in 1985 to less than twice it in 2004.[6] To deal with this situation organizers had to look beyond what Marcela Olivera calls the traditional "mentality of the union leader here, of considering only those who are already organized, those who have a union, of believing that the union card is more important than the people."[7]

So in the 1990s the Fabriles reached out for allies. They built a working relationship with the Chapare cocaleros and offered space for the first office of the Political Instrument for the Sovereignty of the Peoples (later, the MAS-IPSP) in the their downtown headquarters. The Fabriles Federation owns a strategically unique space: the building houses the only grassroots organization located on the plaza. Within it only their Salón Azul is a room large enough for major coalition meetings. No other grassroots institution has this kind of direct access to the plaza, and none of the governmental or church buildings on the square are designed to be in regular relationship with mass crowds. The Water War, and many events that followed, gave the Fabriles' balcony a new purpose at the heart of citywide and regional mobilizations.

A few weeks after the Water War in 2000, May 1 came around again. Hundreds of demonstrators gathered in the south side of downtown at the Plaza San Sebastián and spiraled their way around downtown, ending at the northeast corner of the central plaza. On behalf of a half-dozen unions, the neighborhood committees, the departmental labor federation, and the Coordinadora, they treated International Workers' Day as a time to honor and remember the fallen of Chicago, of generations of struggle in Bolivia, and of the April struggle in Cochabamba.

This memorial was intertwined with hope. The longtime union organizer Oscar Olivera, a spokesman for the movement, celebrated it for breaking a long silence: "We were mute spectators. We watched layoffs and unemployment, the sale and [privatization] of each one of our industries."[8] In the wake of the Coordinadora's victories, many Bolivian activists talked about a new model for struggle. Among them were Raquel Gutiérrez Aguilar and Álvaro García Linera. These two radicals were then struggling with how to reconceptualize revolution. Their attempt, as militants in the Túpaj Katari Guerrilla Army, to start a guerrilla movement in the Altiplano had failed, landing both in jail for several years. They joined the support team for the May 1 People's School in time for the Water War. Suddenly this new coalition was breaking the long impasse. Together with Olivera they synthesized the experience into a political thesis for future organizing.[9] They recognized a "new wave of social regrouping, collective dignity and revitalization of the capacity for mobilization" in defense of "the basic conditions of life . . . such as water, land, housing, public services, gas, oil, electricity."[10] They embraced the desire expressed in the middle of the mobilization to extend assembly-based forms of coordination to the governance of society. "Assemblies of the neighborhood, of the union, of the ayllu, and of the factory," they hoped, would become "a network for deliberating, mobilizing, and managing of public life."[11]

This chapter examines the civic strike (*paro cívico*) as the maximum expression of grassroots pressure, combining the action of workers, urban residents, and rural communities. A revived, direct-action syndicalism operates at the scale of the metropolis or region, interrupting circulation rather than production and seeking greater control of resources and necessities rather than wage gains. This metropolitan multitude acts through the civic strike in the same way unionized workers once acted through a general strike. The same logic has appeared in Venezuela since the 1989 Caracazo, in Ecuador, and in a series of actions in Argentina since 1993. (Earlier, waged and unwaged workers collaborated in civic strikes in Barrancabermeja, Colombia, from 1963 to 1977.)[12]

Like conventional union organizers, participants stage these events in a set sequence: collective organization, striking, escalation, negotiation, and concessions. However, these strikes extend across an entire city, metropolis, region, or nation to address issues occurring at those scales. "Rather than the traditional labor movement," Oscar Olivera wrote, "it was the new world of work that came out into the streets: the unemployed, the self-employed, the young, and the women."[13] These strikes have unwaged workers as key players and make the city or region as a whole into the new ground for class struggle. In so doing they echo visions of "the social factory" or "the multitude" embraced by Italian autonomist Marxists since the 1970s.[14]

Civic strikes combine road blockades, marches, open confrontation of security forces, organizational endorsements of demands, hunger strikes, open public meetings (cabildos), and numerous symbolic actions carried out upon property, persons, and space. Multiple movements collaborate in a series of space-claiming actions, sometimes escalating into a total shutdown of commercial and civic life through coordinated marches, road blockades, enforced closures of businesses, and a general strike. Despite this heterogeneity of actions Bolivians speak of civic strikes as unified objects called either blockades (their most visible form of leverage) or strikes (their organizational form). As they rallied their neighbors to participate, activists called them blockades, peaceful takeovers, the great battle, strikes, or simply mobilization. After the dust settled from the conflicts, they would be remembered as the Water War; the Gas War (or Black October); and the fall of Carlos Mesa Gisbert.[15] Events during the presidency of Evo Morales, such as the 2010 Potosí strike and the Gasolinazo protests (regarding fuel prices) of December 2010 would follow the same pattern. See table 2. Coordinating these actions and agreeing on a process for collective representation poses a series of challenges. Successful mobilization involves both generating effective pressure through these actions (the subject of this chapter) and creating a new collective subject—a "we," a "people"—worthy of representation and capable of negotiating (the subject of the next chapter).

The basic component of large civic strikes is a blockade of a single road, an element of protest that can be set up on its own; it allows protesters to press their claims from a single physical point. In rural areas protesters use physical obstructions—rocks, tree limbs, tires, piles of stones, or constructed barricades—to reinforce a road blockade or to keep a road closed even when no one

TABLE 2  Major recent successful civic strikes

| Date | Conflict | Locations |
|---|---|---|
| November 1999–April 2000 | Water War | C |
| September 2000 | Campesino strike | EA, Altiplano |
| February 2002 | Coca conflict | C, Sacaba, Chapare |
| September–October 2003 | First Gas War | LP, EA, C, S, O, P |
| January 2005 | El Alto Water War | EA |
| May–June 2005 | Second Gas War/fall of Carlos Mesa | LP, EA, C, S, O, P, elsewhere |
| April–May 2006 | Strike demanding development of El Mutún | Puerto Suárez, SC |
| April–May 2010 | Caranavi citrus plant strike | Caranavi, Alto Beni |
| July–August 2010 | Potosí regional strike | P, Potosí dept |
| December 2010 | Gasolinazo protests | LP, EA, C, S, O, P, SC, elsewhere |
| January–May 2011 | Labor strike wave | LP, EA, C, S, O, P, SC |
| September–October 2011 | TIPNIS solidarity strike wave | LP, C, S, O, P, T, SC, Beni dept |
| February–March 2013 | Oruro airport naming strike | O, Huanuni |
| December 2017–January 2018 | Rollback of penal code | LP, EA, C, S, O, P, SC |

*Note*: In the location column major departmental capital cities (Cochabamba, La Paz, Oruro, Potosí, Santa Cruz, Sucre, Tarija) and El Alto are identified by initials. TIPNIS stands for the Isiboro-Sécure National Park and Indigenous Territory.

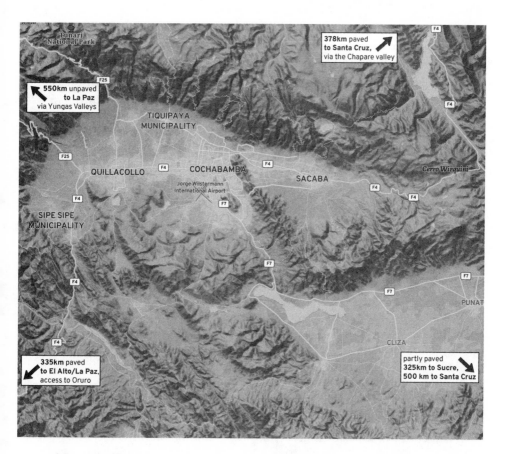

MAP 4  Cochabamba's limited road connections. (Map prepared by Carwil Bjork-James. © Mapbox, © OpenStreetMap)

is around. These blockades can cut off cities, including the capital, from vital supplies of food or fuel. By interrupting the movement of troops, they can alter the outcome of state repression. During the April 2000 Water War in Cochabamba, and a series of El Alto mobilizations from 2000 to 2003, these techniques were brought to the cities and deployed in a way that made state control impossible and that put the state's power in question. When such seemingly modest and local acts are multiplied and coordinated into a larger effort, they can paralyze commerce in a way that is similar to a conventional general strike.

Whether accomplished by simply sitting down in the street, dragging in boulders and tree limbs, or coordinating crowds of thousands to take over key thoroughfares, road blockades bring a sudden urgency to political protest. By blocking the circulation of people and goods, they ensure that the impacts of protest ripple across an entire region. In the next part of this chapter I show how extended blockades impact the economy and the state, forcing the government to negotiate and make concessions. The economic consequences are sufficient to compel a government response, but the political meaning of widespread strikes is equally important. The cooperation of multiple social sectors in a joint mobilization can pose a major political challenge, which I explore in the next chapter.

## Three Simple Road Blockades

June 17, 2008: Several dozen members of an Altiplano peasant community have come to La Paz. A man in a ragged jacket and trousers and a woman with a black coat and multicolored skirt stand on opposite curbs holding between them a white sheet that says, SINDICATO AGRARIO EX FUNDO / ACHUMANI 2DA SECCIÓN PROVINCIA MURILLO / TIERRA Y TERRITORIO (Agrarian Union of the Former Achumani Estate, Second Section of Murillo Province—Land and Territory) and nothing more. The group has come to urge an indictment in the murder of the local leader Martín Silva Choque, whose death was part of a simmering land conflict on the outskirts of La Paz.[16] Clustered together, all face down the steep street that leads past the Ministry of Justice; most wear bowler hats (a standard element of *de pollera* dress for formally attired women of indigenous ancestry) or leather caps (the men) and present themselves as an unmoving block. This impression is reaffirmed by the many women at the rear of the group who have gathered their skirts and sat down in a solid, fearless bloc. They sit with their backs to what would usually be oncoming traffic but are safe because no motorist could even imagine continuing through this section of the roadway. Their faces and banner address the Prosecutor's Office. As I arrive, a police officer walks casually past them and on up the hill, on his way to somewhere else.

This peasant gathering in downtown La Paz was the first road blockade I encountered in Bolivia, and its unassuming simplicity and far-from-aggressive posture reflected how commonplace and accepted blockades had become in the country. In the United States I had repeatedly witnessed police barking orders to clear the streets for automobile traffic and the willingness of inconvenienced motorists to threaten the lives of Critical Mass cyclists or antiwar protesters

FIGURE 9  Rural residents of Achumani, a district of La Paz, blockade the street in front of the Ministry of Justice to demand investigation of an allegedly political murder.

for blocking traffic.[17] So I was struck by the routine nature of this interaction, and the treatment of this event as legitimate protest rather than exceptional confrontation.

A week later, on June 23, three of us ascend a highway that is eerily empty from the tropical town of Coroico to La Paz. Foreigners, we stare at the majestic valley below as we pass above the line where the tropical tree cover of the Yungas gives way to pure rock. An earlier iteration of the Coroico–La Paz road is infamous as the world's deadliest roadway. This, its modernized successor, is more secure, but it is still marked by hairpin turns, intruded upon by fallen boulders of a terrifying scale, and undermined by landslides. Where the road has fallen or washed out, drivers let their wheels dig tracks into the mud and gravel, and they peer out the sides of their vehicles to avoid falling off the edge of the road.

Today, however, the road is nearly silent. A half-dozen unions orchestrate companies of minibus drivers on this route, but not one is in sight. Bike tours have been canceled, and the taxi driver we found cruises empty roads and easily steers clear of both the rock faces and the treacherous edges. Once we are finally inside La Paz, however, the driver comes to a stop at the cause of all the earlier silence. Residents of the northeastern District 13, organized through forty-six neighborhood councils, have plugged the main arteries through their neighborhood with stones and their collective presence. They are calling on the municipality to meet an eight-point platform of demands concerning crime, public works, and water provision.[18] With traffic at a standstill, dozens of people walk—their goods bound for market stacked on their heads, bundled in fabric on their backs, or dragged along in suitcases—across the vehicle-free stretch of urban pavement, littered with rocks and occupied by protesters gathered in the middle. Rather than run the blockade, the minibus operators—who routinely circumvent fallen boulders and washed-out segments of cliffside roadways on the Highway of Death—suspended service for the day. Was this collusion with neighbors, endorsement of the strike's demands, fear of reprisal, or simply a political culture that respects the right to mount blockades? It's difficult to tell. Either way their compliance extended the impact of a neighborhood blockade across an entire region.

I encountered another isolated blockade in late March 2010 on a highway between Potosí and Sucre. This time workers at a waste disposal yard on the road aired their grievances by blocking the region's main thoroughfare. Everyone on the road had to stop: passengers on large buses and in small minivans, riders on the flatbeds of trucks, and truck drivers carrying goods large and small beneath the plastic tarps on their trucks. Hundreds of people were stuck, more every minute. Unable to pass the workers' human and physical barrier, our bus driver simply pulled to a stop and shut off the motor, first explaining that there was a blockade ahead. Then he allowed time for the situation to shift. About ten minutes into this indefinite pause, he suggested that walking past the blockade was an option, "if you wanted," because surely there were buses on the other side. After another fifteen minutes of gathering belongings, negotiating our suitcases out of the cargo compartment, and walking uphill past the dozens of parked vehicles, the situation did shift. A detachment of national police in olive-green uniforms and holding clear plastic shields had insisted the blockaders open the road. Hundreds of passengers filed back to their original buses and went on their way. Nothing suggested that police had actually detained any of the blockaders. Nor was it clear whether any of their demands had been met.

These commonplace blockades are not the stuff of epochal political conflict. As in a demonstration, those affected by an issue act publicly to make it visible, participation is limited, and the effects are not immediately visible. The bystanders at these events did not have their lives seriously interrupted, and the police force may have debated at leisure whether, and how, to intervene. Yet the ways these actions were organized, the familiarity to Bolivians of the interrupted roadway, and the widely distributed knowledge of how to arrange a roadblock are behind history-making events of the twenty-first century, from the Water War to the present.

## Scaling Up to a Civic Strike

At the Water Fair Christian Mamani, the community leader from Santa Vera Cruz in the Zona Sur, begins to walk me through the various tactics he and his community used during the Water War. "What we in the Zona Sur decided was to blockade absolutely all of the roadways providing access to the city. And nothing circulated for almost two weeks, nothing had circulated," he tells me. Economic life ground to a halt. "Nothing. The markets: closed. The shops: all of them closed."[19] This, of course, was a major feat of collective organization.

The simplest mechanism for strengthening a blockade is a rotation system for protesters to be physically at the blockade site. Rural organizations, water committees, and unions all routinely manage the attendance and collective work of their members. They have learned to adapt these systems to coordinate who shows up and participates in protests, including blockades. While in many countries a day of protest ends with a rallying cry from the stage and gradual dispersal into knots of friends seeking each other out, Bolivia is different. A crowd that stood shoulder to shoulder in a plaza or marched in orderly columns through the streets will organize into small clusters. Peasant union federations visiting Cochabamba carry hand-lettered signs with the names of their local and subcentral unions of the Chapare or the High Valley. But most days these clusters have no signage and recognize one another by sight: they are teachers at the same primary school, workers in the same division or worksite, neighbors on the same committee. Their organization may have brought a diamond-shaped sign or banner to represent itself during the march, but now the time for representation has passed and everyone knows where to go. And everyone knows this will be the moment they must register their attendance.

Attendance requirements are part of a union culture of obligatory participation. There are several mechanisms: a responsible official or volunteer may have an attendance list, she may distribute preprinted stickers for participants to bring to their next organizational meeting, or she may extend a notepad for each attendee to sign. In the stationery shops of La Paz these pads are custom printed and sold alongside retail invoices and school attendance charts. Participation in collective actions is understood as one of the obligations of union membership, and union assemblies and steering committees know this when they make decisions. Unions maintain the authority to impose fines for nonparticipation, which is seen as a breach of solidarity. For neighborhood water committees and associations, the purchase of collective goods (a neighborhood's water tank, say, or a roof for the marketplace) and payment of dues are likewise regular obligations of all members.

One way grassroots organizations can create a citywide blockade is to assemble a mesh of quiet solitary blockades. The rural community members, La Paz neighborhood associations, and junkyard workers I described earlier all have small formal organizations that can decide to apply this simple method of pressure and coordinate their actions with those of others. Most groups like these belong to federations organized on a sector-by-sector basis: neighborhood federations, departmental and national campesino organizations, and labor unions.

The flow of power and initiative within these federated organizations is complex. Local leaders stand in an intermediate position, compelled by their base to advance its demands and concerns in the larger organization and expected by the overall leadership to inform and adequately mobilize their base. Lubia Vargas Padilla, a primary school teacher, described how it works while guarding a barricade composed of a few logs stretched across a Cochabamba street alongside the Rocha River. Her school, along with each of the others, sends a union foreperson ( *jefe sindical* ) to the Teacher's Federation, "and he comes and communicates to us. And we look it over, analyzing, we see the problem, and if it really can be addressed if we get involved, and how it would be if we go out [and mobilize], if we are going to the march or not. So in reality we form a consensus among us all."[20] Persuasion operates in several directions: intermediaries convey to members the arguments of union leadership and the enthusiasm or reluctance of the membership base back to headquarters. Workers enjoy the right to determine their own level of participation but also have the social obligation to participate: "If your conscience tells you, 'Caramba, this affects me too,' then you move, you mobilize together with your comrades," Vargas Padilla says. On the other hand, when a wave of activity occurs, those who had held back come along, "practically obligated" by the rest. "It's like this," she clarifies: "When some are fighting for our rights . . . my conscience tells me that I have to get

FIGURE 10   A chalkboard at the Departmental Health Service in Cochabamba on April 13, 2011, communicates the state of strike mobilization: "Comrade! We continue with the Pressure measures for better SALARIES. Today, WEDNESDAY the 13th, we must gather in the [Union] Federation beginning at 8:00 a.m. WE DON'T RULE OUT A TRIP TO LA PAZ. LONG LIVE THE WORKERS!"

mobilized because this is an issue that also benefits me." A grassroots union is neither a system of command nor of individual free will. Officers and workplace assemblies coexist, as do conscience, consensus, and coercion.

A trade union's strength and leverage depend on the choices of thousands of individual members, whose actions can be coordinated by union officials but not fully controlled. Each strike action is a test of officials' "power to convene," which varies with the demand, the leadership, and the momentum of the mobilization in progress. In practice this makes the pattern of multiple waves of mobilization pattern—the one used in the Water War—fairly common. During months of labor mobilization from October 2010 to April 2011, many calls to citywide action were put forward in Cochabamba, some endorsed by only the more militant unions and others by the Departmental Workers' Central (the Cochabamba branch of the Bolivian Workers' Central union confederation) as well. All were meticulously regulated efforts that used the same mechanisms for organizing marches. However, attendance and enthusiasm varied. At the end of an October march participants largely ignored the union leaders making speeches in the plaza, checked in with those taking attendance, and headed home. In the absence of grassroots enthusiasm leaders know to hold off escalation or call an "intermediate truce" until a later date. After two rounds of national labor protests in February and March, however, disruptive efforts by the more militant unions created a sense of forward momentum and mobilization. During the April 2011 strike wave demanding a 15 percent wage hike, the unions moved to channel that momentum into a "blockade of a thousand corners" in departmental capitals. In Cochabamba teachers, public health workers, municipal construction workers, and factory workers followed up days of marching through the city center by agreeing to escalate to blockades on April 14.

Meetings at the Federation of Urban Teachers of Cochabamba, for example, involved hundreds of teachers congregating in the first-floor auditorium of the federation's building on Junín Street, a short walk northwest of the central plaza. The room features a large stage before row upon row of wooden benches and typically serves as a briefing room for the details of the latest cause for mobilization. The union's negotiating team, experts, and secretary of conflicts make presentations using a projection screen. The premobilization talks are practical, lengthy, and filled with technical details about government proposals and movement demands. Details and demands account for more discussion than do exhortations and tactics because, while the demands and offers change, union members know and accept the strategy of steady escalation up a widely understood ladder of tactics (or, "means of pressure"). As Vargas Padilla explained, "The only way that we are heard is this, because we have no other way to speak. . . . We go along dialoguing and dialoguing, and we are not heard. So, if we don't use a coercive method, we achieve nothing."[21]

After the briefing teachers gather in the street, grouped by school and shift, to sign in for the first time. On April 14 this was when the teachers first learned exactly where and for how long they would be blocking a road as part of the multisectoral plan to paralyze Cochabamba. Teachers at each school took on a particular intersection or stretch of roadway and sealed off traffic—using their bodies, chairs, tree limbs, and little else—for the duration of their regular shift. Attendance according to shift was mandatory. The blockades closest to my house on Urquidi Avenue were actually rather tranquil, little more than lines of teachers, sticks, chairs, and debris across the street every few blocks. Their ubiquity dissuaded most traffic, save an occasional motorcyclist who found a gap where no one was paying attention for a moment. As they sat on the curb or folding chairs, participants swapped stories of the more dangerous confrontations a few days earlier in La Paz.[22] More serious assemblages of workers stood shoulder to shoulder to block thoroughfares and bridges in and out of downtown, and by early afternoon these sites were the scenes of debates and insults as motorists edged their vehicles toward the lines, expecting (correctly, in this instance) that the blockades would not continue into an afternoon shift.

The force of popular pressure grows when more people join in, when they erect blockades across more city blocks or rural towns, when multiple sectors collaborate, and when economic interruption extends to a wider area or for a longer duration of time. It is not so simple, however, for unionized workers or some other sectoral organization to carry out a long-term blockade in a major city. Shutting down a city requires more people than are affiliated with a single organization, and keeping a citywide mobilization going day after day requires giving some participants a break. During my fieldwork the transport workers were the only sector to mount a paralyzing mobilization on their own. They, however, use several other techniques to swell their numbers and impact, as I discuss later in this chapter. Even the April 2011 multisector blockades did not completely stop movement, acting instead as an early-morning-to-early-afternoon interruption rather than a comprehensive shutdown. Other than for transport workers, whose workplace is other people's circulation network, scaling up is usually a matter of bringing more people in, through multisectoral alliances and (at the best of times) a wave of mass participation.

## The Water War as a Civic Strike

The Water War's evolution illustrates various mechanisms that make scaling up possible. Its central organization, the Coordinadora, was an organizational hybrid, shaped by the requirements of scaling up effectively. One facet was a coalition that united established sector organizations into an alliance for joint mobilization. Another facet was the unaffiliated activists, who were welcome to join in the continuous and open processes of the Coordinadora, participated in its assemblies and mass gatherings, and worked to generalize participation across the city. The mass participation in the Water War far exceeded the directing grasp of the Coordinadora itself and its adherent organizations. Organizers iteratively learned how to scale up their mobilizations by connecting with entirely new participants.

Some grassroots groups joined in collective mobilizations although they were not originally organized around political action. The Juntas Vecinales in El Alto, the Comités de Agua, and irrigators' organizations in Cochabamba all are examples of once relatively apolitical organizations that became organizing hubs for citywide blockades.[23] When neighbors occupy vacant or once agricultural land on the urban periphery, or hold onto lands they bought through the gray market in property titles, they have no choice but to build tight neighborhood organizations to defend their homes.[24] Sometimes these neighborhood groups engaged in political advocacy, but more often they served as the vehicle for organizing, building, and managing local infrastructure: streets, water systems, sewerage, and (in El Alto, at least) schools and public space. Sian Lazar argues, and Raúl Zibechi agrees, that the twenty-first-century mobilizations were "successful because people drew on their more day-to-day experiences of collective organisation in Juntas Vecinales and sindicatos."[25]

In both Cochabamba and El Alto syndicalist models of organization and working-class political affinity shaped the politics of these neighborhood organizations even before they got involved in street mobilization. Christian Mamani served as president of a rural peasant union whose traditions shaped his community's self-organization. His community of Santa Vera Cruz and a neighboring community jointly organized their water system through the Agua Cruz Water Committee. Water committee officers were responsible for attending Zona Sur–wide meetings and for informing and mobilizing the community.

The first rumbles of the Water War, in November 1999, took the form of serial blockades: "More than a score of blockades comprised of tree trunks, branches, tires, stones, and vehicles were set out from km 6.5 of Blanco Galindo Avenue to Parotani [at km 37]. . . . A similar situation held on the road to Sacaba and the old highway to Santa Cruz."[26] While the Regantes led in establishing these blockades, some water committees of the urban periphery joined in.[27] Since each major highway out of town was a platform for action, periurban residents could demonstrate their solidarity by taking over the closest portion of the road.

While November's collaboration was spontaneous, Coordinadora activists began to organize the committees and neighborhoods for greater participation. At a Zona Sur cabildo abierto, "Oscar and the other leaders of the Coordinadora came to explain," Hurtado recounted. Among the issues at hand, the most persuasive was the water concession's effect on local water systems, he said:

> The thing was that they [SEMAPA and Aguas del Tunari] hadn't invested a single cent to have [our water distribution] system, right? And this made us react. It had been sold to them under the law. So, how could they take possession if they hadn't put forward a single boliviano [the national currency]. Consequently, there in the assembly, we said, "Now, are we going to allow Aguas del Tunari to take ownership of our system?" And all the neighbors said, "No!" "And therefore, what shall we do?" "To the march! To fight it out!"

During and between the rounds of mass action, participants strategized about how to increase their impact, generalizing the lessons of the November mobilization. Reflecting on the January deployment, the Coordinadora found that the union blockades downtown were unimpressive, but the popular outpouring in the Zona Sur had been overwhelming.[28] The water committees barricaded their communities and cut off arterial roadways nearby. Impressed by this, the Coordinadora moved to register these neighborhood councils (*juntas vecinales*) and water committees as a formal part of the organization and soon announced the creation of new committees in fourteen neighborhoods to organize for the February mobilization.[29] As the April strike approached, the Coordinadora envisioned widespread blockades, "with the blockading of streets, avenues, and bridges, in each neighborhood and in each house."[30] The needs of street mobilization became the driving basis for organization, under the charge of "blockade committees" with multiple responsibilities.

## Strategic Impacts of Blockades

Space-claiming protests make an impact by seizing spaces where goods and people flow and changing them into spaces of protest and blockage. Why does interrupting these flows matter? Why does it provide leverage for negotiating concessions from the government? The movements themselves have a clear response to these questions. Through unions and other groups that share their style of organizing, systematically planning and preparing for collective action has become a kitchen-table conversation topic in Bolivia. Workers, whether schoolteachers like Lubia Vargas Padilla, garbage collectors, or doctors, contemplate whether and how long to go on strike for higher wages. People who might see themselves as small businesspeople in other societies—shopkeepers, coca leaf wholesalers, taxi drivers—meet in their unions and plan marches and street blockades. Farming communities, including the irrigation users and coca growers of Cochabamba, have local unions that take on all the economic roles of the traditional village. For all of them striking and making demands go hand in hand.

The May 1 People's School's handbook, *Métodos de Lucha*, describes citywide blockades as "more radical and effective, as well as better suited to the current social circumstances in the country" than workplace-based strikes. The force of blockades, the manual advises its rank-and-file readers, comes "through [their] implications for the overall unfolding of economic and productive activities." The blockade is a tool for winning concessions from the state: "When the productive routes are left disconnected, the government will find itself obliged to attend to the demands of the blockaders."[31]

The leverage of these methods of struggle comes when they affect the economy and public life. Basic measures of economic activity (like gross domestic product, exports, or industrial production) rely on businesses, factories, and roadways to function normally. A workplace strike or a blockade that disconnects workers from their jobs reveals that economic output is the product of workers' time and productivity. Missed work means less economic activity, a quantifiable loss on corporate balance sheets and in national economic statistics. As the political theorist Paul Virilio argues: "The general strike . . . was a formidable invention, much more so than the barricades of the peasant revolt. . . . It was less an interruption of space (as with the barricade) than of duration. The strike was a barricade in time."[32]

In a three-year study José Luis Evia, Roberto Laserna, and Stergios Skaperdas attempted to estimate the economic impact from all Bolivian protests from 1970 to 2005. Their method? Counting lost days of work and calculating their value according to which economic sector was paralyzed. Their calculations yielded an annual average of "slightly more than $60 million" (in 2004 U.S. dollars) in "direct losses" to gross domestic product from lost production by the protesters themselves.[33] This amount, however, was only a fraction of the total cost since many people not on strike missed work. To deal with this the researchers introduced, for each type of protest, a "multiplier effect," the number of people that each protester kept from contributing to the GDP. By far the strongest protests were urban blockades (an estimated multiplier effect of 12.5) and rural blockades (estimated at 10). When a whole city was paralyzed the researchers counted its entire population and added a multiplier effect of 2 because neighboring regions are affected.[34] Accounting for these indirect effects, Bolivian protest imposed about U.S.\$200 million in annual economic costs, about 3 percent of GDP in 2004. This impact rose to nearly 10 percent of GDP at times of peak protest, such as in 1982–85 and 2000–2005.[35] Combine the general strike—"a barrier in time"—and road blockades—barriers in space— and the force of each is greatly multiplied.

The effectiveness of both rural and metropolitan blockades is enhanced by the topography and limited infrastructural development of Bolivia. Mountainous terrain in the highlands and heavy rainfall in the lowlands have made infrastructure construction difficult and costly. Bolivia's road density ranks is the least of any Latin American country, and less than one kilometer in ten was paved at the beginning of the twenty-first century.[36] Interdepartmental highways in Bolivia are few, and until 2014 all were just two lanes wide. As a result heavy transport is bedeviled by delays and interruptions. The country's centers of power need a steady supply of agricultural goods and are thus quickly made vulnerable by interruptions in transportation. Bolivia's limitations in roads, rail, and flight all serve to amplify the impact of what might otherwise be local blockades.

## Amplifiers of Economic Impact: Mobilized Strikes, Looting, and Public Acceptance

Like blockaders, marchers in a strike attempt to multiply their impact by reducing the ability of others to work. It is more difficult to quantify the impact of a march of strikers than that of a blockade, but the fact that Bolivian strikers don't merely avoid work but instead march through city centers surely amplifies their impact. A mobilized strike (*paro movilizado*)—as workers term these traveling protests—may combine marches with public sabotage, looting of goods, and symbolic or effective destruction of the property of political opponents. During my fieldwork actual destruction was relatively unusual, but it was a latent tool that affected the meaning of protest.

February 22, 2011, is the fourth day of the strike by Cochabamba's fixed-route transit drivers demanding the right to increase fares. Government officials had declared a "day of tolerance" for tardiness and absenteeism in official workplaces and schools. Throughout downtown the absence of large vehicles and the march of hundreds of drivers along the main thoroughfares means that traffic is sparse. At about 10 a.m. I am walking alongside the march up Ayacucho. Up ahead, union officials present a well-crafted image to the reporters covering the march. The unions lead collective chants and talk about the economics of fares and fuel with interviewers from radio and television stations. Alongside the march, however, dozens of younger drivers run excitedly onto the side streets to patrol for people they are calling strikebreakers—that is, taxi drivers offering individuals rides around town. (The taxi drivers' union isn't on strike.) The first words the young transit drivers exchange with these drivers are generally "*Hay paro*"—There is a strike. The taxi drivers, aware of the implicit threat, react by shifting into reverse. On the one-way, one-lane streets of downtown Cochabamba, however, some don't have time or room to back up. The young transit drivers on foot flash various metal tools and puncture the tires of these unlucky taxi drivers—just one at times and sometimes all four—and run off. In their wake the drivers and their suddenly stranded riders can only vent their frustrations to one another.

Two hours later the same march is traveling south along the eastern edge of the Cancha, Cochabamba's working-class central market. Sellers of tires, bicycles, and produce line the west side of the street in metal and wooden stalls. The east side is lined with larger, deeper shops on the ground floors of midrise buildings: paint stores that will mix your desired color, providers of building material, sellers of large panes of glass. These are vendors who use the crumbling sidewalks as an extension of their showrooms. Now that the marchers have arrived, however, they are packing up their complex displays and dragging them inside, even as they pull down the metal gates that seal their businesses shut at night.

It's not that any looting is actively taking place. The most active young men in the crowd are still concentrating on pursuing renegade drivers on the side streets. Nor has the drivers' union made a public call for a general strike or shop closure. But talk and fear of looting circulate in the crowd and among the shopkeepers. Marchers yell toward the sidewalks, "Close your doors!" An older protesting driver, dressed in a blue trousers and a blue button-down shirt, yells to enliven the crowd, "*Hay que saquear*"—We ought to loot. He attracts enthusiasm but no action.

Looting is present in the scene in a way that entangles threat with action, enthusiasm with illegality, and fear with solidarity. The social understanding behind this mix is as follows: The drivers have created an incidental general strike by keeping people away from work. Clearly the shopkeepers are not

FIGURE 11   Striking drivers march through a street market on the east side of the Cancha, February 22, 2011.

among those kept away from their jobs, but from a certain point of view they *ought to have been*. During a real general strike marchers would be reminding everyone of the need to close their businesses in solidarity. Shopkeepers in Bolivia understand that a militant crowd may enforce such a demand with damage or looting to businesses that "break the strike." In the case of this day's encounter, the unity of purpose between the two groups is loose at best and entirely feigned at worst. From what I can see, no one in the crowd actually moves to punish noncompliance, but neither do any of the shopkeepers confront the crowd about its imposition. Once the march moves on, they roll their shutters back up and resume business. The practical result, of course, is that it's a bad day to buy things on the march route, and the multiplier effect for the strike is a bit higher than it might have been otherwise. Symbolically, this exchange turns each sector-specific strike into a little bit of a general strike.

Two days later Cochabamba's drivers carry out a further escalation. On the morning of February 24 they drive their minibuses and passenger vans into the central zone and turn Cochabamba's main roadways into a giant parking lot. Drivers woke early to fill all the lanes of streets with the simplest but heaviest blockading objects of all: their vehicles. The intersection of Ayacucho and Heroínas looks like a still photograph of midday traffic as motionless, driverless buses sit in the middle of left turns they would never complete. Circulation was far more paralyzed than during the drivers' marches; private taxis simply didn't have enough connected roadway to run their fares around the blockades; and downtown streets were depopulated in comparison with typical workdays. (The *transportistas'* vehicle blockades are a somewhat exceptional tactic; few sectors have access to this kind of blockading material.) On the deserted central plaza only pedestrians were about. Elsewhere a vacant calm prevailed: few businesses opened, and the streets were silent without the roar of motors and the bustle of commerce. At Heroinas and Aroma, near the market and the bus station, drivers played an impromptu soccer game in the street.

## Blockades and the Food Supply

Major blockades don't hit just the pocketbooks of the city and the accounts of businesspeople; more urgently they hit the population through their stomachs. To explain the impact of the Water War, Christian Mamani started with vegetables: "We're talking about potatoes, oca [a sweet yellow tuber crisscrossed by magenta grooves], all kinds of tubers, and . . . even corn and *choclo* [an oversized variety of corn]." Food becomes the language through which economic pressure is exerted, felt, and remembered. Mamani continued:

> All of the tubers that arrive into the city of Cochabamba do so through the Zona Sur. . . . And I remember that even we ourselves felt this means of pressure. Not even we ourselves could reach the center of the city, nor could those in the center reach us. And some neighbors needed to buy some vegetables, and so we loaned vegetables from one of us to the next, and we went to find the [rural] unions and see if someone might be able to sell us an onion, a tomato. And this is how we kept up this means of pressure, which was quite harsh. The families, the mothers, the housewives had to seek out—as I say—the food which they will cook today. And there was just one meal for the rest of the day.

These effects were expected consequences of the carpet of blockades across the metropolitan landscape, and the Coordinadora's communiqué on March 30, 2000, urged preparation for the supply shortages that would accompany mobilization: "Supply yourselves with food, water, medicine, lanterns, radios, and everything which may be necessary in accordance with the experience of past struggles."[37] Conversely, the giving of food was also a central symbol of public support for the mobilization. "It was an act of solidarity," remembered Marcelo Rojas, adding that "when in all of Cochabamba there was no food, in the main square, we didn't lack food, we didn't lack beverages, we didn't lack water, we didn't lack anything."[38]

Coordinated blockades have repeatedly resulted in urban food shortages, which are at once a dramatizing element of the sense of crisis they generate and a challenge in terms of planning logistics and sustaining commitment. In September 2000 three different grassroots movements brought a new round of conflicts to a head in synchronous actions across the country, generating an unprecedented disruptive effect. The teachers' union strike included a march from Oruro to La Paz, while the highland peasant union confederation mobilized nationwide roadblocks, and the Six Federations (the coca growers) demanded the government break its commitment to coca eradication and the planned construction of three new U.S.-funded military bases in the Chapare.[39] The blockades lasted from September 11 to October 7. Felipe Quispe Huanca, the leader of the rural workers, described that month as reaching a new level of mobilization: "I have been impressed by the force and massiveness of the uprising, and it was because the *mita* and the *ayni* functioned, the communitarian form of struggle and organization functioned.[40] For example, thousands of community members came out of the valleys; I couldn't do anything else but cry. . . . Those who had come out . . . gave me their hands . . . the thin people, malnourished, but all of them in the road with their ponchos."[41] As the mobilization continued, there was a shift from mere blockades to mass gatherings, fifty thousand in Achacachi alone, of people eager to advance on La Paz.

In the capital food began to grow scarce in both working-class and elite neighborhoods. This had a great impact both politically and psychologically. As Felix Patzi emphasizes, "For the first time since [Túpaj] Katari and [Zarate] Willka, the dominant class was affected by the campesinos in a direct manner," in its very bodies.[42] The government moved to airlift supplies, only to face blockades outside the airport led by El Alto housewives. In the end the state was obliged to concede certain demands, including the cancellation of the military installations.

Patzi argues, "The blockade revealed before national society and the international community the role of small-scale rural reproduction in the national economy and the dependence of the cities on the rural economy."[43] In his attempt to discourage a national blockade wave in March 2005, President Carlos Mesa suggested the burden of blockades falls hardest on recent migrants to the cities "who live from day to day, who eat from day to day, and who go down from El Alto to La Paz . . . to assemble each day the food for their children."[44] Ironically, however, the informal proletariat of the urban indigenous has often been better able to weather the economic disruptions of the blockades and general strikes, in part because it relies on a different set of commodities for its daily life. The tubers Christian Mamani spoke of, as well as chuño (the freeze-dried potato product made by the Quechua and Aymara communities) and quinoa, are goods traded in large quantities and stored for slow and steady use. During the September–October 2003 blockade in the Gas War, Patzi writes, these practices reinforced "the idea of the savings-oriented indigenous and the white squanderer" (an inversion of dominant racial stereotypes): "The indigenous had accumulated impressive *quintales* (hundredweight sacks) of chuño and quinoa, through which they were unaffected by the blockade. The whites, accustomed to buying only for the day's consumption, were severely affected by the measure."[45]

Everyday perseverance, preparation, and thrift, however, are not the only strategies for outlasting hunger during a blockade. Rather, as blockades have become a more frequently used protest tool, participants have made weathering their impact part of planning for major mobilizations. During the 2010 Potosí strike for regional development, the Potosí Civic Committee modulated its call for total blockades during most days with two-hour or half-day interruptions during which commerce could occur and supplies could be bought. Similarly the strategy of repeated twenty-four- or forty-eight-hour general strikes allows for limiting the survival impacts of a mobilization while maintaining much of its economic force.

## Paralyzing Commerce and Infrastructure

It's not just workers and consumers who are held up by mobilizations but also commerce and connection. Goods sit in trucks motionless on highways or pile up or rot in storage facilities for lack of transport. Tourism is put on hold and long-distance travel suspended. Beyond the monetary losses this disconnection entails, it is also a reversal of a main government achievement: the integration of national territory into an easily traveled, unified space. Infrastructural technologies are frequently invoked as symbols of state sovereignty, successful modernization, and national unity.[46] Blockades show these achievements to be tenuous, fragile, and subject to local consent rather than a projection of the central government's power.

Regular functioning of the economy, free-flowing commerce, and undisrupted infrastructure are important to the government's international standing. The *Métodos de Lucha* handbook observes: "The worker, contrary to what the government proclaims, never loses with the strike or blockade: it is rather the government that ends up discredited before the instructing angels from the North [who must assent] for it to receive the qualifications, cosignatures, and credit to keep open for business [*lit.*, for usufruct] the economic emporium into which the Bolivian state has converted itself."[47] Alongside an anticolonialist swipe at foreign economic advisers and Bolivia's economic dependency, this passage addresses the real significance that international perceptions of conflict hold for Bolivian state decision makers. The ability to avoid or control protest disruptions, and to fulfill privatization contracts, is operationalized as "maintaining a favorable investment climate" and "ensuring the rule of law." In the global economic order a national government's first duty is to guard against disruption.

Consider President Mesa's televised speech of March 6, 2005. Mesa took several minutes to personally address Abel Mamani, of the El Alto Federation of Neighborhood Councils, who was then organizing blockades to eject Aguas de Illimani from his city in a reprise of the Cochabamba Water War. In Mesa's speech the craziest element of "the carnival of crazy men" was Abel Mamani's threat to blockade the La Paz–El Alto airport:

And, what is it that you are proposing, Sir Abel Mamani? Let's take over the El Alto International Airport. Three days ago, a group of lawless people [that is, civic strikers] sought to break one of the wire fences that control the El Alto International Airport and go onto the tarmac and interrupt the flights. You, who I suppose . . . would want a modern El Alto, who I suppose would want a city of El Alto which grows and produces, but at the same time who wants to take over the international airport.

You know what would happen when a group of lawless persons takes over an international airport? The international rating of that airport falls, and we will not see again a flight from American Airlines, or Varig, or LAN Chile, or any international line whatsoever, covering the city of El Alto and the city of La Paz.

And so, what we have built over years and years and years we throw into the garbage in a second, and what does it matter to you?[48]

What he said offers a window into what keeps a Bolivian president awake at night. It illustrates at once the power of international technocratic standards to set state priorities and the truly compelling leverage available by interrupting those elements of the economy that are of highest priority to foreign investors.[49]

## The City at a Standstill: The Space Created by Blockades

While a single blockade can shut down a major transport route, adding many more across a broader space can radically shift the feel of a city, replacing the routines of day-to-day life with either an eerie calm or a dramatic space of confrontation. Marcelo Rojas remembers how in April 2000 blockading crews carpeted the central city. Working outward from his own group, which was in the Plaza 14 de Septiembre, "we began to create other groups on each corner"—his hands create a virtual map on the desk between us—"[and] we began to surround it, to make circles, as far as Aroma and the stadium. It was all these groups of people, and to enter the plaza you had to pass as many as ten groups." This fabric of interruption extended "out to Aroma, San Martín and all that side, to Ayacucho, from Ayacucho out to Lanza, and across [the Rocha River] and absolutely nothing could enter from that [far] side [of the river]. It was quite impressive."[50] What impressed Marcela Olivera was the desire to put up blockades absolutely everywhere: "For example, Quillacollo, on that avenue—I don't know if you've been to Urkupiña"—a massive religious festival that takes place every August 15. (I *have* been to it. That avenue floods with several hundred thousand dancers, pilgrims, and visitors processing or watching the procession to the Calvary shrine of the Virgin Mary of Urkupiña.) And in April 2000 "that avenue was blockaded," she continued. "Who wants to go to [the] Calvario [sanctuary] then, right? But there wasn't anything else to blockade, and so the people had blockaded that." And so the blockades extended westward through Quillacollo and east through Sacaba, "in all of the Zona Sur."[51]

During a civic strike the many points of blockades are connected by spaces of immobility that become part of the territory of the strike. The general cessation of economic activity creates the sense that everyone is participating: "It was not only Cochabamba in the fight, but also it was the Chapare; it was the

Altiplano. All of Cochabamba committed itself, [set up] blockades. It had gone like that, growing quite well," Ángel Hurtado recalled. It's this sense that animates people to blockade alleyways and festival esplanades, that led "a group of ladies in [ritzy] Cala Cala, at the end of Avenida Libertador, to slash the tire of a gentleman on a bicycle," and that drew everyday Cochabambans to find nails and break glass to lay out across their roadways.[52] In small acts the collective effort can be applied everywhere, and in the silenced streets its effects can be seen everywhere. Christian Mamani recalled that during the April phase of the Water War, "no vehicles circulated on the highways. From eight, eight-thirty in the morning, nothing circulated at all. We were all in the struggle, we were all in protest. . . . Because in all of Cochabamba, absolutely all of the center of the city was filled with tear gas." With broad enough participation extending over wide enough space, a blockade ceases to be something done by a mobilized few to the rest of the region, and the entire city, department, or country becomes part of the strike.

Conflict and confrontation transform urban spaces. In the midst of a prolonged civic strike, state forces—the police and military, principally—withdraw from contested blocks or regions in an effort to concentrate their forces. The suddenly unpoliced spaces they leave behind become a sign of the limitations of state power. As I show in the next chapter, these open spaces are filled with alternate forms of sociality: intense solidarity, democratic decision making, and claims of sovereignty voiced from the street. With the roads made impassable to soldiers and trucks, writes Álvaro García Linera, the state appears "as an inept intruder to whom geography and time become alien and uncontrollable forces."[53] When the state turns to repression, it arouses still greater adversity. The logic of the roadblock pushes the community toward the deepening construction of political autonomy. Routines of daily life are disrupted, time and location are subjected to participants' own initiative, and collective decisions are made in movement forums like unions and cabildos.

## The Right to Interrupt

Thus the leverage that blockades bring to bear is exerted upon economic activity, connectivity, and the capacity for state control. These are priority areas for the state in its own rhetoric and central to major theoretical interpretations of the modern state. Michel Foucault's description of modern governance highlights how the state takes on responsibility for the management of the economy, including overseeing its growth, and for regulating and facilitating both the provision of basic needs and the mechanisms of "the circulation of goods." Both the "material network that allows the circulation of goods and possibly men" and "the facilities and encouragements that will allow the circulation of men and things" come under this new state's purview.[54] For James Scott the modern state is a system for "transforming [territory] into a fully governed, fiscally fertile zone." This process is "made possible only by distance-demolishing technologies (all-weather roads, bridges, railroads, airplanes, modern weapons, telegraphy, telephone, and now modern information technologies including global positioning systems)."[55] Whether we understand the state as a manager of the economy, a logistical manager of civilian life, or an instrument of territorial rule, a mass blockade undoes—at least temporarily—the primary work of the state.

As I have shown in this chapter, on most days both protesters and other city residents contribute to the impact of blockading tactics. Motorists, police, bystanders, and even those people who have their lives interrupted often defer to these interruptions rather than work actively to circumvent them. It is precisely when transport unions cancel their scheduled routes, when bus drivers idle their motors on highways, when city officials declare a "day of tolerance" for workers who can't get to their workplaces, when shopkeepers shutter their doors that a barricade in the streets becomes a small space of a general strike. Further, when people defer and accept these tactics, they often do so as potential users of strike tactics. Recall the Coroico–La Paz bus drivers whose daily work requires circumventing boulders on the highway but who respected the neighborhood blockade in La Paz. People defer to and accept these tactics because on another day they might carry out a strike of their own. Each small group, from a neighborhood council to a primary-school teaching shift to an outlying neighborhood, can grasp the nearest choke point to demand what they need. The understanding of these direct-action tactics as a form of striking, and the choice to respect rather than defy them, is a form of labor solidarity, of mutual recognition by potential strikers. They grant one another the right to strike and help make sure those strikes to hit hard.

(On the other hand, it isn't so hard for people acting collectively to push back against a blockade. Motorists can try to push through blockades, forcing strikers to work hard to stand their ground. Even transit drivers, whose vehicles give them an enormous tactical advantage, have faced retaliation from neighborhood groups boycotting their services or blocking their routes.)[56]

This right to interrupt, and the respect that people accord that right, are a cultural—and sometimes legal—extension of the repertoire of contention. The legal right to strike, to immunity from prosecution for union activity, and to blockade roads as part of strikes are widely acknowledged. Despite extreme conflict between the state and unions, seven requests to indict strikers for impeding public transit were refused by Bolivian prosecutors between 2000 and 2003, in recognition of the right to strike.[57] If the repertoire is about the routinization of forms of protest, that routine is not just about the choices of protesters but about the ways other social forces acknowledge and respect that routine. Inside the repertoire tactics like people blocking roads and "mobilized strike" marches are linked to a political culture of direct-action syndicalism, in which any social grouping may exercise that right to strike and deploy such tactics.

Still, something more sets a small number of civic strikes apart. Not only is the daily life of the city at a standstill but the mobilization claims the right to speak on behalf of the metropolis: the city itself is on strike. The remarkable capacity of a city or nation to act as a whole, to dissolve internal differences to end a generally detested situation, to proclaim a collective *no* is not the result of a certain type of organization. It has elements that come about through the process of mobilization itself and that persist only as long as the political impasse of which they are a part. In the next chapter I look at how that particular kind of unity is built and how the protesters at its forefront assert not just the right to bargain with the state but also the right to govern themselves.

## CHAPTER 4

# The Sovereign Street

*How Protests Become "the Voice of the People"*

> *We had to take the plaza because doing so is very symbolic. Always,*
> *in all the revolutions, the first thing that happened was taking*
> *the plaza.*
>
> —MARCELO ROJAS

**M**arcelo Rojas, then a politicized young adult from Cochabamba's central zone, remembers the February 2000 "taking of Cochabamba" as his first major political action and as what "lit the spark" for the Water War.[1] He joined the early-morning crowd on February 4 with his neighbors and the bricklayers who worked for his uncle, a crew that expected police hostility and marched with bandanas over their faces to hide their identities. Farmers defending their irrigation rights led the march from Tiquipaya (the town immediately northwest of Cochabamba) to converge with another from Vinto and Quillacollo at the Víaducto, a bridge that passes over Blanco Galindo Avenue two kilometers west of downtown. It was there, after the marches combined, that they encountered the police. Protesters faced an unprecedented challenge from the well-armed antiriot Special Security Group, a police unit brought in from La Paz. Rojas and other marchers then participated in two days of street confrontations.

Protesters tossed back painfully hot teargas canisters and used cloths soaked in vinegar, soda, and even urine to protect their eyes and noses from the effects of the gas. They learned to watch the direction of the wind and pick strategic paths to approach police lines where the gas would drift back on the officers who threw it. The protesters gathered debris into makeshift barricades on the streets. To advance they hurled stones and fireworks at police lines and urged the crowd to surge forward, moving block by block toward the central plaza.

West of downtown the police established barricades first at the Quillacollo Bridge and then at the Plazuela of the Corazonistas. At each site the determined crowd eventually overwhelmed the police while advancing toward the central square.

Amid the chaos of tear gas and repeated confrontations, Marcelo joined a handful of other unarmed militants on the frontlines. Previously strangers, they did not see one another's faces or learn each other's names until the street battles ended. When Rojas grabbed a Bolivian flag that had been dropped by a boy in the thick of the gas and held on to it after being pushed against the wall by a police officer, Rojas became known as "Banderas" (Flags), a name still used today in his union office, where he serves as president of the workers at SEMAPA, the once-again public water utility.

At five minutes to eleven on the night of February 5, 2000, Bolivian security forces gave up their defense of Cochabamba's central square, the Plaza 14 de Septiembre. Hundreds of police, who had waged a two-day battle to keep protesters out of the square, regrouped into a thin line along the balcony-lined north face of the plaza, guarding the departmental palace, or Prefectura. In just two days they had fired more than seven thousand canisters of tear gas and fired ten thousand rounds of rubber bullets to enforce a ban issued by then-prefect Hugo Galindo on the Coordinadora's plan to flood the city with protesters and "take Cochabamba."[2] Minutes earlier the government had agreed to renegotiate the hated water contract, return fees to the precontract level, and release arrested protesters, the Coordinadora's demands from the previous night. All sides had agreed to the "immediate and simultaneous pullback of police, military, and marchers," but there was no holding back the celebratory emotion of the victors who poured into the square.[3] Within minutes the troops were standing face-to-face with about two thousand joyous Cochabambans. They bore the signs of a hard fight and still wore bandanas wet with vinegar. They whooped, they chanted, "We have won!" and they shouted demands for the release of their comrades. Then they doffed their caps and began to sing the national anthem and Cochabamba's departmental anthem. The bulk of the crowd marched around the four corners of the square.

Ceremony had intruded on confrontation, and this ceremonial component is significant. As Robert Bellah reminds us, "We know enough about the function of ceremonial and ritual in various societies" to listen to "what people say on solemn occasions."[4] Central plazas in Bolivian cities are spaces of state pageantry. When soldiers parade to mark national independence, when plazas are decked with garlands to greet foreign dignitaries or for the swearing-in of an official, or when the National Congress meets in an honorary session, central plazas are the chosen setting.[5] They contain all these memories and therefore amplify the historical import of events held within them. Accordingly, rebellious action in the plaza is recognized as symbolically potent, and governments and their police forces have often actively strategized to prevent certain marchers and mass movements from gaining control of the space.

The Coordinadora's communiqué of February 6, 2000, written in the joy of the takeover, expresses what the space meant for them:

> We entered into the Plaza after two days of battle, just as we said we would, jubilantly, to say that Cochabamba does not yield, that our water is not for sale, to take back the right to speak [*recuperar la palabra*] and democracy; and finally, to show that when it comes to water, it is we who will decide, that we are not disposed to submit to what ministers, businessmen, and international financial institutions dictate. That is what the Cochabamban population of the city and the country has done, forcefully and decidedly, accompanied by us.[6]

"The goal was to throw out Aguas del Tunari," Rojas explained, adding that, before that day, "we knew we couldn't because the government was defending it very strongly." The public seizure of the plaza, however, changed things. "We broke through the gap, we broke through the police [and from there], we said, 'Let's negotiate,' because they knew we had overcome the police, and the riot squads."[7]

Note what has shifted in his account: in his words the government's defense of the Aguas del Tunari contract blurs with its security forces' defense of the central square. In space-claiming protest tactical outcomes—control over space, access to symbolically important places, and impacts on commerce—matter. Political collectivities step into the streets as particular bodies, and through their struggles for practical control they assert political claims and win. The government's political position drove a physical stand against street protesters, and when the physical stand failed, the political stance retreated as well: the contract was now up for renegotiation.

The stories Bolivians tell about these transformative events reveal how mass protest can symbolically stand in for collective political entities like Cochabamba. Space-claiming protests generate opportunities for just this kind of description: narratives that literally describe on-the-ground events but meta-phorically call forth larger political shifts. Already on the morning of Febru-ary 5, 2000, *Los Tiempos* had started using *Cochabamba* as a synonym for the Coordinadora and its allies, as in "Cochabamba decided to continue protests." A headline in the paper on April 14 read, simply, "Cochabamba bent the arm of the government." Identification of the whole city with the protest had solidified into journalistic fact. Nothing is uniquely subjective or wild-eyed about this kind of narrative: it is the one offered by protesters and their adversaries, local media, and social scientific accounts. Protesters, elected officials, reporters, edi-torial writers, and academics declare that a street protest *forced* a policy change or *overcame* the government's resistance.

This chapter looks in depth at moments when street action precipitated a rethinking of Bolivian political relations. In the first half of this chapter I ana-lyze the experiential and practical bases for deeply felt unity in protest: the collaboration of multiple social sectors in successful protest, the physical neces-sity of cooperation and empathy in the process of confrontation, and utopian feelings of oneness even amid bitter physical combat. Examining the Water War in dialogue with participant observation of protest in 2010 and 2011, I look at how mass public participation in large-scale protests generates a profoundly felt and empirically grounded sense of unity. Blockades seem to be everywhere (as I describe in the last chapter) and protests seem to involve everyone. This felt and demonstrated unity arose through three forms of space-claiming protest: con-verging marches, battles for streets and the central square, and massive cabildos that make a powerful claim to political power.

In the second half of the chapter I consider the nationwide upheavals in 2003 and 2005, when protesters advanced a claim to national sovereignty over and above that exercised by the elected president. Protest gatherings and seemingly endless waves of mobilization not only defied repression but controlled the cir-culation of goods and stymied the work of security forces. At times they isolated and stranded lawmakers or prevented legislatures from holding their sessions. When the crises of September–October 2003 and May–June 2005 ended, pres-idents (Sánchez de Lozada in 2003 and Mesa in 2005) stepped aside, leaving their successors to negotiate directly with protesters for time to govern in peace, which both Mesa and Rodríguez did. By surviving and resisting repression and intervening in the process of presidential succession, the Bolivian street won surprising official recognition of its claims to sovereignty.

## Collective Actions and Collective Emotions

Like Rojas's description of the battle for the plaza, many political perceptions that emerge from mass protest are simultaneously emotional and analytical. Scholars of social movements increasingly recognize emotions as relevant to the power and impact of protest. Rather than an irrational and inherently unpredictable aspect of social life, emotions turn out to be guided by experience and events. Indeed, "collective identities, in fact, are nothing more or less than affective loyalties."[8] Depending on the extent to which mass protests generate both political and emotional loyalties, they can have a transformative effect on politics. Felt experience shapes political reality.

Anthropologists have long known that intense collective experiences, when people assemble in large groups and feed off of one another's energy, generate a sense of heightened significance. Émile Durkheim saw commonly felt emotions, reaffirmed in public gatherings, as the foundations of social and political life.[9] He described the "collective effervescence" of revolutionary politics as akin to those feelings that surface during ritual.[10] In *The Ritual Process* Victor Turner famously identified rites of passage in east African indigenous societies as moments when participants mock the usual authorities, blur normally rigid categories, and exalt those with the least power. Youths becoming adults through these rituals collectively experience liminality, a time of being "betwixt and between," stripped of status and rank, outside social structures, and dissolved in raw *communitas*, or "togetherness itself," with their comrades.[11] Taking Durkheim's insight one step further, Turner saw disruptive political events, like May 1968 in France, as liminal, antistructural situations in which social values and structures can be remade.

During periods of intense mobilization, tens or hundreds of thousands of Bolivians meet in the streets of cities to engage in strenuous space-claiming protest. They throng plazas, breathe tear gas, and share in the vulnerability of their bodies to batons and rubber bullets. Confrontation displaces conventional patterns of public behavior, and protesters defy authorities rather than defer to them. Protesters battle police and mock prefects and presidents. These mass gatherings, marked by shared effort, bodily engagement, and physical risk, are emotional places. Becoming part of a crowd, listening to music while marching, collaborating physically against a common adversary, and sharing reflexive emotions (whether the pain of breathing tear gas, the fear of violence, or the joy of overcoming adversity) all heighten solidarity and love within a group. Jeffrey

Juris, describing large antiglobalization protests, argues that affective and bodily experience links individual and collective sentiment: "Mass mobilizations, and [direct] actions in particular, largely operate through affect, amplifying an initial emotion, such as a sense of injustice, and transforming it into collective solidarity. The awareness of bodily co-presence induces particularly strong sensations."[12] The result, Juris finds, is affective solidarity: shared emotional experiences that drive mutual identification as allies experience danger, uncertainty, relief, play, and joy in tandem.[13]

People carrying out mass collective protest experience affective solidarity through the tactics they choose and the repression they endure. Through the experience of holding space against determined adversaries, participants model to one another (and to themselves) popular unity, collective power, and capacity for sacrifice. And in these protests space matters. Protesters and governments alike concentrate their efforts on which bits of urban space are claimed or lost, blockaded or opened up, entered or defended from entry. Two kinds of uncertainty overlap: what will happen next physically and what will change politically. This can create a situation in which actions have a heightened meaning, where the tactical is political.

While participants may claim the right to speak on behalf of the country, it takes more to convince observers and adversaries. Street actions become politically meaningful only when, in the eyes of the larger society, they represent a legitimate constituency and its political aspirations. This reframes them as an expression of popular will, not acts of vandalism. When the usual means of state coercion prove unable to restore order in the streets, policy makers are forced to reckon, and negotiate, with an emerging, unconventional political force. At times of intense uncertainty state control itself appears threatened by a rival power in the streets. This is the situation Leon Trotsky termed *dual power*, when "essentially incompatible governmental organisations—the one outlived, the other in process of formation . . . jostle against each other at every step."[14] People on the streets find that their actions are making history.

## Convergence on the Streets and Emotional Unity

The February 2000 street battle to enter Cochabamba's central square was one example of what Charles Tilly calls the "struggle for control of crucial public spaces in validation of claims to political power."[15] But what makes these spaces crucial? What meanings do protesters claim as they enter and take control of particular public spaces? In a suggestive article Tilly draws attention to two ways that powerful meanings are embedded in places: First, "routine political life, including . . . parades, parliaments, public ceremonies, and the like . . . endows different places with symbolic significance, which is then available for adoption, parody, or transmutation by participants in transgressive politics." Second, the protests of the past changed the significance of the spaces they claimed. They created new layers of meaning there: feelings of ownership, power, triumph, and sacrifice.[16] That is, past and present uses of urban spaces leave behind a set of available meanings to be invoked by protesters.

During my fieldwork I accompanied scores of protests and documented their routes, which typically connected two focal points of activity. I expanded this in-person survey by regularly monitoring press reports of protests. Typically the originating point represented a space of power or organization for the group mobilizing, while the destination was symbolic of state power. (Only twice did a march begin at a central governmental plaza and end up somewhere else and then only to lead into an actual meeting.) Map 5 illustrates the principal origin sites of marches in Cochabamba during my fieldwork from July 2010 to May 2011. The originating spaces were sometimes actual places for organizing: Cochabamba's urban teacher federation, campesino federation, the departmental workers' federation, and cocalero union headquarters all have large first-floor auditoriums designed for premarch briefings of their membership. Often, however, they were places that evoke popular mobilization and working-class community: the Ceja in El Alto, Plaza San Francisco in La Paz, or the outskirts of the Cancha in Cochabamba. Many of these spaces of popular power are organizational headquarters. Streets and plazas—especially Plazuela Busch and Kilometer Zero of Avenida Petrolera—allow for even larger crowds to amass in preparation for marches, mobilized strikes, and blockades.

The march from places of popular power to places of official governance can produce an electric connection between two disparate forms of power: a move from our territory to theirs. The process energizes participants first with the experience of gathering in a place that is their own and then with daring to confront their rulers. If the political order were well respected by the grassroots, marchers could simply act as petitioners, carrying their needs and demands to accountable leaders. However, the relationship with government is rarely so straightforward. Popular mobilizations can refuse to recognize the government's

MAP 5   Major points of origin and routes of marches in central Cochabamba. (Base map prepared by Carwil Bjork-James. Map tiles by Stamen Design, under CC BY 3.0. Data by OpenStreetMap, under ODbL.)

primacy or legitimacy; sometimes protesters openly challenge the government's right to speak for the people or seek to shake the rulers from their space.

The destination of marches in central Cochabamba was consistent. A typical march in 2010–11 ended in the Plaza 14 de Septiembre, the city's central plaza. On occasion as many as three demonstrations were using the plaza at once.[17] Sometimes marchers came to the plaza to directly address—or, more often, to demand to address—officials in the departmental palace or city hall. Only a handful of marches sought out decision makers elsewhere in the city.[18] The vast majority of those I observed used the central plaza as their public platform for making demands even of the national government, which has no office there.

When multiple movements unite behind a common demand, they often organize multiple marches from different origin points but with a common destination. This approach shows the breadth and diversity of public support for a cause. The many groups in these marches either fold in (*plegar*) to long processions, with each group behind its own banners, or arrive separately at the plaza and bring their banners to the front of the crowd. The handful of people behind each banner represents in miniature the united front among organizations by literally stand shoulder to shoulder. Rather than stating demands, most banners simply identify a constituency ("Cochabamba Federation of Health Workers, Presente!" or simply "Tarata District"). "We are gathered here, students, workers of the Caja de Salud, teachers, retirees, factory workers, neighborhood councils, to ratify in a unified form—," declares a speaker at a labor cabildo I attended in April 2011. His language was commonplace: multiple grassroots sectors coming together, united but separately organized. He said in words what marchers say with their use of urban public space.

While the Coordinadora's organizing work mobilized thousands of Cochabambans behind common demands, only when these diverse groups met, rallied, and fought together in the streets did they demonstrate to the world, and themselves, that they were "the Cochabamban people." "The indignation was not ours alone," as Eliana Quiñones Guzmán said, "but rather that of the whole city, in all of Cochabamba."[19] To achieve this requires melding sectors of the public together despite their differences, an act of social alchemy achieved through space claiming.

The grassroots mobilization began as a sector-by-sector effort, with each organization assigned particular spaces to blockade. In the process of mobilization, however, new organizations joined in and those already on the streets developed novel working relationships. "One could go and join with any movement; there was fighting with the police in every sector," Christian Mamani remembered. "It didn't matter whether you were with this organization or that one; the thing to do was confront them."[20] Through the February and April battles the multisector coalition became a functional self-organized multitude capable of contesting the streets of downtown and keeping the major thoroughfares blocked.

Even years later participants remark upon the transcendence of boundaries of class or ethnicity.[21] Strategically participants perceived that longtime social adversaries had formed a winning coalition and felt affective solidarity with these unexpected allies. To explain this, Gabriel Herbas, a Coordinadora spokesman, spoke of "Moors and Christians"—that is, "the popular sectors" and "moneyed people" who met one another in cabildos in the plaza.[22] They also met during days of frantic confrontation. For Christian Mamani this unity was expressed through collaboration on the practicalities of on-the-street struggle: "Those of us from the Zona Sur would come in caravans to join the fight, and those in the central zone, those who lived downtown, were charged [*encargado*, the word for a community-assigned responsibility] with giving us water, vinegar to combat the [tear]gas. They threw old mattresses and sheets of paper [for fuel] so we could burn tires."[23]

In Cochabamba divisions of class and race (mestizo vs. indigenous) predominate and are mapped onto the split between a middle-class center-north of the city and the larger, poorer, more indigenous Zona Sur. Oscar Olivera celebrated a new relationship between class and power in the Water War: "There were the rich from the northern part of the city . . . but this time something was different. This time they marched behind the slogans of the poor, instead of the other way around—the way it usually happens—with the poor marching behind the slogans of the rich."[24] I asked Marcela Olivera who was in the streets during the conflict, and she replied, "I think there was [someone of] every kind. There in the assembly of the Coordinadora, you could better identify the organizations but in the end in the streets, there were people coming from their houses who didn't have any organization." She remembers more aggressive actions by the wealthier locals as well: "The bank workers were the ones who passed out newspapers to burn in the streets. I remember how right here [four blocks from the plaza] the *vecinos* [neighbors but implicitly middle-class ones] were making Molotov cocktails. Not the miners, not, *damn!*, the factory workers either. It wasn't the coca growers. It was the vecinos who were preparing Molotov cocktails."[25]

The ongoing street confrontations involved both women and men, across wide spans of age and class status. However, men predominate in photographs of the frontline confrontations and made up the majority of those most severely injured.[26] A young woman dressed in the skirted chola style of Bolivia's central valleys was photographed while lobbing a stone at police lines with an equally traditional slingshot and became an icon of collective participation in the resistance.[27] A more systematic study of women's participation listed the following as major tasks they carried out: "serving as roadblock delegates or chiefs"; "carrying rocks, wire, etc., to enforce a blockade"; "cooking in communal kitchens"; "keeping watch"; "providing protection against tear gas"; and "responding to police repression with sticks and stones."[28] During confrontations "street brigades of men and women from the ranks of the unemployed, the poor, youths, and vagabonds" worked together and "demonstrated incredible discipline," write Rocío Bustamante, Elizabeth Peredo, and María Esther Udaeta.[29] The acceptance of the urban poor, down to the shoe shiners and homeless youth who are stigmatized glue sniffers, accentuated the cross-class solidarity of the large movement.

For Marcelo Rojas the partial differentiation of roles by age and gender did not reduce the amount of unity and equality within the struggle, "because the children fought just like me. . . . The women with their valiance, the youth with their strength, the men with their spirit, the elders with their experience, the aged ones. All of that came together there."[30] Ángel Hurtado saw both his neighborhood and his city come together in the days of street fighting during the Water War. As the February and April battles went on, more and more people descended from Barrio Primero de Mayo to confront the police downtown. In the city the people from the barrio sent little "commissions"— handfuls of neighborhood youth—to keep track of people and make sure the injured were attended to, even as neighbors became dispersed among various points of confrontation. Hurtado describes the small-scale aid offered by local residents to Zona Sur residents who came downtown to protest as "the growing consciousness of the people" who "had just recently gotten involved." Remembering a man he didn't know who was felled just ahead of him from rubber bullets, Hurtado was moved to speak of unity: "He fell, and what are we to do? We can't just go over him. We had to lift and carry him away quickly. That is, it was of no concern who [he was] . . . that there was a strength, a solidarity that was unique in that place. There, there were no left, right, or center parties, no tall or ugly, no Indian or gringo, nothing at all. All of us were one. That is what we learned as well."[31]

"All of us were one": Unity comes as a revelation. Rather than an achievement, it feels like an insight into our true selves. The tangible experiences that provoke this realization (and the things my interviewees described to evoke my understanding) were of several different genres. What was tangibly happening at these moments of unity could be shared suffering, such as the sting of tear gas, or shared risk, such as the possibility you would be shot, or acts of material aid from one person to the next (even quite minimal ones like sharing a newspaper or an onion). Yet all were taken as signs of deep bonds and the lack of separation between people. The commonality among these experiences, I argue, is shared vulnerability and embodied mutual aid.

"We came to know each other well in the daily work in the streets, in protest, on marches," Quiñones Guzmán remembered. "So, we joined the collective struggle, which belonged to everyone."[32] In the melee, unlike in the meeting, each body shares the same vulnerability, has the same needs, and must engage with others on a one-to-one basis. Such experience is "undifferentiated, egalitarian, direct, spontaneous, concrete, and unmediated," precisely the kind of bonds created through communitas.[33] Solidarity, lived through intense experiences, can presage potent shifts in political relations.

## The Emergence of Regional Collective Subjects

On February 4, the first day of unarmed combat across downtown Cochabamba retreated to an uneasy calm after dusk settled. Bonfires burned in the streets while police on motorcycles loosed tear gas on the city's cafés.[34] Speaking in the Plaza Colón, five blocks north of the central square, the three spokesmen for the Coordinadora laid out their conditions for negotiation. The day's fighting, which sent scores of wounded to Hospital Clínico Viedma, had hardened their position. But it had also brought the establishment Civic Committee around to their side. Only a day earlier the committee had urged people not to join in taking the city, but its leader now urged the government to back down and was working late into the night to organize new means of pressuring it to do so. The Departmental Federation of Neighborhood Councils called for citywide road blockades for the next morning.[35] United in the streets, these three organizations now stood shoulder to shoulder.

Over time the mobilization broadened with the addition of newly politicized organizations (especially the water committees), the tacit endorsement of numerous civic organizations outraged by the price hike, and the unmediated assent of tens of thousands through the cabildos and the unofficial referendum. Finally, the activity of the street confrontations themselves gave the alliance a territorial character: Zona Sur blockaders, young "water warriors" from across the metropolis, and the central zone supporters who gave them food, aid, and comfort began to perceive themselves and one another as representing their communities. And in their collaboration, numbers, and acts of unity, they took on the mantle of representing a regional subject, a *Cochabambinidad* (Cochabamba-ness) that the region spoke as one.

At heightened points in mobilization, collective political subjects merge into commonplace narratives. The Coordinadora, Cochabamba, and the upheaval became mutually identified when "all of 'cochabambinidad,' with very few exceptions . . . gave itself over" to a unified political demand (as *Los Tiempos* editorialists would recall a dozen years later).[36] On June 9, the final day of the 2005 upheaval, which I describe later in this chapter, "Cochabamba cabildo-ed," according to a headline in the daily *Gente*. This Cochabamba was embodied in a multitude made up of "tens of social, neighborhood, labor, and shopkeeper institutions, among others," who "determined to begin acts of civil resistance." In an unusual journalistic move, the article attributed quotations to the speakers as a collective rather than to individuals, naming six with their sectoral affiliations.[37]

Language makes it easier for Bolivian cities to take on this role of collective subject. *El pueblo* literally means both "the people" and "the town," and *el pueblo* may appear as combative actor ("El pueblo took over the plaza," meaning certain protesters did), as public opinion ("El pueblo [a reference to the city] rejects the rate hike for water"), as the owner of common resources ("The gas belongs to el pueblo"—that is, Bolivians as a whole), and as a mix of all these ("Goni has fallen; el pueblo has won").[38] Since five departmental capitals share the names of the larger departments, Cochabamba or La Paz, for example, can be used to identify a region where peasants and urban citizens are united. The Altiplano and El Alto came into their own as political subjects through high-profile uprisings.

This felt unity was in some ways my most surprising research finding. After all, these were moments of profound political conflict, combat, suffering, and victory. Narratives of the grassroots upsurge tend to emphasize a class-defined protagonist—whether that is the working class, the impoverished urban periphery, or the indigenous peasant—or the overcoming of the specific subordination of indigenous peoples. (This is how the Left has long told the story of revolution, after all.) The grassroots upsurge in Bolivia was all of these things, but it claimed its political legitimacy from moments of collective action in which these divisions seemed to be transcended. People in movement asserted their right to sovereignty from the widely shared sense that they were "the people," that their breadth extended to everyone.

There are important points of resonance between this notion of the people and the imagined community of the nation as described by Benedict Anderson. The elements Anderson emphasizes—anonymous personal sacrifice, a deep continuity that endures longer than any one political force, and comradeship among equals who need not know one another personally—all are affirmed by mass protest. This is particularly true when, as I will show later in this chapter, demonstrators mix the ceremonies and ceremonial spaces of state rule with political protest. While protesters sometimes put the nation of Bolivia at the center, they also identify themselves with long-subordinated indigenous nationalities or insist on a plurinational Bolivia that encompasses multiple ethnic groups. Space-claiming protest thus becomes a tool for both claiming and reimagining the political community of Bolivia.

## Cabildos: Claiming the Power of the Plaza

"This thing about the cabilidos didn't begin with the Water War," Marcela Olivera explained. "Cabildos were there since before the Republic." When the plaza is taken over, it is often to make a claim of popular sovereignty. The town halls in Spanish colonial towns usually were called cabildos, the word also used for the council of officials who met inside the town halls. That council was the most horizontally organized of the institutions of colonial government, but it was composed of local elites throughout the period of Spanish rule. These exclusive cabildos nonetheless convened larger gatherings—cabildos abiertos—for a wide variety of decisions.[39] Members of the public gathered in the city hall, the cathedral, or upon the central plaza itself on a Sunday, the day residents of the outlying countryside were most likely to visit the city.[40] "In the plaza, everything was decided," Olivera continued. "It's like the plaza [is where] all of the powers are brought together. And so it's is a space of power disputes that aren't merely symbolic but also physical."[41]

Every Bolivian schoolchild learns of the cabildos abiertos convened during the struggle for independence from Spain. The names of central plazas memorialize moments of departmental or national independence struggles, when these gatherings were used to proclaim independence.[42] The commonsense meaning of a cabildo abierto is a mass gathering that puts the will of the government in question. The term has been invoked at moments of revolutionary crisis across twentieth-century Bolivia.[43]

Today's cabildos abiertos are large-scale mass meetings that combine the tasks of demonstrating the mass support for a movement and making decisions about its direction. What sets these meetings apart from others is the open call for participation and attendance. Pivotal cabildos in the run-up to the Water War were held in the Zona Sur, bringing together neighbors who committed to joint mobilization. These gatherings brought water committee representatives and other neighbors together on sports fields to hear calls from the Coordinadora to mobilize.

The largest cabildos of the Water War took place in the Plaza 14 de Septiembre. "We convened [the public] through the radio, through media that were totally accessible," Herbas, the Coordinadora spokesman, recalled in an interview. These open calls brought in thousands of wealthier citizens with few or no connections to the organic grassroots organizations of the urban outskirts. A cabildo abierto is nothing if not a show of numbers and political strength. A protest can become so large and diverse that it conveys a common popular sentiment, even to political adversaries. With rich and poor both affected by the privatization of the water supply, "things heated up and we had an enormous support, and soon the Plaza . . . would end up completely full."[44]

Assemblies, large and small, are the linchpin of grassroots political ethics in Bolivia, the mechanism by which the collective will is revealed and leaders are held to account.[45] Even within this tradition the Coordinadora's leadership made an unusual public commitment to the will of the people assembled. Herbas recalled that "effort was always made to ensure that the important decisions were collective ones. We were especially careful that, for example, entering into some mobilization, or taking some definitive measure, or that type of things, had to be a decision assumed by the assemblies."[46] For Eliana Quiñones Guzmán this horizontal process made the decision collective: "It wasn't someone who said it. . . . The people decided in the assembly, and so it was done. . . . And when the people decided, 'We're going to blockade,' *everyone* came out to blockade."[47] Collective decision making prompted collective participation.

The Coordinadora's leadership, guided by assemblies of grassroots organizations, attempted in turn to guide the movement from the balcony. Marcela Olivera described these efforts: "When there were cabildos in the plaza, the structure, the assembly of the Coordinadora, would meet beforehand, and they would say, 'What are we going to do?,' 'What are we going to say?,' or 'What is the strategy?,' right? And then they would go out on the balcony and offer a little bit of this direction, right, and would say, 'Okay, we're going to do this.' And then the people would sort of decide by means of applause or by booing." However, Herbas recalls that the crowds at cabildos radicalized the Coordinadora's agenda by using chants from street level to push for breaking the contract: "The cabildo was demanding greater things, that Aguas del Tunari must go." Meanwhile, at the bargaining table the Coordinadora spokesmen tried to offer "a certain serenity . . . not an intransigent stance but rather an openness to negotiation."[48]

In spite their leaders, the results of the cabildos were relatively consistent: the crowds pushed the Coordinadora's leadership to take a stronger stance. Generally, the Cochabambans in the plaza demanded a maximalist agenda for negotiations (annulling rather than modifying the privatization contract) and applauded an overall strategy of blockade-based pressure and mass public ratification of the Coordinadora's legitimacy. That hours of clashes in the streets were sometimes required even to meet in the plaza surely led the crowd to harden its stance.

During the April mobilization, as government and Civic Committee representatives gathered in the Prefectura, a team of Coordinadora negotiators found their way inside too. The two establishment forces literally refused to give them a seat at the table, while hundreds of protesters in the plaza refused to let them out the front door. The demand for negotiations was spatialized. When the Coordinadora's leadership was called into negotiations three turbulent days later, the leaders held fast to the idea that the cabildo had to have the final say on any agreement and refused to guarantee that blockades would be lifted once a draft was agreed upon.

Cabildos both credibly claim to speak for the people as a whole and exercise a practical sovereignty over the city through the actions they coordinate. While claiming the space of the plaza, they effectively govern all the spaces shut down by blockades and all the workplaces shuttered by strikes. The government's tangible loss of control over urban space and flows of vital necessities (like food, fuel, or water) puts its claim to control in question. While defying government attempts at repression, protesters stand as a physical negation of the orders to silence their mobilization. "At the culmination of the struggle," Oscar Olivera told interviewers for the film *The Corporation* (2003), "the army remained in their barracks, the police also remained in their stations, the members of Congress became invisible; the governor . . . resigned."[49] The plaza also grew in ritual and political significance. When the army sharpshooter Robinson Iriarte shot the teenager Víctor Hugo Daza dead in the street, a crowd carried his body a half-dozen blocks north to the plaza. The next day his funeral attracted about forty thousand mourners who walked from the plaza to the General Cemetery.[50]

At such a moment a sufficiently large and effective cabildo appears to express another grassroots sovereignty opposed to that of the state. The grassroots govern the street protests, channel demands, vote on negotiating proposals, elevate their own leaders, and honor the dead. Oscar Olivera told the filmmakers: "There was no 'legal' authority"—his hands draw quotation marks around the word—"The only legitimate authority was the people, who were in a cabildo, who were in the plaza, and who made their decisions in large assemblies, and who in the end decided about the water." It was dual power made visible. The experience of mass organization offers a taste of a different kind of politics that might one day become the norm. "I think people, all of us, young and old, could taste," Olivera concluded, "could quench our thirst for democracy."[51]

All of this is not to say, as some have argued, that cabildos abiertos are hives of direct democracy. While the cabildos are at the apex of this assembly-based, directly democratic tradition, in practice they offer far less horizontal participation than smaller gatherings or the assemblies of unions and neighborhood committees.[52] (For an example of the bare minimum of direct democracy in a cabildo, see box 5 on pages 132–33.) Bolivian urban squares did not have the kinds of long-term, self-organized protest camps that would later characterize the Arab Spring, Occupy, and the Spanish and Greek antiausterity movements. Given their size and lack of internal structure, large Bolivian cabildos are essentially rallies with decision-making power.

The Coordinadora, with its multiple assemblies, organizing committees, and assembly-led affiliate organizations, did constitute an impressive directly democratic form of organizing. But forms of organization differ greatly from mobilization to mobilization in Bolivia. In cases where established organizations predominate, officers in formal vertical structures may have significant power to speak on behalf of their movements. Yet even in these cases the common collective understandings—that the membership as a whole decides, that leaders are often corrupt, and that movements have the right to bypass or replace their leaders—all push power toward the base level of organizations.[53] Cabildos abiertos are places where movements can speak together; to understand how this voice is assembled, you must look beyond the plaza to a larger network of meetings, conversations, and movement-building spaces.

## Toward National Uprisings

As the Water War progressed, and as Cochabamban activists joined in national mobilizations in later years, this claim to sovereignty became more and more developed. The mobilization's signature slogan—"The Water Is Ours!"—put the idea of public ownership of resources at the center of the dispute. Activists appropriated the idea of "national patrimony" and contrasted their stance with those of politicians they labeled *vendepatrías*, those who sold out their country. These moves were part of a shift from particular demands about resources and policies to general demands about economic and political direction. Ángel Hurtado recalled: "We began simply with the matter of water, to lower the rate and throw out Aguas del Tunari. But it grew; the position of the organizations grew. And it was no longer simply the water, but instead it was the Constituent Assembly, that Goni must go, or first that Banzer must go and so must Aguas del Tunari. And from there we put forward political questions, right? And it was not only the water. It was something much more—it matured then."[56]

Hurtado's slip about Gonzalo "Goni" Sánchez de Lozada is revealing—Hugo Banzer was the president of Bolivia at the time of the Water War, and Sánchez de Lozada succeeded him. Hurtado's recollection of the Water War makes the later demand to oust Goni, which came during the Gas War in 2003, part of a single continuing process. Carlos Mesa Gisbert, the vice president until Goni's October 2003 departure, had the distinction of seeing his presidency begin and end with blockades of capital cities. A new round of protest in May 2005 would end in his resignation.

Blockades and civic strikes, converging marches and cabildos—the key elements of protest I have highlighted so far—continued to be the vital structural elements of the 2003 and 2005 conflicts. What made these mobilizations so consequential was that they replicated blockades and strikes on an even wider geographic scale, while the twin cities of El Alto and La Paz became the sites of convergence for delegations from movements across the country. The patterns of multiple coalescing marches and of protest itineraries linking grassroots spaces to governmental ones held again. Three spaces in particular,

## Box 5. How a Cabildo Speaks

On February 18, 2011, several public sector unions—urban and rural teachers, and health workers for the public health service and the Casegural pension system—and some factory workers and retirees participated in a joint march that was part of a nationwide strike wave demanding higher pay. The Trotskyist-aligned teachers in La Paz marched in with signs demanding radical economic measures (EXPEL THE TRANSNATIONAL CORPORATIONS!), revolutionary political steps (WORKERS AND PEASANTS TO POWER!) and wage increases (SALARY INCREASES IN ACCORDANCE WITH THE FAMILY BASKET!). Like many marches, this one culminated in a joint rally, filling the plaza atop the newly reconstructed Mercado Camacho, which overlooks the central park in downtown La Paz. Thousands of workers gathered in that square, and speakers

FIGURE 12 From atop a small platform in the Plaza Camacho in La Paz, labor leaders address a crowd on February 18, 2011, to pledge the formation of an inter-union strike committee. The sign above the speaker reads, SALARY INCREASE IN ACCORDANCE WITH THE FAMILY BASKET, while the label on the prop to the right is EMPTY FAMILY BASKET.

from each of the unions present made fiery speeches from a platform that jutted out into the crowd. Journalists thrust cameras, tape recorders, and digital devices into the air to capture their words, while two loudspeakers on tripods made the shouted arguments audible to the entire crowd. This was the cabildo abierto of the Inter-Union Strike Committee (Comité Intersindical), an alliance of unions pressuring the Bolivian Workers' Central union confederation from the left. The decision-making aspect wasn't particularly prominent, however. The Casegural health worker union leader's speech was ending when he added, "Now, this cabildo has got to put forward some important resolutions on all that has been spoken about by the compañeros. Given this situation, help me by shouting." Crowd shouts of ¡Que viva! (Long live!) and ¡Abajo! (Down with!) were just the acclamation needed to approve this sentence of resolutions: "Long live the unity of all the workers! ¡Que viva! Down with hunger and misery! ¡Abajo! Down with the country-selling government of Evo Morales. ¡Abajo! Down with the traitorous [union] bureaucracy. ¡Abajo!"[54] The Inter-Union Strike Committee was able to elaborate this approval into a twelve-point resolution.[55] Despite the abbreviated approval and the lack of debate, there was nothing in the longer document that hadn't been said from the podium: the speakers had in fact explained that by the "unity of the workers" they meant an interunion alliance to hold strikes. To put "hunger and misery" behind us, the transnational corporations would have to be expropriated without compensation. Nor could one easily discount the enthusiasm of the crowd and their frustration with both the national government and the leadership of the Bolivian Workers' Central union confederation. While this was by far the most compressed process I observed, it reflects the relative absence of participation and deliberation in many large cabildos and cabildos' dependence on continued mobilizing power and circumstance, rather than their approved language, to have real effects. This gathering reflected not so much the feelings of the crowd as the organization of a pact among unions to press for mobilization. In the end, despite the words from the podium and in the resolution, this cabildo will be remembered as one step forward in a strike wave that crested not with the fall of President Evo Morales but with a modest wage increase two months later. (For more on this strike, see chapter 7.)

FIGURE 13 The main road entering La Paz from El Alto passes through the Plaza San Francisco, a massive space for popular gatherings. A new multistory public market was under construction when this photo was taken in June 2008.

El Alto's Ceja market, La Paz's plebeian Plaza San Francisco, and its formal Plaza Murillo, were the points of focus. The Ceja ("Brow" or "Rim") market is perched on the edge of the bowl-like valley that contains La Paz and is the core of an open-air marketplace that stretches for blocks in several directions. Protesters gathered there have several options for descending to La Paz, including the downhill Autopista (highway), whose tollbooth presents a ready target for antigovernment anger.

No space is as emblematic of the Bolivian political upsurge as La Paz's Plaza San Francisco. The Church of San Francisco (now a basilica) was built from 1549 to 1581 to serve the indigenous-majority town across the river from early colonial La Paz. The Choqueyapu River, which once separated indigenous people from the Spaniards in La Paz, now runs in a culvert beneath the city's principal roadway, a six-lane thoroughfare that descends from El Alto. Working-class vendors fill the streets above the plaza with their tables, booths, and blankets in an open-air market that extends for many blocks uphill. Across from the basilica stands the eight-story high-rise belonging to the Factory Workers Union Federation of La Paz Department, built in the early 1970s.[57] Between the indigenous popular cathedral and the proletarian syndicalist union headquarters, four decades of Bolivian popular movements have gathered their forces in the capital.

A half-dozen blocks uphill the Presidential Palace (Palacio Quemado) and Legislative Palace stand on La Paz's main plaza, the Plaza Murillo. Although contained within the street grid of the old city, it still offers an expansive space around its central fountain for official processions, passersby, and pigeons, and it contains a chock-a-block cluster of official monuments. This plaza was itself disputed terrain in a long history of popular revolts stretching back to the 1809 independence struggle and its leader, Pedro Domingo Murillo, for whom the square was named.[58]

In 2003 and 2005 people gathered for cabildos in both the Ceja and Plaza San Francisco, while marchers along the Ceja–San Francisco–Murillo trajectory (as well as into elite sectors of the capital) could imagine themselves carrying grassroots legitimacy with them into more rarefied spaces of power and privilege. Cabildos of unprecedented scale and diversity brought as many as two hundred thousand people into the Plaza San Francisco to demand and win the ouster of two presidents.

## The Gas War of 2003

During the three-and-a-half years between the Water War and late 2003, a steady drumbeat of mass mobilizations rocked Bolivia. Protesters often won tactical victories, as in the peasant protests of September 2000 that secured a seventy-two-point agreement for rural development, but the government's promises remained unfulfilled. Or they pushed back government initiatives, as in the February 2003 revolt sparked by a new tax, only to see them rise again. Gonzalo "Goni" Sánchez de Lozada, the architect of Bolivian neoliberalism, had won the 2002 presidential election with a scant 22.5 percent of the votes in a crowded field of candidates. Goni built a governing coalition committed to privatizing state assets and pursued a broadly unpopular plan to export Bolivia's gas through a pipeline to a Chilean port. Seemingly in anticipation of mass pushback against its plans, the government moved to criminalize blockades and other direct-action protests in August 2003.[59]

The 2003 Gas War erupted from a cascade of actions by various unions and associations pressing a wide array of demands. Particularly important within this broad sweep of actions were a peasant movement making demands about agrarian issues and for greater indigenous autonomy; a national alliance of organizations pressing demands against the privatization and export of gas; the massive mobilization of residents of the poor city of El Alto; and the late support of largely middle-class demonstrators and political elites through an October hunger strike. The many disparate sectors and causes in Bolivia, including both sectoral demands and more generalized fears about the loss of national wealth, the lack of industrialization, official corruption, and violence by the military and police, finally had reason to come together, and they made possible a historic mobilization.

Beginning on September 2, seventy-five leaders from the Unified Union Confederation of Rural Bolivian Workers (CSUTCB) and urban movements in El Alto marched from Caracollo toward the capital.[60] From September 6 to 8, three thousand marchers trekked fifty kilometers from the shores of Lake Titicaca to El Alto (where the two marches merged) to demand government action on the seventy-two-point agreement that had been reached in September 2000. There, five hundred to one thousand Alteños and peasants joined Felipe Quispe Huanca, a leader of the Pachakuti Indigenous Movement, in a hunger strike that began on September 10 at Radio San Gabriel. Meanwhile a government proposal to build a foreign-owned pipeline to export gas through Chile (long the object of nationalist ire for its possession of Bolivia's lost coastal territory) aroused widespread indignation. Five days earlier grassroots organizations and political parties like the MAS-IPSP, meeting in Oruro, had formed a Coordinadora for the Defense and Recovery of Gas for a national mobilization that they already were calling the *guerra de gas*.[61]

The gas coordinadora called a nationwide strike on September 19. That day an estimated sixty thousand people streamed from six locations into Cochabamba's Plaza 14 de Septiembre "in defense of the gas," where representatives of the Bolivian Workers' Central union federation, Fabriles, cocaleros, peasants, professionals, and veterans of the 1932–35 Chaco War spoke from the balcony.[62] In La Paz a large but festive morning demonstration, during which demonstrators dressed as oil barrels danced and waved a wiphala, contrasted with a military show of force that put three rings of troops onto the streets to defend the Plaza Murillo.[63] Transport drivers, teachers, and war widows in the city of La Paz, CSUTCB-affiliated peasants and agrarian colonists in La Paz Department, indigenous peoples in the north of the country, and the Potosí Civic Committee all conducted simultaneous strike actions, each with local demands.[64]

Campesinos in the CSUTCB organized road blockades around El Alto and La Paz from early September. When the national government sent antiterrorist troops to break the union's blockade in the Altiplano town of Warisata on September 20, bloody confrontations left at least six people dead, including one soldier.[65] By bringing death to Warisata, the military focused attention on a community with impeccable credentials in campesino organizing that had also sent numerous indigenous volunteers into the Chaco War. That previous generation's sacrifice in defense of the gas-producing region of Tarija, alongside the current generation's sacrifice for the rural indigenous cause, made the town a symbol of the overlapping struggle of Altiplano campesinos and opponents of gas privatization.

The regional labor federation Central Obrera Regional–El Alto and the Federation of Neighborhood Councils (FEJUVE–El Alto) organized a series of marches, roadblocks, and civic strikes, paralyzing public transit, blockading arterial roads, and closing access to outside regions beginning on September 29 and escalating to an indefinite civic strike on October 8. Once again participants made the ever-multiplying blockades and La Paz–bound marches into a public symbol of solidarity. Six thousand merchants marched from Oruro, three thousand miners left from Huanuni, and more than a thousand cocaleros departed from the Yungas. Three hundred marchers left Cochabamba, bound for Warisata, on a "march for life, gas, and the right to a job."

In short, a dizzying array of groups were converging their marches and synchronizing their strikes by the beginning of October. The various groups put forward a platform in opposition to the export of natural gas and the new tax code and in favor of joining the Free Trade Area of the Americas. Organizations pledged not to make separate agreements with the state and to support one another's demands. And following the deaths in Warisata, all forces called for the resignation of President Gonzalo Sánchez de Lozada.[66] In Cochabamba the water committees of the Zona Sur began mobilizing to set up blockades in solidarity. It was less a matter of direct interest than solidarity. As Marcela Olivera recalls, it was a way "of saying, 'They are killing people like us over there. Why don't we do something about it here?'"[67]

As part of the El Alto civic strike, protesters blocked gasoline tankers bound for La Paz. On October 11 the military organized a convoy to break the blockade. Hundreds of soldiers and Special Security Group riot police escorted the tankers from the oil refinery in Senkata on the outskirts of El Alto. Thousands of Bolivians faced off against the troops, throwing stones and dynamite. The soldiers deployed tear gas, fired rubber bullets, and then opened fire with live ammunition, killing dozens of people on a route that stretched across El Alto. (It's worth noting that what prompted the government's deadly escalations on September 20 and October 11 was the interruption of food and fuel deliveries and the stranding of international tourists.) The violence shocked the public but failed to intimidate protesters. Alteños dug trenches and felled trees, lampposts, and pedestrian bridges to obstruct principal roads through their city. Hugo Torres, the secretary of conflicts for the La Paz factory workers' union, recounted to me "those difficult moments, when no one could be sure of their own life. . . . Our obligation was to defend, on one hand, our own lives and those of our family but also, on the other hand, to fight once and for all for everyone and to stop the massacre."[68]

After that deadly October weekend, Vice President Mesa distanced himself from the government. The killings also generated middle-class outrage, expressed through a second wave of hunger strikes led by Ana María Romero de Campero and the Permanent Assembly of Human Rights.[69] As churches opened their doors to host hunger-strike pickets, more than a thousand people swore off food at eighty-three sites in eight departments.[70] Members of the National Congress also joined the hunger strike, including Elsa Guevara, the ranking legislator from the MIR Party, which was part of the president's governing coalition.[71]

The protesters had convinced elites that they had the Bolivian public on their side. Hugo San Martín, a congressional deputy in Sánchez de Lozada's party, said on October 14, "Governability is not just a matter of having a majority in Congress, it is legitimacy before the population. This is the end of one stage of democracy and the beginning of a second, with greater public participation."[72] Cochabamba prefect Manfred Reyes Villa, a coalition partner of the Sánchez de Lozada government, also abandoned it. While visiting the presidential palace, he told the media, "I have come to tell the president to listen to the Bolivians. We cannot go against the current. What are we waiting for? Greater spilling of blood?"[73] According to one report, direct pleas by Romero de Campero and security adviser Juan Ramón Quintana to commanders led the military to warn Sánchez de Lozada that they would return to their barracks.[74]

Finally, on October 16 about two hundred thousand people joined in five converging marches that flooded La Paz's Plaza San Francisco and the streets around it. The labor leader Jaime Solares began the early afternoon cabildo by proposing more hunger-strike committees, trenches, and barricades, but, as *La Prensa* reported, "the demonstrators were tired of speeches: 'Let's go into action,' they demanded." Responding to the mood like a seasoned Bolivian grassroots leader, Solares urged them to surround the government palace and the Plaza Murillo, vowing, "We are not going to lose this social war. . . . We are not afraid of this butchering government."[75] The street battles that followed extended for hours and continued until the police cut electricity and left the streets in darkness.[76] The massive gathering was the final mobilization before Sánchez de Lozada's resignation on October 17 and his immediate departure to exile in Miami.

## 2005: Intervening in Succession

In 2004 President Carlos Mesa reclaimed the initiative with his own proposals for a constituent assembly and a referendum on Bolivia's gas resources. Mesa called for the referendum to be held on July 18, 2004, to authorize a middle way on the issue of gas nationalization and export plans. His government proposed to reestablish the state-owned gas corporation YPFB, put gas resources under nominal state ownership, and allow gas exports by private companies to be taxed by as much as 50 percent; the private companies would then be only "operating partners" in the extraction of state resources. Cochabamba's Coordinadora, El Alto's Regional Labor Confederation (COR–El Alto), the Bolivian Workers' Central union confederation, and CSUTCB opposed the referendum outright. All four organizations urged abstention or null votes (spoiled ballots). Labor and peasant leaders prepared blockades for the day of the vote. However, the MAS proposed a more subtle tactic: voting yes on three questions about nationalization but no on two questions about gas export.[77] Unlike its allies, the MAS preferred to channel popular energy to the ballot box rather than construct alternate forms of politics. The contrasting stances divided the grassroots Left, and Mesa's five points won majority backing of those voting, though boycott efforts dampened voter turnout. Only in 2005, after Alteños fought their own Water War to reverse privatization of their municipal water company, did these forces come back together in the streets.

The national crisis in May and June 2005 reprised the 2003 Gas War, but the entire process was accelerated. On May 2 an enormous crowd of Alteños, led by the local workers' confederation and neighborhood council federation, marched on the Senkata refinery, the scene of the bloodiest day in 2003. Departing from the Ceja market area on the rim of the Altiplano, the crowd stretched for about three miles before the last marchers left their starting point. The peaceful and symbolic action kicked off a call for nationalizing the country's hydrocarbons.[78] Two weeks later the same forces were marching on downtown La Paz, threatening to close the National Congress. Heliodoro Equiapaza, vice president of FEJUVE–El Alto, told the press, "We want the president to fulfill his promise of October 18, [2003]. . . . He said the gas would be nationalized and industrialized, and that he would not betray the city of El Alto."[79] Numerous sectors joined the Alteños in their demands, first within La Paz Department and later across the country. Teachers were already on strike, and labor federations gathered in Santa Cruz, Sucre, and Potosí to plan a national wave of pressure. Paceño legislators began a hunger strike within the Chamber of Deputies. An indefinite general strike in El Alto began on May 22 and with only one respite (May 27 to 30) continued to constrict supplies and transport in and out of La Paz until the end of the crisis on June 10.

New elements in the 2005 protest included a wide variety of infrastructure takeovers, which were concentrated in the oil and gas sector at the center of the dispute. Protesters occupied seven gas fields and closed the valves at several pumping stations.[80] Other direct-action strikes occurred in the heavy transport sector as well as in the nationalized cement and beer industries. Road blockades multiplied in the final days of the conflict, reaching 119 on June 9.[81] Marches on the Plaza Murillo became continual and threatening. President Mesa recounts, "Thousands of demonstrators made a ring of iron around the Plaza [Murillo], marching for hours with strong dynamite explosions and the intent to defeat police control so as to take over the Parliament."[82] On June 2 the National Congress was unable to meet because its building was surrounded and MAS-IPSP delegates opposed the session. These actions expanded the tactical repertoire of popular protest, and they moved the protesters closer to securing direct implementation of their demands.

Bolivian presidents had long taken their mandates from the streets, but here the street was ready to take it back. Unlike 2003, a change of faces in the Palacio Quemado was not even on the agenda of the protesters; at the top of the list of grassroots demands were, instead, the nationalization of gas and the convening of a constituent assembly to redefine the governing model of the country. From the palace in La Paz, Mesa tried a number of responses: denouncing the mobilizations as tantamount to a coup d'état on May 30 and signing supreme decrees authorizing both a constituent assembly and an autonomy referendum for the eastern departments on June 2. The president made pleas in an effort to turn public support against the blockades and proposed to resign if he didn't receive the public's backing to govern. (A similar gambit, including a formal resignation letter that the National Congress did not accept, had resolved a protest crisis in March 2005.) Finally on June 6 he announced, "I have done what I can so that Bolivia can manage to fulfill an agenda that is the agenda of all. . . . I believe that I have the responsibility to say that this is as far as I can go," and offered his definitive resignation.[83] Mesa directed police to keep protesters from key locations but did not authorize bloodshed.

The country was suddenly without a president, and all sides turned to the battle over succession. Second in line to the presidency was the right-wing president of the Senate, Hormando Vaca Díez, who publicly and privately vowed to confront protesters without hesitation or limits. The senator secured a working coalition for a new government. According to Mesa, Vaca Díez also sought American backing, promising U.S. Ambassador David Greenlee that "immediately upon taking power, he would bring order; he calculated that in three days the country would be under control. Greenlee believed him."[84] In negotiations sponsored by the Catholic church, Vaca Díez refused to cede his right to the presidency, leaving Mesa with no guarantees when he resigned on June 6.[85]

With La Paz under protesters' control, Vaca Díez announced that the National Congress would move its sessions to Sucre. The official capital was effectively neutral ground between the leftist-indigenous-grassroots mobilizations of the previous five years and the autonomy push from the senator's native Santa Cruz. But Vaca Díez needed Congress to formally convene and accept Mesa's resignation so that power would pass to him. MAS-IPSP and the legislators from the Pachakuti Indigenous Movement demanded that both Vaca Díez and the head of the Chamber of Deputies renounce their right of succession—in favor of the neutral Supreme Court president Eduardo Rodríguez Veltzé—before any session could start.[86]

The grassroots quickly shifted its focus of mobilization to Sucre, coordinating a convergence of campesinos, teachers, and students from across Chuquisaca; cooperative miners and ayllus from Oruro and Potosí who had been organized

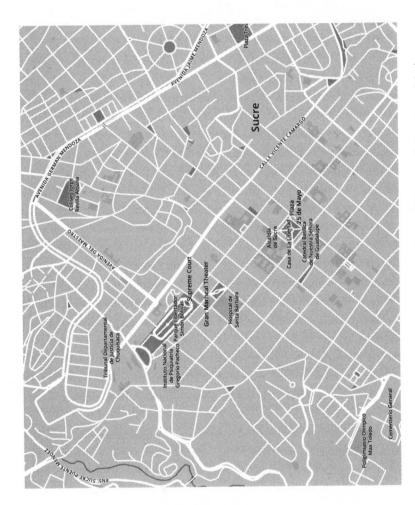

MAP 6 Central Sucre. (Map prepared by Emma Banks. © Mapbox © OpenStreetMap)

by the National Council of Ayllus and Markas of Qullasuyu; and urban protesters from Sucre itself. Protesters replicated their strategy from La Paz around Sucre's central Plaza 25 de Mayo. The outnumbered police confined themselves to defending the blocks around the square from encroachment by protesters. Within the plaza on June 9 legislators met in cafes and restaurants and counted votes. Some urged Mesa's representative, Jorge Cortés, to open the cordon "to permit the people to enter the plaza and pressure the Congress."[87] Sucre's mayor, Aydée Nava, was at the forefront of organizing middle-class hunger strikes to urge Rodríguez's succession as president.

By June 9 there were ninety-four hunger strikes across the country as fervor for direct action escalated.[88] Campesinos blockaded Sucre's four main land exits, to Potosí, Santa Cruz, Oruro, and Cochabamba. That night military troops outside the city killed Juan Carlos Coro Mayta, a leader of cooperative miners from Potosí, ratcheting tensions higher.[89] Security officials informed members of Congress that the police were on the verge of being overrun.[90] Grassroots protest disabled and isolated Sucre's airport (through an air traffic controllers' strike), while the military high command tried to dissuade the Senate president from his claim. Several centrist political parties withdrew support they had promised to Vaca Díez.[91] Finding himself politically stranded, Vaca Díez conceded the presidency between 9:00 and 9:30 p.m. Just after midnight Eduardo Rodríguez took the presidential oath with an extraordinarily narrow mandate: to hold elections in December 2005. While Rodríguez's succession brought a quick end to protests in Sucre and across the country, the new president had to personally appeal to movement leaders in El Alto to end the city's blockades.

Evo Morales was not instrumental in the agitation that brought down Mesa, though Morales led congressional opposition to a Vaca Díez presidency.[92] Furious that Morales had supported the 2004 referendum, El Alto workers had even threatened "to submit [him] to community justice" should he betray the alliance formed in March 2005.[93] Still, Morales would spend the succeeding months and years securing his administration's identification with the waves of unrest that had characterized 2000 to 2005. Morales kicked off his presidential campaign in the Plaza San Francisco on October 12, his body clothed in movement symbols: "A YPFB mining helmet, a staff, and a whip given to him by indigenous authorities."[94] Morales took as his primary mandates the recuperation of Bolivia's gas resources, the expansion of indigenous and campesino land rights, and the convening of a constituent assembly.

## The Sovereign Street

In the afternoon heat of a sunny Cochabamba day, Christian Mamani, the community leader from Santa Vera Cruz, is telling me about the struggle for downtown during the Water War. Suddenly, he shifts his emphasis from the experience of protest to its political significance:

> We confronted the army, and we had some tragic losses of some of the youths. But the fight was really about how can a state, how can a government, as the representative of the people, of a nation, not have to be accountable to the nation? That was the dispute. If the people want for the decree to be annulled, then it must be annulled. Because the voice of the people is the voice of God. . . . I believe that it is we the people who forge our own destiny—it is not economic interests or the personal interests of those who govern. . . . That was what the fight was about and I think that we were all conscious of that.[95]

A decade after the events Mamani focuses his memory of the Water War on an intensely political question, the right of "the people" to "forge our political destiny," to have the government be responsive to them, to understand that the people's will is sovereign. He describes that will as sacred, precisely in the sense described by Émile Durkheim: "Society . . . consecrates things, especially ideas. If a belief is unanimously shared by a people, then . . . it is forbidden to touch it . . . to deny it or to contest it."[96]

Revolutionary events take place in times of uncertainty in the balance of power. Bolivia's political culture, forged through generations of social upheaval, links the embodied collective experience of protest to the political foundations of a social order. Grassroots movements, assemblies, the language of militancy and protest all are part of that political inheritance. Occasionally new levels of mobilization exceed the traditional upper limits of popular power, while mechanisms of repression and control seem newly ineffective. Suddenly it seems obvious that physical actions, the very things being planned and decided upon in gatherings on the street, can affect the political future. Simultaneously the very things that make these moments so extraordinary to live through—communitas, liminality, shared danger, and unprecedented affective solidarity—allow the emotional flexibility to reinterpret the political order. The collectivities that are the protagonists in the country's revolutionary tradition can suddenly become constituent parties within the new political order.

Sovereign crowds differ from ordinary political demonstrations because they are challenging rather than appealing to the state. Charles Tilly and other scholars of contentious politics argue that social movements organize conspicuous displays of worth, unity, numbers, and commitment (which he calls WUNC). In turn, states recognize these signs of democratic legitimacy and modify their policies accordingly. Conceived this way, social movement campaigns neither undermine nor question the authority of the state.[97] But what if grassroots movements see themselves not just as claimants before the state but as a rival power to it? What if they claim a bit of sovereignty for themselves? The mobilized communities described here do use their unity and numbers to illustrate their claim to represent the public as a whole. To create the shared impression that everyone is part of a mobilization, however, they also highlight diversity among themselves and carry out geographically expansive protests. And they demonstrate effective practical sovereignty over urban spaces and persistence in the face of state violence.

In summary a mobilization claiming sovereignty has worth, unity, numbers, and commitment but is also diverse, widespread, irrepressible, and in control.[98] When all these elements combine, a popular upheaval can effectively claim to be an alternative power deserving to replace the existing government. The largest cabildos in 2003 and 2005 claimed to represent Bolivia as a whole and actually exercised power over vast interruptions of daily life, capital streets, and the legislature's ability to meet. In the cabildos participants came to see coordination of different sectors as the way to realize the grassroots democracy they were increasingly demanding. Most shockingly these claims garnered respect and recognition even from state officials. Carlos Mesa and Eduardo Rodríguez both appeared before demonstrations to ask for their support. In 2005 and 2006 Evo Morales and Álvaro García Linera felt compelled to do the same thing, incorporating the Plaza San Francisco in their inaugural ceremonies. Each of these state leaders went out of his way to acknowledge and seek the approval of the sovereign street.

The moments of street sovereignty described in this chapter were exceptional. They emerged at times of unusually broad participation in protest, of unlikely coalitions, and of widespread (and apparently contagious) willingness to take exceptional risks. And they emerged in moments when the government was temporarily stripped of its democratic credentials by the apparent disconnect between its policies and the desires of the mobilized public. These sovereign crowds are more like strike committees than governments: they govern the protest but not the country, the metropolitan strike rather than the metropolis. Sometimes their term of office may extend for days or even weeks, forcing them to coordinate more and more of the necessities of life, but that term ends almost immediately when the protesters demobilize. But the limits on the sovereign street's power are uncertain, and protesters have turned many of their demands into reality, from the revocation of Bolivia's Water Law 2029 to the resignations of presidents.

In this chapter and chapter 3, I have shown how the sovereign crowds of the 1999–2005 grassroots upheaval challenged the political authority of the government, particularly when the crowds' message of grassroots sovereignty was amplified by the political geography of the spaces they claimed. However, many of the same mobilizations also spoke from a subordinated racial position: indigeneity. In chapters 5 and 6, I will shift focus to this racial dimension of claiming urban space.

## CHAPTER 5

# "We're No Longer Just Tenants"

*Indigenous Bodies Defiantly out of Place*

I n the midst of a crowded gathering in Cochabamba's Plaza 14 de Septiembre, the central plaza, in January 2011, a neatly dressed man takes the microphone to explain why "we" must defend the coca leaf. Marcelo Guzman, a self-employed electrician, is a ruddy-skinned urban Cochabamban whose large, forceful hands grip the microphone and his wooden flute. His thin spectacles sit below the beige brim of his hat and tuck into his salt-and-pepper hair. In his speech he weaves coca and the indigenous wiphala flag into a story of the previous twelve years of political struggle. Coca growers arrive in the narrative with the Water War: "Thanks to the campesinos, to our brothers, thanks to the cocaleros with their wiphala [colorful flag] who came to the city to defend our water, which is the water of life." Coca, he says, is what we chewed on the hard march to La Paz. "The coca leaf made it so that we could arrive with greater force to our destination so that they would hear us." As he speaks, the entire decade from the Water War through the fall of Goni and the struggles over the new constitution become a single path that a common "we" have walked, chewing coca all the while. Culture and politics, and likewise physical and political adversity, prove difficult to separate. Soon he reaches the crescendo of his speech, a synthesis of activist historical memory, coca's physicality, and the urban-rural alliance.

> Let's not forget that with the wiphala we arrived in government and in power, with the new political constitution of the state. It has cost us tears, it has cost us

suffering. . . . And now, compañeros, we can feel happy, for we have recovered our true home. We're no longer just tenants, now we are the owner of our homeland, and for that, comrades, we ought to feel proud. Compañeros, help me in saying: *Jallalla* Bolivia, *Jallalla* the sacred coca leaf.[1]

The affirmative Aymara chant Jallalla, the checkered-rainbow wiphala, and the dried green coca leaf all mark the indigenous face of recent Bolivian struggle.

The traditional crop is also the raw material for the lucrative narcotic cocaine, and integration in that global market, and the drug war combating it, would reshape Bolivian life. Beginning in the late 1970s highland Andean settlers brought coca plants to valleys of the Chapare, whose altitude (around three hundred meters above sea level) is two thousand meters lower than that of urban Cochabamba, and created a vast growing operation for the leaf. While far behind Colombia and Peru in coca leaf production, exports of coca and its illicit derivatives provided as much as 6 percent of Bolivia's gross domestic product.[2] For three decades Chapare coca growers resisted U.S.-backed eradication efforts that were part of the War on Drugs. Where many indigenous movements claim a unity of people, land, and culture, the cocaleros center their claims on the "sacred leaf," leaving aside the land, which they or their parents settled.[3] In the 1990s and 2000s the Chapare cocaleros and campesinos from the valleys marched alongside workers and poor city dwellers who increasingly recognized a cultural, familial, and political affinity with them. The cocaleros also built alliances with lowland indigenous peoples whose focus was self-rule and self-sufficiency. In a society that has long disrespected and excluded them all from its central decisions and its places of highest esteem, the subordinate racial status of indigenous Bolivians binds many particularities together.

Like the crowds at peak moments during the grassroots upheaval, Bolivia's indigenous majority is plural and multilayered but capable of concerted action. At such moments common opponents, symbols like the wiphala and concepts like refounding the country as a plurinational society enabled them to come together, and gave them hope of "recovering our true home." As indigenous collective subjects, these crowds claimed the right to redefine Bolivia, putting aside whatever parts of the state they rejected and reconfiguring politics to accommodate indigenous self-rule, an end to the impoverishment of the indigenous majority, and equal social status for indigenous individuals and cultures. They proposed a plurinational Bolivia that would mirror their plural mobilizations.

Understanding the impact of their mobilizations requires unearthing these underlying feelings about race and space in Bolivia. I begin with a single practice—the historical requirement that indigenous people yield the sidewalks to their whiter compatriots—and explore a web of associated meanings: servitude, ownership of space, restrictions on comportment, and absence of political voice. I show the differences in the governing of cities and rural areas, and in elite spaces of literate colonial officials and the surrounding spaces governed by their written words, all of which embedded race in geography. In recent decades being both urban and indigenous—like many of my interviewees—has become not just thinkable but a critical position from which to participate in grassroots politics. Despite this transformation, this hierarchical ordering of urban space remains intact.

When they gathered in city centers, indigenous Bolivians entered the urban spaces where their subordination had long been organized and enacted. Just as urban and rural mass protests unsettled the established geography of power, indigenous crowds disrupted Bolivia's racial geography. When indigenous people appear unbowed and represent themselves politically in the public spaces at the heart of the city, their presence creates drama. They violate their racial exclusion from space to speak from the centers of power but against the state as constituted. This potential for disruption is not new; as I will show next, it was used masterfully by the Cochabamba-led campaign for agrarian reform after the 1952 Revolution. Indeed indigenous people's takeover of spaces in central Cochabamba still incites strong emotions. I use a 2011 Cochabamba protest to illustrate how collectively living out indigenous culture in public space can be a richly political act. (As I show in chapter 6, when leftist protesters, many from outside the city, occupied the elite thoroughfares north of the city center in early 2007, they elicited a fierce and violent reaction.) These three examples all show how race-based understandings of urban spaces can powerfully amplify the importance of protests within them.

## The Emotional Power of Racial Geography

"Forty or fifty years ago, our ancestors didn't have the right to walk on the sidewalks," President Evo Morales remarked during his first inaugural address. He remembered: "Early this morning, I saw some of my brothers and sisters singing in the historic Plaza Murillo, the same Plaza Murillo where . . . forty or fifty years ago, we didn't have the right to enter. . . . That is our history."[4]

The obligation to yield the sidewalk and exclusion from the plaza were just two of many restrictions. Racial segregation had once been legally enforced in La Paz, Oruro, and even the small mining town of Huanuni.[5] These rules were emblematic of indigenous Bolivians' exclusion from public office and the ballot box—in effect, politics itself. This limit was now brought to an end in the most dramatic way possible. Portraying the speech, the Morales biographer Martín Sivak wrote, "In gestures and words [Morales] embodied the campesino who had come to the most important post in the city."[6] From the time of his 1997 election as a deputy in the National Congress, he was one of a handful of *indígenas* there and therefore was a living transgression of traditional Bolivian order.[7] This made him "a permanent official target . . . the perfect and long-wished-for enemy," subject to public accusations and private humiliations.[8]

Now President Evo Morales used his first turn at the podium to make the troubling historical memories of exclusion a public issue. Understanding Morales's remarks requires considering what such rules mean and why they are historically important. First, the obligation to yield the sidewalk is an intimate racial marker. Indigenous passersby who stepped down exposed themselves to greater amounts of dirt and discomfort in the often-earthen roadway, providing a margin of protection, safety, and deference to the anonymous, but they privileged creoles or mestizos they passed. Stepping down resonated with the assignment of (some) indigenous servants to the role of *pongo*, the personal servant who slept outside the doorway (hence the Quechua term from *punku*, door), giving up their comfort and cleanliness to provide immediate service to the master. The obligatory gesture of stepping off the roadway is thus a racialized generalization of the relatively common condition of indigenous servitude.

Anticolonial and Black writers from Frantz Fanon to James Baldwin to Audre Lorde have proffered in their works testimony that illustrates how public encounters with race powerfully shaped their personal identities and the limits racism can place on equal enjoyment of the public sphere.[9] The sidewalk rule inscribes a relationship between the mestizo or creole person who remains on the sidewalk and the indigenous woman, man, or child who is socially obligated to descend to the gutter. Both parties to such public interpersonal interactions were compelled to internalize the racial roles and characteristics involved in repeated interactions. As Susan Ruddick argues, encounters scripted in this way instruct those who experience them in their unequal worth and their vulnerability to violent enforcement of their obligation. She writes that "such encounters deeply scar the psyche, inscribing in the very bodies of people their understanding of themselves and their place in a racialized hierarchy."[10] In present-day Bolivia the street remains a place for face-to-face discrimination, where "the high-class women [jailonas] look at you badly" or strangers "insult the *pollera* and the color of one's skin."[11]

While not always immediately obvious, these kinds of rules have an intense spatial dimension. In their text or practice they define and demarcate spaces where mestizos and creoles are respected and yielded to in special ways. Many of Bolivia's segregation laws and conventions applied especially in the main plaza, its adjacent streets, or a specific radius around it, or else to spaces of convenience like streetcars and elevators. They were applied especially rigorously in spaces understood as belonging to creoles and mestizos, in the city and its center, not the marketplace or the rural village. Through such interactions the deferring indigenous person is compelled to yield not just passage through but ownership of public space to the dominant creole. The indigenous child who watches her parents give way to a passing creole would rapidly learn that this part of the city did not belong to people like her.

Law and custom assigned mestizo/creole ownership without excluding indigenous people entirely. Indeed the subordinated presence of the oppressed may be a more powerful sign of the power of the dominant than would banning the oppressed. Self-possessed indigenous bodies were regulated through restrictions on transit ridership, occupations, and eligibility for civic life. In the late 1800s Cochabamba prohibited indigenous people from "singing, dancing, or playing their instruments within ten blocks of the plaza."[12] In 1925 President Bautista Saavedra declared that indigenous men could not enter the Plaza Murillo in traditional dress.[13] Service was acceptable; self-representation was forbidden.

This pattern of scripted or regulated encounters, microaggressions, and internalized power differences is replicated in other urban interactions, which can be most striking to foreign observers. Unlike the sidewalk rule, most are played out around class. Indeed class, comportment, and geography largely constitute the racial difference between *cholos* (urbanized Indians, imputed to have European blood) and *indios* (rural "full-blooded" Indians). Carter Goodrich, a midtwentieth-century American visitor, offers a brief panorama of Indian (as opposed to cholo) occupations: "Whenever Indians appeared in La Paz before the revolution, they kept mainly to the back streets, dressed in an extremely ragged clothing, or drove llama trains loaded with llama dung to serve as fuel in their masters' town houses. Some of them served as bearers of burdens."[14] (Even his sympathetic language reflects a geographical displacement: cholo workers are "town dwellers" and feel "at home" in the city, while Indian domestic servants and porters "appear" in the city without residing in it.) Porters' lives were also circumscribed by rules of comportment. Goodrich continues, "One of these [bearers of burdens] appeared at our office in the hotel staggering under a wooden box of supplies which, according to the stenciled label, weighed well over 200 pounds. This he had carried upstairs on his back since Indians were not allowed to use the elevator."[15] The Argentine literary scholar Alicia Ortiz, who traveled to Bolivia in 1952 to document the revolution, had her own racial encounter with a porter at her hotel: A hotel employee pointed the porter out on the street ("*aquel bicho* [that critter]") and advised her of a maximum fee ("It's enough. These are abusers."). She observed the man in detail, "ragged and with indescribably tattered clothing," "his gait faltering under the weight of the suitcases . . . the lack of energy from his malnourished nature." Still, she handed him the prescribed amount. His haggling consisted of four words, "It's not much, mama," spoken with "a plaintive voice, that voice of the submissive servant that the Indian directs to the white person." She did not yield, and he emitted a "discordant wail, a kind of prolonged and deep sob" and "leaves suddenly without another word."[16]

Both Goodrich and Ortiz deploy these accounts to sum up in a moment, as Morales would do again in 2006, the contours and impact of racial power on the bodies and selves of indigenous peoples. The limits placed on Bolivia's indigenous majority, and the pain they caused, had many parallels across Latin America and beyond. Rules of sidewalk deference were applied in Tlacotalpan, Toluca, and Chiapas, Mexico, and to Africans and African Americans in apartheid South Africa and in the United States, the North as well as the South.[17] They originated as part of a broader set of forms of deference (removing hats, bowing heads, averting the gaze, etc.) that subordinates of many kinds had to follow. These rituals conflicted directly with the ideal of equal participation in a public sphere. As these examples illustrate, the rituals of deference became sore reminders of exclusion from that sphere and/or flashpoints for groups contesting that exclusion. While experienced immediately in these embodied interactions, this power was constructed and embedded in the cityscape through centuries of history.

## The Spatiality of Racial Power in Bolivian Cities

"Let's not fall into illusions. The cities have always been enemies of the Indian," declared Julio Butrón Mendoza, a peasant organizer from the high valley outside Cochabamba, in his memoir of the 1952 Revolution. In his account the urban area appears as a space totally hostile to the indigenous countryside: "It was in [the cities] that we carried out the services of *pongueaje* and *mitanaje* [rotating household servitude for men and women, respectively]; it was also in the populated centers where we were most devalued and where we suffered humiliations of all kinds like the ridicule of our dress, our skin color, our gross attitude, and our ignorance. In the cities there was not a single friend of the Indian. Only enemies. Only exploiters. Only landlords (even those who never owned even a square meter in property nor a single *colono* [unpaid laborer tied to the land])."[18]

Throughout Bolivia's colonial and republican history its elites constructed social hierarchy by assigning access, ownership, and roles in certain spaces on the basis of race. Yet even Spanish colonial cities were not in fact creole islands in an indigenous sea.[19] Instead, colonial cities were miniature reproductions of the urban-rural hierarchies of identity, power, and labor, crisscrossed by streets on which creole elites, mestizos, and indigenous all walked. The urban creole–rural indigenous polarity was an internal feature of towns and cities, of the segregation of residential and public spaces. The geographical boundaries of the creole/mestizo city were not the outer limits of towns but lines between zones of restricted behavior, respectful comportment, and role. The geography of power and the geography of race were analogous: governing spaces were coded as white spaces, within which indigenous politics were an aberration and indigenous servitude was routine.

When governing is a race- and gender-exclusive task, the governing body is presumed to be racially privileged and male, a standard that Nirmal Puwar calls the "somatic norm." "Specific bodies have been constructed out of the imagination of authority," she writes.[20] This association, made silently so long as there are no exceptions to exclusion, becomes visible when no-longer-subordinate people enter the exclusive space or take on the forbidden role. That transgression of boundaries arouses powerful emotions, which can include fear, anxiety, disorientation, and revulsion. The number and presence of the out-of-place bodies are amplified in importance and seem to threaten the structure of division altogether.[21]

## Urban and Indigenous Come Together

While *urban* and *indigenous* have long been taken as opposites in Bolivia and much of the rest of Latin America, they have recently begun to overlap to an unprecedented degree, qualitatively changing the racial cast of the Bolivian metropolis. On a Friday night in Cochabamba you may be invited to a *k'oa*, a gathering where coca leaves are burned with other objects, sometimes to seek good luck for new projects and sometimes merely to celebrate community and offer gratitude. These everyday practices correlate with indigenous identity since many (but surely not all) upper-class Cochabambans disdain coca chewing. Cochabamba swelled as new residents built the neighborhoods of the Zona Sur, and its neighboring cities knitted together into an urban conglomerate spanning seven municipalities. In most Bolivian cities poor periurban dwellers outnumber the entire pre-expansion population of their cities, and most self-identified indigenous Bolivians now live in rapidly growing urban areas.[22] The migration from the countryside and the sharply downsized mines, and the collective struggles to establish these settlements, generated structures of community self-organization and a political consciousness in the urban periphery.[23] Meanwhile ethnically conscious political movements led these collectives to increasingly think of themselves in indigenous terms. As Sian Lazar found in El Alto, many periurban residents are invested in an "indigenous identity . . . based upon the mixing of the rural and the urban" and grounded in their neighborhood, their union, and their rural community of origin.[24]

Christian Mamani and his community of Santa Vera Cruz went from living in part of the rural countryside to the urban outskirts by staying put. Cochabamba simply grew around them. Mamani traces his family as residents there for four generations. Santa Vera Cruz, once best known for a patron saint's festival, was a place where "over the passage of years, families established themselves and at the beginning, we all knew one another."[25] On the other hand, the adjoining Nueva Vera Cruz was built alongside Avenida Petrolera beginning in the 1980s. Together the two communities built common water infrastructure managed by a single water committee. In collaboration with a half-dozen other neighborhood associations, they worked under the Quechua-named alliance Yaku Pacha to safeguard their environment by closing the nearby polluting municipal dump.[26]

María Eugenia ("Mauge") Flores Castro, a young Cochabamba urban activist who has cultivated alliances with rural organizations, is aware of the traditional opposition between urban residence and indigeneity but defines herself as Aymara. Like President Morales, she first experienced discrimination and mocking in relation to her identity at school. School or university is where Bolivians most often experience discrimination, according to a 2015 survey.[27] Morales has described his own childhood traumas, associated with urban space as a whole, in these terms: "When I first went to school in the city, the other children would laugh at me and call me ugly because I was Aymara. If I spoke my language, they would laugh and know I was Indian, and at that time I didn't speak Spanish, so to avoid being laughed at, for a long time I didn't speak at all."[28] Flores Castro describes her experiences of racialization as "more subtle" and masked but deeply paternalistic: "People always seemed like they felt sorry for us, when they spoke of us or spoke directly to us, right? Even my own comrades and friends; I've seen this relation they have with people of my skin color or of my origin." At other times the words were clearer—"They would mess with you in school [saying] 'the Indian, the backward, is the worst'"—but came from humble origins themselves. "Many of these people are children of campesinos and they deny their own origins. They negate them."[29]

In time Flores Castro built a defiantly indigenous identity as someone too brave to disavow her own roots in the face of such slights. In this fragment of her narrative she explains this through familial and community connections to rural communities:

> I grew up in the city, but my identity is Aymara because my parents are Aymaras. My family is Aymara; they live in the countryside. And, well, identity is not only acquired by where one lives, right? Rather, one acquires identity through the values one acquires. Beyond language, beyond whether you live in a certain place, you are from there and you are indigenous, and [to say that] if you live in the city, you totally relinquish your culture is a lie, isn't it? So I came to the city [here she speaks metaphorically; she was born in Cochabamba] but . . . I was raised under the values of the Aymara culture. My mother has nourished me, has given me the values of the community, shall we say. So therefore I identify myself as Aymara. Of course, before I did not [so identify] because of the discrimination.[30]

This shows how the rural countryside structures Andean identity, defining "the community" as a font of values that can be preserved and transmitted in the city. However, many people, like Flores Castro, take up a full identification as indigenous while remaining urban, overcoming what they read as a discriminatory impulse to give up this part of their biographies.

## The Shock of Arrival: Peasant Crowds in the 1952 Revolution

Indigenous crowds in urban plazas have long been a potent political symbol. In November 1944 the military socialist government of Gualberto Villarroel lifted all legal prohibitions on indigenous people entering plazas. At the time the newspaper *La Calle*, which backed the Revolutionary Nationalist Movement (MNR), celebrated "the happy conclusion of an intolerable regime which has been exercised since many years back."[31] In the wake of the 1952 Revolution, indigenous campesinos unmade their status as feudal serfs in the countryside, and one of their biggest tools in this fight was staging a massive presence in city centers. In his memoir, subtitled *Passages of the Indian Face of a Revolution*, Butrón Mendoza recalls:

> From April 1952 to August of the following year, we brought to the cities thousands of campesinos from all the provinces and all the rural corners of the country, sometimes with music of panpipes and other instruments, other times with rifle and machine gun blasts, concentrating ourselves in their plazas, streets, and sports fields. . . . We entered the city those times we thought necessary, boldly displaying [*ostentando*] our number and our weapons in its avenues and most travelled streets, firing our weapons towards the sky, at some known houses of feudal lords, or at public buildings. We crossed the city from one extreme to the other, expounding our human force and our decision to assume the defense of our rights against all who opposed the resurgence of the Indian.[32]

Indigenous peasants marched (sometimes bearing arms) in state parades, demonstrated to underline their grievances, queued up to meet bureaucrats, and simply inhabited the public plazas where they had previously been shunned. Their appearance was at times a joint effort of rural indigenous organizers and the ruling MNR party, and their presence alone was a dramatic statement.

Carter Goodrich, a technical support mission leader for the United Nations, was among those impressed with the peasants' "human force," which he saw (from the vantage point of La Paz) as tightly connected to the MNR government:

> More spectacular were the processions of tens of thousands of campesinos from all over the country that were brought in to La Paz by truckloads. . . . Each group carried banners bearing the slogans of the revolution and, in some cases, of the attack on *analfabetismo* (illiteracy), and it was usually preceded by its own band playing panpipes or native drums or other instruments. Some of the men, and even a few women, carried guns. In each unit the first rank or two of the marchers typically included the village leaders with their staffs of office and others in the native costume of their region. The procession, which formed an ethnologist's or at least a photographer's review of the indigenous population of the country, moved for

hours through the main streets of the city and ended in either the Plaza Murillo or the Stadium where the president rendered an account of his stewardship.[33]

The MNR proudly showcased the indigenous symbols used in these rallies and at the 1953 signing of the Agrarian Reform Law in Ucureña. A government publication celebrating "ten years of revolution" highlighted the flying of the wiphala and captioned a photo, "The 'pututu' [a shell or horn-based wind instrument] of campesino liberation is allowed to be heard."[34]

Amid the general presence of mobilized Indians in the city, their takeover of central governing spaces stood out. Alicia Ortiz observed:

> The multitude flows constantly towards the Plaza Murillo, as if this were the center of gravity of the city. Indians, who previously did not have access to the plaza, for it was prohibited for them to cross certain boundaries, as if this were the holy city of the czars, now fill it to the brim [la colman] with picturesque coloring. They sit down on its benches, crowd themselves on its steps, or remain standing before the Palacio Quemado, watching as if the solution to their destinies, incarnated in a certain person, might surge from its interior from one moment to the next. They arrive from the northern zones of the Altiplano, from the shores of Titicaca, with their multicolored woolen gorros with earflaps, and their tremendous ponchos of vibrant colors; they arrive from the valleys of Sucre and Cochabamba, with their wide felt hats like steel helmets, their pants cut at the knee and their long hair on their shoulders; they arrive from Potosí with their hats like black plates and their ponchos like dark tunics with crisscrossed stripes.[35]

By many accounts so many mobilized indigenous bodies attracted not just photographers and ethnological curiosity but fear. Goodrich detected a "traditional vague fear of Indian revolt" among both liberal and conservative elites. Even the unarmed gathering of Indian leaders for the 1945 Indigenous Congress had prompted upper-class Paceños to bury their silver and prepare weapons for defense.[36]

What the marching indigenous peasants wanted was the redistribution of the lands on which they worked. Their marches and rural uprisings would culminate in comprehensive agrarian reform in August 1953. The very demand was tantamount to incitement against the prevailing racial order. It "awakened fears that ran deep," as James Malloy observed: "The relationship between the Spanish-speaking culture and the suppressed Indian culture was pervaded with

mutual hate, distrust, and fear. To many, the city was the repository of civiliza-
tion and the hacienda its outpost. With the hacienda destroyed, what was to
stop the hate-filled Indian horde from sweeping over the cities in a paroxysm
of revenge?"[37] While no horde was materializing in the cities, Indian organizers
did make calculated use of these subterranean fears. Their discipline in urban
demonstrations showed a capacity for restraint that defied stereotypes that
ascribed them a violent nature. Yet at the same time they were aware of the visceral reactions they provoked. The peasant organizer Butrón Mendoza recalls:
"We made a daily presence of Indians in the city, although the people protested
the nerve-wracking frequency of the gatherings, the presence of weapons, and
even our odor. In reality, this was the point. That they should have us present
even in their dreams and their nightmares and would not forget about us at any
moment, whether sympathetic or otherwise; better, that they should be fearful
of our number, our objectives, and our activity."[38]

One striking facet of these accounts by travelers, local politicians, protest
leaders, and protest participants is that all recognize the political significance
of indigenous presence in these spaces. Not only their political presence (as
demonstrators, militia, or petitioners) and their self-presentation as claimants
but their collective enjoyment of these urban spaces (wearing indigenous dress,
staring at walls, and just being there) are read by all as a political act.

## Marching on the Cities

Since the early 1990s lowland and highland indigenous movements have deployed
the tactic of mass indigenous arrival in urban spaces with transformative consequences. The 1990 March for Territory and Dignity was a defining event in the
Bolivian indigenous movement. CIDOB—then the newly formed Confederation of Indigenous Peoples in the Bolivian East (Confederación de Pueblos Indígenas del Oriente Boliviano)—organized a thirty-four-day trek from Trinidad,
Beni, to La Paz demanding "an autonomous territory of our own."[39] The march
advocated the recognition of indigenous territories governed by local residents
and secured government approval for four such indigenous territories, including
what was then the Isiboro-Sécure National Park. The initial core of three hundred marchers swelled to eight hundred lowland indigenous people by the time
they reached La Cumbre, the chilly high point of the road uphill from northern
Bolivia to the capital, and then merged with a crowd of thousands of Quechua
and Aymara supporters.[40] These highlanders accompanied the march into La Paz

and backed the protesters' successful demand for the country to sign the International Labor Organization Convention 169, on the rights of indigenous peoples.

As a spatial tactic, these national marches (CIDOB has organized nine so far) have three functional parts. First, a cross-country convergence brings multiple organizations into a single mobile community that works out solidarity and shared politics day by day. Second, the route brings marching activists into contact with scores of local communities and rural workplaces along the way, including the towns that host them nightly as they set up camp. Third, if and when they enter the destination city, the marchers come together with urban allies and hold joint protests, sometimes in the form of a plaza encampment that remains until their demands are met. Marches are long, slow events that are attention gathering rather than disruptive. They can't paralyze economic life, but they do seize symbolically important spaces. Compared with road blockades, then, the march is better suited to numerically smaller sectors with high moral authority. For the lowland indigenous movement this moral authority comes from the ancestral claim indigenous peoples have on national territory and the history of racial violence against them.

In 1992 indigenous and campesino organizations mounted symbolic resistance to the Columbus Quincentennial. They prepared separate events, often designated as takeovers (*tomas*), in the cities of La Paz, Sucre, Potosí, Cochabamba, Oruro, Trinidad, Santa Cruz, Tarija, and Llallagua (the last is in Potosí Department). The campesinos of Chuquisaca planned a five-hour "encirclement," accomplished by marches on each of the four access roads to Sucre. Frantic newspaper accounts raised the specter of violent attacks ("The Rebellion of the Quechua People Has Begun," *Hoy*, September 29, 1992), only to be tamped down by assurances from the movements involved that their mobilizations would be peaceful.[41] An impressive crowd of twenty thousand converged on Sucre where "at the sounding of *pututus*, they began the *acullico*, or chewing of coca, in honor of the Pachamama [Earth Mother deity]."[42]

Nicole Fabricant's description of the Sixth Indigenous March in 2006—in which the Landless Peasant Movement participated—emphasizes the ties that are built among different communities through these physical acts. She focuses on the "communities of pain" that emerge from their shared suffering and the various forms of self-organization that arise to make the operation function—ensuring that participants present an ordered image to the public and that everyone is fed—and to allow for collective decisions about demands and negotiations.[43] The far-flung ethnic groups represented in the CIDOB, and the indigenous-peasant-landless movement as a whole, have built ties of solidarity in part through these acts of common effort, sacrifice, and autonomous organization.

At their strongest these marches combine several elements to provide meaning and force to their space claiming. Their suffering on the road functions through the logic of nonviolence. It reveals their commitment to the cause and willingness to put their bodies at risk. When they convince the public that their suffering is not justified, it also becomes a visible representation of the historical violence against them. In the city they bring their bodies to where they are most out of place and simultaneously to where the state's power and presence are in their most concrete form. Finally, the ballooning of their marches with periurban and urban supporters demonstrates that even this minority movement has numerous and diverse supporters. In these moments indigeneity unites small groups of lowland peoples with the vast populations of the highlands. The exchange offers the lowlanders more political weight and the highlanders greater moral legitimacy, even as it illustrates how the political system has left both out.

This lowland-highland collaboration had lasting effects, both advancing an indigenous agenda through the Bolivian political system in the 1990s (despite neoliberalism) and reorienting Bolivian highland peasant politics around the language of decolonization, autonomy, and indigenous rights. After the cooperation in 1990, CIDOB would be joined by highland peasant organizations—the Unified Union Confederation of Rural Bolivian Workers and the rural colonists' federation—in further mobilizations and in alliance with a widening agenda. Moreover these marches of minority lowland peoples also shared itineraries of protest and templates for action with other rural movements entering the cities to make demands. Marches into the cities, particularly from the Chapare to La Paz, have been a primary tool of the coca growers of the Cochabamba tropics. Marches of rural indigenous people kicked off mass participation by Alteños in the 2003 Gas War, and later marches knitted the country together in that common effort. As I discuss in chapter 6, a diverse, largely indigenous march on La Paz provided the final impetus for authorizing a plurinational constitution in 2008.

## The Electrifying Impact of Indigenous Presence

A different, more cultural, kind of indigenous protest can remake public places into exhibitions of cultural force. In January 2011 the Morales government was conducting a diplomatic effort to revise international drug laws that treat coca

FIGURE 14  A coca grower from the Federación Chimore in the Chapare offers a handful of coca leaves during the coca chew-in in the Plaza 14 de Septiembre on January 26, 2011.

leaf chewing—a widespread practice throughout the Andes with practical, medicinal, and cultural importance—as an illegitimate vestige of the past that must be eliminated. In an effort to bolster the campaign's impact, the coca growers' unions and the government organized a massive public chewing of coca leaves in Cochabamba's central square and on the La Paz avenue where the U.S. Embassy stands.

I spend January 25, 2011, in Cochabamba's central plaza. The presence and different habitus of so many coca-growing campesinos transforms the plaza. The main spaces have been filling up since my 9:00 a.m. arrival. Coca growers are seating themselves in the various pathways, spreading out square cloths covered with leaves, breastfeeding their babies, sitting on the paved walkways, lounging on the ground, crossing into the normally rigidly preserved green spaces, and turning the grass into a place to relax. There they are joined by city youth, now that it's clear that these boundaries will not be enforced today. As I walk through the plaza the foremost feeling is of human density, of having to walk slowly, bumping into others, of continuous interaction. In this informal takeover of Cochabamba's central plaza, indigenous farmers interrupt the routines of urban space. The usually ordered plaza, accustomed to demonstrations, is made into a market, a gift-giving space, a place of quotidian living and leisure for primarily rural indigenous people. The crowd of observers on the stage reverses the normal order of a traditional political rally. This is a cultural occupation as much as it is a political one.

"We are here to *acullicar, pijechear* [chew coca] as peoples, as indígenas campesinos. All of us together," explains Leonilda Zurita Vargas, a cocalero leader and head of the Movement Toward Socialism–Political Instrument for the Sovereignty of the Peoples (MAS-IPSP) in Cochabamba. "What we want is the decriminalization of our sacred leaf." Performers, politicians, poets, and members of the crowd moved to make a speech do so from a microphone in the part of the plaza opposite the city hall. Among them is Marcelo Guzman, who is urging urbanites to stand with the coca growers. Speeches and performances are made on the ground, while the stage that was brought in acts as a place for people to cluster as part of the audience while watching the performance. In fact, however, most people are not watching the performance, and the loudspeakers are barely even noticeable on the opposite street. If the voices from the main stage had a variety of messages, and the booths of the vendors emphasized the benefits of coca (as did individuals I encountered), the message of the masses in the square was simpler: "We grow coca. We chew coca. And we are many."

It is not always easy to perceive the political meaning of a protest through these, the simplest elements of protest: number; density; inhabiting a formal space in a way that one's own rules of bodily comportment are at the fore, rather than the usual official ones; letting coca growing, distributing, and chewing speak for themselves. But in situations like the coca-chewing protest, they rise to the surface. Rather than concentrating attention on speakers who provide the meaning of the demonstration, this event has speakers who are projecting overt political language alongside the much larger enactment of a politicized lifeway. The point of the protest, after all, was that coca chewing is embedded in a living culture that will not give it up. The lived implacability of a day spent being indigenous in public view illustrates immovability. The public location reminds everyone that this implacable culture now inhabits the spaces of representation that once excluded them.[44]

## Being Indigenous in Public Space

The 1952–53 campesino protests, CIDOB plaza occupations, 1992 indigenous takeovers, and 2011 coca chew-in share the common element of people *being indigenous in public space*.[45] By this I mean this characteristic is not merely a coincidence of ethnicity and location but a self-aware performance that is carried out strategically. Protesters deploy their own indigeneity out of its usual place, relative to the geographies of state and of race, to challenge the political and racial orders of society.

My interpretation of these acts as deliberate arises from the ways that participants choose to perform their indigeneity. People present themselves as indigenous in Bolivia by a variety of markers: dark skin color, short stature, limbs and torsos shaped or dirtied by physical labor, use of indigenous languages, ethnically marked dress, and formal symbols of belonging to indigenous communities. Along this spectrum, the more physical elements are the most difficult to change at the moment of presentation. They are also radically insufficient to necessarily convey indigenous self-identification and social status, particularly in central Bolivia where a mestizo-identified elite often appears phenotypically indigenous in body.

In 1952 and 1953, however, the indigenous bodies that circulated in the city centers of Bolivia suddenly became noticeable, and thereby noticeable as indigenous. They did so by breaking with rules of deference and the routines of labor to appear in mass demonstrations and congregate outside governmental offices. When they "remain[ed] standing before the Palacio Quemado, watching," they ceased to be the politically voiceless porters of the hotels and became political subjects making a claim. Similarly the addition of more chosen elements of indigenous identification—traditional costume, musical instruments, the wiphala, and pututu—makes being indigenous in public space an explicit act. Indigenous political actors can use these overt symbols explicitly to direct the attention of their viewers to their indigeneity, in a way that would be impossible with bodily features alone.

Indigenous imagery is often incorporated in the structures of social movement organizations, particularly campesino unions and indigenous organizations. By wearing traditional dress in an official capacity, these actors insist that others recognize them as indigenous. They are refusing to act in a way that accepts traditions of creole/mestizo presentation as necessary to interact with the state. When they do so in traditionally elite spaces, they are taking steps to redefine who may be considered capable of government and political self-representation. It is certainly no coincidence that symbols of indigenous self-rule—staffs of office, the wiphala, and the pututu—are brought into this performance.

Many of the space-claiming protests described in chapters 3 and 4 made being indigenous part of their self-presentation in public space. The Cochabamba Water War, which was carried out by a broad urban-periurban-rural coalition, foregrounded indigeneity in its chosen symbols. The Regantes' mass-mobilizing capacity in its indigenous-identified base and its reliance on *usos y costumbres* (traditional rights to resources and forms of self-governance) as the moral basis for its water claims facilitated an indigenization of the Water War.[46] Mestizos and indigenous-identified urbanites also deployed indigenous symbols in the Water War, to illustrate the primordial importance of their claims and their unity with the Regantes, campesinos, and cocaleros. By invoking indigeneity, Cochabambans were able to move the discussion to issues of the human relationship to the environment and commodification per se rather than advancing only class-based claims. As Robert Albro argues, "Cultural heritage is an effective means to form and revitalize the moral community of a popular, collective politics" and a "coalition-building device across historically indigenous and popular political projects."[47] Being indigenous can be made into a political statement.

## Indigenous Presence from the National Revolution to the Plurinational State

The overlap of racial and government power and their accompanying exclusions and embodied subordination have long created a field of tension in Bolivian cities. Each generation of mobilized indigenous people that has marched into a Bolivian downtown has activated that field, throwing out sparks as they arrive. The reversal of long-internalized rules, the transgression of the racial and political order, has left behind an electrifying sense of that order's fragility. The sudden presence of large numbers of indigenous people in ruling spaces makes manifest their exclusion from the power organized from these places. Further, fearful elites may wonder, If indigenous bodies cannot be controlled in this most central and precious of spaces, will systems for controlling them function at all? Thus their presence raises the prospect of a shifting social order. Observers and participants share the sense that everything can change in terms of power because the usual rules on the streets have been broken. Indigenous crowds marching on the plazas, sitting on manicured greens, and taking up space with their undisguised presence have aroused hope and revulsion, and sometimes both simultaneously.

Between the visiting campesino crowds of 1952–53 and the mobilizations of the twenty-first century lay a series of historical transformations. The long-standing opposition of indigenous and urban has been supplanted by the irruption of indigenous identity inside the cities. Migration, the revival of indigenous self-identification, and demonstrated solidarity of rural and urban popular sectors have redrawn the map of indigeneity. The indigenous city dweller and campesino recognize their shared roots and have built up experience collaborating during takeovers of downtown streets. In the 1990 March for Territory and Dignity, the 2000 Water War, and the 2011 Coca Chew-In, to name just a few examples, urban and rural residents have joined in common actions. Together they have made La Paz's San Francisco Plaza and Cochabamba's Plaza 14 de Septiembre their own.

The MNR and its military successors stood apart from the indigenous people they claimed to represent, a relationship expressed through assembled crowds, paternalistic rhetoric, and the language of a pact between peasants and the government. Even as it paraded indigenous supporters in their traditional regalia, the MNR sought to supersede the category of "Indian" altogether. Later generations of indigenous organizers would remember the 1952 Revolution more for the effacement than the mobilization of indigenous identity. In the twenty-first century, in contrast, space claiming by indigenous people was part of a drive for self-representation and (frequently) recognition of their right to autonomy. The concepts of the plurinational state and decolonization involved simultaneously removing colonial dynamics of power from the interior of the state apparatus and devolving power to indigenous collectivities. Also, unlike the MNR of the 1940s, the MAS-IPSP was founded as a campesino party. By the nature of its membership, the MAS-IPSP government placed indigenous-bodied people in spaces of power and transgressed a history of excluding indigenous peoples. In the next chapter I show how the Morales government worked to transform certain state spaces in its effort to define them as representing plurinational self-rule.

Overcoming colonial domination, and the colonial legacy of racialized power (what Anibal Quijano calls "the coloniality of power"), is a common project that brings together many different indigenous positions, all different kinds of indigenous peoples.[48] So long as it lay in the future, the plurinational project for remaking Bolivia enabled a sense of unity in diversity. However, defending one's particular indigenous standpoint, restoring the world as it might be had the colonial state not intruded, is not necessarily so unifying. As I show in the next two chapters, once indigenous peoples moved from being an opposition force in the streets to occupying formal positions of power, more and more of these differences in political projects became visible.

## CHAPTER 6

# Who Owns the City?

*Race and Space During the Catastrophic Stalemate*

ucre, the "city of four names," was founded as La Plata ("City of Silver of New Toledo") in 1538 and made the capital of the Spanish colonial Audiencia de Charcas, the future Bolivia. A small city (fewer than 16,000 residents in the 1770s) with great political responsibility, it oversaw a vast territory and the enormous silver wealth extracted from nearby Potosí (where as many as 160,000 people lived in the early 1600s).[1] As the colonial capital La Plata hosted institutions of the Crown, the Catholic church, and the Universidad Mayor, Real y Pontificia de San Francisco Xavier de Chuquisaca, the third university to be established in the Americas.[2] By the late eighteenth century, colonial elites throughout Bolivia were discarding their colonial loyalties and contemplating seizing sovereignty from the royal government.[3] The university was one of many regional centers for agitating for independence, and residents claim the city's 1809 call for independence (*Grito Libertario*) marked the start of the continent's separation from Spain. As Chuquisaca, it became the first capital of independent Bolivia (in 1825) and took the name of the war hero and president José Antonio de Sucre in 1839.

However, the seat of government moved to La Paz following the 1899 civil war. Twenty years later a Bolivian geography almanac observed: "Sucre, isolated, deprived of railways, without appreciable commerce, etc. seems to have lost half its population."[4] Sucre stagnated, illustrating how cities can rise and fall with their administrative importance. While the populations of La Paz and

Cochabamba nearly quadrupled between 1900 and 1950, reaching 267,000 and 80,795, respectively, Sucre saw more modest growth, reaching just 40,128 inhabitants at midcentury.[5]

Today central Sucre is a UNESCO-designated World Heritage Site and serves as a sort of monument to the lettered city. Despite its recent growth and the presence of Bolivia's highest courts, Sucre feels much more like a provincial capital. The city lacks the high-rise buildings that dominate central La Paz and dot central and north Cochabamba. Instead, Sucre's core district has the feel of an old Spanish colonial town. Narrow cobblestone streets ascend the sloped area around the central plaza, which is flanked by plastered walls topped with ceramic roofs or ornamental gray stone. The uniform aesthetic is like the interior of a time capsule. The Victorian-era Central Park and the metal-and-glass modernism of a handful of governmental buildings (including the Supreme Court) that surround it stand as interruptions of the city center's timescape.

The central plaza of Sucre, surrounded on all sides by blockaders in June 2005—workers, teachers, miners, and campesinos—welcomed those same sectors back in August 2006, this time as part of a body to rewrite Bolivia's constitution.[6] Most of the 255 members of the Constituent Assembly who gathered in Sucre identified with an indigenous people, half spoke an indigenous language, and one in five was a grassroots leader.[7] This remarkable assembly's sessions began with twenty thousand observers: an "enormous quantity of indigenous people and campesinos who . . . dominated the urban center with their presence, breaking the especially tranquil rhythm of life in the capital city."[8] Their presence at the center of national life was a dramatic reconfiguration of race, place, and politics.

The assembly's opening ceremony on August 6, 2006, was accompanied by the formal protocol and official ordering of space that marks Bolivian state functions: police guards, neat lines of white chairs, lines of soldiers in ceremonial dress. Carla Valcarce recounts, "Suddenly there appeared a hundred indígenas and campesinos dressed in their best finery who took possession of this VIP area. The red ponchos, the knotted cords, the tricolored (Bolivian) and wiphala (indigenous) flags glowed against the white backs of the seats. Truly I felt that change had begun."[9]

In chapter 5, I discussed the dramatic role played by indigenous people entering public plazas in both Bolivia's "second revolution" in 1952 and the twenty-first-century upsurge in protests. The mass presence of indigenous peoples in state spaces during the Evo Morales presidency echoes the crowds summoned by the Nationalist Revolutionary Movement (MNR) when it arrived in power in 1943 but with a vital difference. Where the 1952 Revolution presumed a creole/mestizo culture would continue to set the standard for state practice, the MAS-IPSP government proposed a redefinition of state institutions as plurinational spaces.

Under the MNR Spanish-speaking urban dwellers continued to staff state offices. The Ministry of Peasant Affairs, on whose grounds indigenous petitioners camped as they waited for assistance, pledged, "The Indian has served us for four centuries. Let us devote the next 50 years to serving him." Its practice, however, maintained the line between the creole/mestizo state (us) and campesinos no longer designated as *indios* (them). Just four Indian peasants attended the 1953 National Convention of the Revolutionary Nationalist Movement, and the writer Alicia Ortiz observed three to be silent and inhibited during the meeting. While there, they may have heard Ñuflo Chávez Ortiz, a Santa Cruz lawyer who headed of the Ministry of Peasant Affairs, argue that the commission on Indian issues should be composed of creole/mestizo intellectuals rather than Indians themselves, whose "backwardness" would have made them ineffective.[10]

The opening day of the Constituent Assembly reveals the rather different approach taken for creating the plurinational state in 2006. This was part of the series of moments in which grassroots movements lent legitimacy to the new MAS-IPSP government. Yet it was also a day for the same movements to directly appropriate the spaces and symbols of state and to enter them as participants and decision makers. Before dawn, reports José de la Fuente Jeria (a staff member at the Center for Research and Promotion of Farmers), the first march designed to influence the Constituent Assembly had already begun. A women's rights coalition carried placards and chanted as members marched into the Plaza 25 de Mayo. In the plaza the delegation from Evo Morales's hometown of Orinoca, "impeccably uniformed and musically equipped," waited to be the lead element of the day. De la Fuente Jeria describes them as "a kind of receiving commission for 'their' president, a type of community guard, and above all a way of making their dominion felt musically over the political process and the Constituent Assembly." The procession of indigenous and campesino marchers before the assembled dignitaries on white chairs lasted into the night. De la Fuente Jeria was left with this impression: "The indigenous—those for whom we [who work in support institutions for indigenous and campesino rights] have become accustomed to speaking as we demand their rights in the abstract— were *there*, more secure and implanted than anyone else" (emphasis added).[11]

Beginning with Morales's inauguration, the MAS-IPSP has frequently used, reappropriated, and redesigned spaces belonging to the state. These acts remade both formal and informal governing spaces in an effort to realize a structural and symbolic refounding of the country. In essence plurinational politics requires a plural performance that fills the space of politics with cultural diversity. In the National Congress, the Constituent Assembly, and the cabinet, grassroots leaders wore their ethnically distinct *polleras* and sweaters, bowler hats and miners' helmets. Movements claimed state spaces with official authorization and did so in a way that extended their earlier space-claiming protests. They flooded the city with crowds, made decisions during movement summits, and found ways to be ostentatiously indigenous in official spaces. Outside these newly occupied spaces, space-claiming protest took a new form: defending these plurinational spaces from the attacks of others and continuing to pressure government entities that opposed the remaking of Bolivia. Surrounding the state, metaphorically and sometimes literally, were vast gatherings of thousands of movement participants, organized by sector and full of demands.

This shift in the ownership of state space touched off dramatic resistance from the country's right wing. In the three-year power struggle from 2006 to 2009, indigenous members of the Constituent Assembly, rural protesters in Cochabamba, and the wiphala in city plazas all became targets of the opposition's ire. In Cochabamba and Sucre right-wing mobilizations often mirrored the forms previously used by the leftist grassroots. At every stage the Morales government worked with social movements to mount public mobilizations around the constitution until it was finally adopted in January 2009. Beyond the ballot box ceremonial escorts, defensive vigils, cabildos, street confrontations, rural blockades isolating right-leaning cities, street confrontations, mass marches, and finally the encirclement of the National Congress were among the forms of space-claiming protest deployed during this period. This chapter explores the left-right deadlock as a period of active mobilization and countermobilization, of disputes about the right to urban space, and of intracivilian violence.

## Symbolically Embodying Indigenous Self-Rule

From the beginning the Morales administration fashioned the symbolism of the executive branch to reflect long-standing calls for indigenous self-rule. In an unconventional investiture ceremony at the Tiwanaku archaeological site, he "donned the replica of a 1,000-year-old tunic similar to those once used by Tiwanaku's wise men, was purified in an ancient ritual and accepted the symbolic leadership of the myriad indigenous groups of the Andes."[12] The choice of site, Morales's dress, his anointment by an indigenous priest, or *amauta*, the ceremony, and Morales's staff of office were intended to define him as the authorized leader of the country's indigenous peoples. Koen De Munter and Ton Salman describe the ceremony as the first of many "pluricultural civil practices" that correspond to a newly plural approach to political participation.[13]

Prominent grassroots activists catapulted into leadership while publicly embracing their indigenous identity. Morales's first cabinet included the Quechua domestic worker and union leader Casimira Rodríguez as minister of justice; Abel Mamani, the Aymara president of the El Alto Federation of Neighborhood Councils, as minister of water; and the Aymara campesino organizer David Choquehuanca as foreign minister. When the team of sixteen assumed their offices, Choquehuanca declared in Aymara, "Uka jacha uru jutasjiway"— the great day has arrived.[14] Across multiple ministries the new administration undertook a systematic effort to prepare indigenous activists to staff the administrative apparatus of the state.[15] The central government grew by 89 percent in the first decade of the MAS-IPSP government, and municipal and departmental governments grew even more dramatically.[16] A 2013 survey found that 45 percent of Education Ministry functionaries and 63 percent of those in the Chuquisaca departmental government self-identified as indigenous.[17]

At ground level the new government threw open the doors of the state to a more diverse public. The Cochabamba neighborhood leader Ángel Hurtado recalled: "Before, they didn't even allow the ladies *de pollera* to be in a [government] office, one couldn't even enter with a sombrero into an office. You had to be dressed in a [Western] men's suit to enter, right? It was prohibited to wear sandals."[18] The MAS-IPSP had brought women *de pollera* and men wearing miners' hats into the National Congress, and into the everyday offices of the administration, thereby redefining state spaces as open to everyone. Speaking Spanish, like wearing a suit, would no longer be a requirement to access state services. Morales urged all state functionaries to learn an indigenous language, a requirement written into the new constitution. Most dramatically limitations and fees for government identity cards were eliminated, bringing many new voters into the electorate; 5.14 million Bolivians were eligible to vote in 2009,

40 percent more than in 2005.[19] For Hurtado the lowering of barriers to indigenous voices and bodies was the prime example of "a government that is doing some measure of justice."[20]

## The Constituent Assembly as Indigenous Space

Many voices had called for a constituent assembly to redefine the constitution and the country, but their visions for the body were not identical. The Pact of Unity, a multimovement alliance that began to coalesce in 2002, articulated a vision for a movement-based, nonpartisan constituent assembly in its earliest proposals.[21] The pact had generated this vision through mass gatherings of hundreds of activists and a larger set of organizations, as well as during cross-country marches and the countrywide mobilization of 2003. Grassroots advocates for a constituent assembly imagined a body outside Congress and a political party system that could undertake a comprehensive reenvisioning of Bolivian politics. They saw such a body as an alternative to political parties and as an extension of local assemblies and cabildos.[22] For Eliana Quiñones Guzmán, an activist in several political collectives, "The idea was that the majority would participate in the assembly from their own sector, their reality, from their people—indigenous peoples, campesinos, workers, men, women, children, et cetera—they would all be participating to build a vision of a new country."[23]

At climactic points in mass organizing, when popular disruption chased presidents from office, movements imagined a constituent assembly would emerge from the mobilizations themselves, rather than be chosen at the ballot box. Raquel Gutiérrez Aguilar describes "a thorny debate" during the October 2003 mobilization: "Should the state convene it, or should the mobilized population and its organizations be able to convene a constituent assembly on their own?"[24] This would also follow the example of the 1970–71 Popular Assembly when workers, students, and peasants met in the National Congress building and spoke on behalf of their sectors. At a minimum activists expected that any legally recognized organization—not just political parties—would be permitted to offer candidates, as they did in the 2004 regional elections.

The MAS-IPSP, however, had a more centralized vision. The party used negotiations in the National Congress to propose itself as the primary vehicle for representing the grassroots Left in the constituent assembly. The compromise text restricted elections to slates chosen by existing political parties. The MAS-IPSP then integrated social movement organizers and leaders in its electoral slate. The convening law worked out between the MAS-IPSP and the opposition parties in government created a 255-member Constituent Assembly to draft a constitution in Sucre while the National Congress continued to meet in La Paz.[25]

When its vision for a grassroots constituent assembly chosen by the grassroots was ignored, the Pact of Unity organized its own constitution-drafting process and to the best of its ability sought to impose the results of its more open process on the assembly.[26] It convened a series of meetings among member groups and allies, culminating in the National Assembly of Peasant and Indigenous Organizations, held in Sucre just before the official Constituent Assembly's inauguration. The hundreds of delegates who attended this unofficial grassroots gathering crafted a crucial mandate: "The organizations and some constituents had [made] it very clear that this Constituent [Assembly] was that of the organizations, and that the organizations must be there, supporting and participating," recalled the public intellectual Raúl Prada Alcoreza, who had been elected to the Constituent Assembly.[27] Many others elected to the Constituent Assembly were members of pact member organizations and were termed *organic* assembly members from the movements' perspective.[28] Other sympathetic members of the Constituent Assembly, even MAS-IPSP affiliates, were considered allies, a second tier in the pact's strategizing.[29]

On August 5, the final day of this mass meeting of movement organizations, both organic and allied members of the Constituent Assembly were invited to sign an "Act of Commitment" pledging to use and defend the pact's draft in their work. The draft they devised would be one of the most influential sources of text for the Constituent Assembly, which ultimately produced a constitution with 411 articles. In return, the assembled organizations pledged to "maintain a vigil over the action of the constituents to guarantee the re-founding of Bolivia in the framework of a Plurinational State."[30] This act at a movement summit helps clarify the meaning of the state ceremony the next day. When indigenous men and men in traditional dress took their place on the VIP stage as members of the Constituent Assembly, they carried these political commitments with them. These constituents (as members were called) and their supporters signaled by their actions that they were not just ethnically marked bodies but political claimants with a tradition of collective mobilization. One could even say that the political agenda of the movements became embodied in their ethnic and class presentation and their racially marked bodies as they stepped into a space that had long been defined against the poor, peasant, and indigenous.[31]

The formal sessions of the Constituent Assembly were held in Sucre's Grand Marshall Theatre. The building, which is under the auspices of the San Francisco Xavier University, was built in halting stages from the late 1800s through the 1950s. Across these decades of redesigns, its builders kept their focus on emulating precedents from European high culture. And yet, within weeks of the opening, the organic constituents were treating the Constituent Assembly as a space of their own at the heart of the state. Khantuta Muruchi and Andres Calla observe that "the changes [in Bolivia] mean the possibility of coming into and taking possession of the spaces of political power which had been denied them until now."[32] Inside the walls the elected constituents introduced indigenous symbols (like traditional dress and symbols of office), indigenous languages, and grassroots movement practices into the activities of the assembly. Yet there was also overt racism: times of "strong confrontation, of insults, provocation, and fighting," as one constituent recalled.[33] Constituent Isabel Dominguez rose to address the body in Quechua, only to face insults from a right-wing constituent who shouted, "Quiet, Indian, so long as you don't speak Spanish, get out of here."[34] Indigenous constituents were outside the somatic norm for occupants of power, called the traditional qualifications for governance into question, and upset the alignment of government service with class privilege. Their charged appearance in these spaces unsettled the identification between state and racial power, eliciting direct resistance.

Nonetheless, the inversion of state space, from hostility to indigenous presence to embodiment of it, led to an inversion of the spatial orientation of leftist grassroots protests outside. "We of the Chuquisaca campesino confederation, had the assignment of providing security," recalled José Santos Romero, then a peasant leader within the Sucre municipality. "From the first moment the Constituent Assembly was installed, we were on top of [their] very security . . . day and night."[35] Movements mobilized not to surround and cut off a legislative body (as they had in June 2005) but to hold defensive vigils around it. The Chuquisaca campesinos and lowland indigenous peoples held one such vigil in November 2006; the Indigenous March embarked for Sucre in July 2007; and about two hundred supporters formed a ring of defense against right-wing protesters from November 19 to 21, 2007. Such outward-directed vigilance was a key form of collaboration between leftist grassroots movements and the Morales government.

## Bodies out of Place: Indigenous Presence as Disruption

While the display of diversity was vital to illustrate the unprecedented breadth of the grassroots Left's protests from 2000 to 2005, and the transformative aspirations for the Constituent Assembly, the same crowds were given a rather different meaning in the years that followed. The so-called catastrophic stalemate (*empate catastrófico*) between the Morales government and the right-wing opposition divided the country and fractured the metropolitan areas of Cochabamba and Sucre along geographic and racial lines. The right-wing opposition movements would refigure indigenous protesters as people contaminating the city, making it dirty and backward, as uninvited guests, and finally as invaders. These interpretations reactivated the dichotomy of the urban mestizo versus rural indigenous, energized race and class divides within the cities, and punished those who stepped out of place.

When the stalemate began, the Bolivian Right was in a state of organizational flux. Its national political strength had largely collapsed after two presidential resignations and a poor showing in the 2005 elections. Nevertheless, neoliberal and right-wing politicians retained considerable institutional resources: control of the Senate; a significant minority within the Constituent Assembly; and the leadership of five departmental governments. They organized these forces into a backlash that counterposed regional autonomy and the proposed plurinational order.

In the four Media Luna (half moon) departments (Santa Cruz, Beni, Pando, and Tarija), the right-wing movements spoke of a "Camba nation," named after the term for mestizo-criollo lowlanders.[36] For those who embraced it, the term Camba denoted a peculiar kind of *mestizaje* (miscegenation) that preserves white physical features while adding to creole men's valor and women's beauty. Self-identified Cochalas—residents of Cochabamba—and mestizos in Sucre drew distinctions between themselves and the indigenous they supposed were from rural areas, whom the mestizos would confront on the streets. The regionalist Right mirrored three elements of the indigenous grassroots Left: a push for decentralization, the language of autonomy, and the orchestration of massive public gatherings—cabildos—to articulate their demands. Ruben Costas's Civic Committee for Santa Cruz (Comité Pro Santa Cruz) called a cabildo on June 22, 2004. Costas used the gathering to propose a "June Agenda" of the East in opposition to the October Agenda advanced by leftist grassroots protesters in the West, which he claimed was one of "blockade, centralism, and violence."[37]

MAP 7   Departments of Bolivia and their capitals. Pando, Beni, Santa Cruz and Tarija comprise the Media Luna. (Map by the United States government.)

In 2006 Costas worked with the prefects of Tarija, Beni, and Pando to form CONALDE, the National Coalition for Democracy. With CONALDE as the central voice demanding negotiations with the national government, region replaced party as the organizing principle of opposition.

At the end of 2006 the Constituent Assembly was deadlocked in trying to decide whether its voting procedure would require a two-thirds vote to approve each article of the future constitution or simply a two-thirds vote in support of the document as a whole. (The MAS-IPSP had won a simple majority of 137 seats; together with reliable allies, it controlled 158, or 62 percent.)[38] The four Media Luna prefects backed this demand and called mass public meetings for December 15 to back their stance. The prefects asked attendees at each of those cabildos to voice their approval for departmental autonomy, rejection of the new constitution, and the formation of a "Junta Autonómica Democrática de Bolivia" (a Media Luna government-in-waiting) while swearing to defend the decisions undertaken at these cabildos.

In Cochabamba, Prefect Manfred Reyes Villa (who had been mayor during the Water War) presided over his own cabildo on December 14. The meeting was held on the Prado, a wide shaded promenade that stretches from the Plaza Colón (a modern square that is home to a municipal government building and the department's congressional delegation) to the Plaza de las Banderas, a traffic circle surrounding numerous flags and a fountain. The location was away from the usual sites for political protest in Cochabamba, in a part of town lined with corporate offices, upscale restaurants, and high-rise apartment buildings. Just across the Rocha River lies the pricey neighborhood of Cala Cala, with its football stadium and numerous nightspots interspersed with residences. By holding the cabildo there, Reyes Villa was tacitly acknowledging the geographic split in the city's political allegiances. While Media Luna leaders were denying any interest in separatism, Reyes Villa went off script, offering his support for the "independence" of the eastern departments.

Leftist grassroots movements in Cochabamba were outraged by Reyes Villa's support for the opposition. Twenty-four hours later social sectors that supported the national MAS-IPSP government mobilized in the Plaza 14 de Septiembre. For the next five days the urban labor confederation, urban leftists, neighborhood associations, and the department's campesino and cocalero movements led an escalating pressure campaign centered on vigils in the central square. Rural movements blocked major highways around Cochabamba while protesters clashed with police in the city. Larger gatherings were held on December 19 and January 4. During an extended confrontation between protesters and police on January 8, thirty-one people were injured and leftist grassroots protesters set fire to the massive front door of the prefecture. Maria Eugenia Flores Castro, then an activist with Indymedia Cochabamba, recalled that a new rhetoric was emerging that denounced campesinos as a contaminating presence: "They began talking about the public monuments, and how 'these campesinos' dirty our streets. 'They dirty them, they spit out their coca, right? They dirty our gardens on the Prado.'"[39]

Then, on January 10, the leftist grassroots movements occupied the Plaza de las Banderas. It was a self-consciously symbolic move, provocative in its location but tactically subdued. While Cochabamba's Civic Committee (aligned with Reyes Villa) called off a cabildo scheduled for the same location, its supporters marched and circulated in the neighborhoods south of the river. María Eugenia saw them, "They said they were coming to evict and throw out these foreigners, these strangers who are invading." As she remembers it, "The strangest thing was that . . . they were armed, they had shields and sticks, boards that had nails at the end of them, right? Who puts a nail on a stick? There's an objective, right? To break heads."[40]

The night of January 10 an unsigned open letter from "the TRUE COCHABAMBANS" ran as an advertisement in the daily newspaper *Los Tiempos*; the letter set an ominous deadline for progovernment protesters. It read, in part, "The people of Cochabamba ratify the time allotted to the political movements which disturb the healthy coexistence in our city to cease their actions and return to their places of origin by noon on Thursday, January 11. If not, we hold the Central [i.e., the Morales] Government responsible for any violent event that might bring mourning upon the Cochabamban and Bolivian family."[41]

On January 11 groups of predominantly young men, many of them affiliated with a civic movement youth organization, gathered on the north side of the Río Rocha. In the Plaza de las Banderas a more "heterogeneous grouping, including women, the elderly, children, and men," gathered.[42] Both sides were physically prepared for some kind of confrontation, but the weapons carried by the civic movement were far more lethal than the youth organization's. Critically, only the civic movement brought firearms. Police on the bridges kept the groups apart until about 3:30 p.m., when the police either were overcome by the civic movement protesters or stepped aside and allowed them to come south (witnesses reported both scenarios).

The most dangerous moments occurred in the next thirty minutes. Juan Ticacolque Machaca, a forty-eight-year-old coca farmer, was shot dead on the plaza; he was one of seven people who suffered bullet wounds. Just meters away the campesino Luciano Colque Anagua, forty-one, was beaten until his skull fractured; he never recovered and died in a hospital on February 25. The melee extended throughout the street grid from the Plaza de las Banderas south to Avenida Heroínas, another conventional marker of the boundary between north and south Cochabamba. At about 5 p.m. Christian Daniel Urresti Ferrel, a seventeen-year-old participating with his family on the civic movement side, was beaten to death in a street brawl with campesinos.[43] Hundreds were wounded on both sides. Despite some moves toward de-escalation in the week that followed, the conflict in the city remained unresolved until Prefect Manfred Reyes Villa was recalled from office by popular vote in August 2008.

María Eugenia Flores Castro, who was at the Plaza de las Banderas and who was wounded in the melee, has had a lot of time to think about the conflict and how it was framed. To her the recasting of protest as invasion came down to a small-scale intrusion by the grassroots Left into spaces that elites thought they owned: "The Prado is a symbolic space for the zone of the rich, as is the Plaza de las Banderas. It's a symbolic space, right?—because . . . it's their space. And when the campesinos occupied it, it was as if they were taking away that space from them. . . . When they arrived at the point that symbolizes them and where they meet, where they drink, where they stroll the streets—which is the Prado—that really was the limit. And from there, they began to speak of invasion."[44]

A student at a private university and civic movement activist, Adriana Gisselle Harasic Rojas, would have had to agree with Flores Castro's description. In a letter she wrote on January 12 Harasic Rojas declared,

> Yesterday in a march which all of us Cochabambans organized . . . we tried to take back our city, which is being destroyed and burned by campesinos. We all went out and . . . we valiantly retook the well-known Prado, the Plaza Colón, our streets in the middle of the city. . . . We were filled with anger, rage, and negative feelings because we see our city destroyed, our beautiful gardens trashed by a group who calls themselves "pueblo," by a group who says they are Cochabambans. I bet that of the whole disgraced lot of them, not one knows our hymn, nor knows our history, nor loves our city as we love it.
>
> No one has the right to step upon our gardens, to set fire to our cultural patrimony. Things cannot remain like this, we cannot let them invade our city and do whatever they want, no sir!! Nobody touches COCHABAMBA, damnit!![45]

Attempts by indigenous protesters to claim and speak from traditionally elite spaces prompted resistance and outrage. The civic movement's physical moves to expel the protesters were accompanied by racial insults and rhetoric that disavowed the right of indigenous protesters to occupy urban spaces. In Adriana Harasic Rojas's letter, which was widely circulated and reprinted by *Los Tiempos*, the process of exclusion is evident through her use of "the people of Cochabamba" to define other (poor, indigenous) people as false Cochabambans. The boundaries of the first-person plural *we* became tightened and rigid at precisely the same time that the civic movement pressed a political demand for autonomy on behalf of the entire department. The only way to accomplish this was by disqualifying their leftist grassroots adversaries as being "pueblo" and, above all, by preventing them from exercising their claim to be "the people" in the central spaces that matter most symbolically.

## Invaders and Traitors in Sucre

Sucre is known as the White City, officially for the whitewashed walls of its well-preserved institutions. Whiteness of a different kind is also part of Sucre's colonial legacy. Sucre's upper class preserved racial stratification almost as it preserved its colonial architecture and street grid, as markers of its status to be cherished even if outsiders might regard them as anachronistic. The landholding elites generally conserved their creole racial purity until the 1953 Agrarian Reform, after which many took their remaining wealth out of the region entirely. In the decades that followed, they were replaced by mestizo families that were deeply attached to the Cochabamba's Lettered City heritage.[46]

Nonetheless the city expanded dramatically with the post-1985 relocation of miners and urban migration of peasants, until its population numbered 215,778 in 2001.[47] This wave of new arrivals faced all the challenges of periurban expansion as well as hostility from the city's elite institutions. There is a sharp contrast in ethnic identification at the city's edge: 54 percent of urban residents of central Chuquisaca identified as Quechua in the 2001 Census, but fully 91 percent of residents in the rural areas of these municipalities did.[48] Sucre's recent arrivals altered the racial balance of the city but did not change the identity of those in the upper echelons of its main institutions. Leaders of entities like the university, Civic Committee, and municipal government were deeply unsettled by the grassroots leftist movements that shook the country in the early 2000s and arrived in large numbers once the Constituent Assembly opened in 2006.

Sucre's civic movement mobilized in 2006 behind the demand that the Constituent Assembly return Sucre to its nineteenth-century role as capital of Bolivia. Convinced that a return to its status as the sole capital—and the transfer of executive and legislative offices—could restore the city's greatness, the elite formed the Inter-Institutional Committee of the Interests of Chuquisaca to lobby for this change. The local newspaper *Correo del Sur* made the case that "given the undeniable confrontation between east and west" it was "unviable" for La Paz to continue being the seat of power.[49] The Inter-Institutional

Committee asked local candidates of all parties to reaffirm the region's historic claim to being the true capital of Bolivia, and all naturally obliged. Soon, however, Chuquisaca's labor and peasant movement began to disavow the committee's use of pressure tactics to make demands on the central government.[50] Instead of backing an August 2006 civic movement protest, a hundred campesino leaders—together with some municipal workers and Chuquisaca's prefect, David Sánchez—marched in support of the MAS majority within the Constituent Assembly.[51] A struggle had begun about who spoke for Chuquisaca.

Inside the frequently deadlocked Constituent Assembly, Sucre's bid for full-capital status became a point of paralysis. Opposition politicians from the lowland East rallied behind Sucre's "full capital status" proposal, while the MAS attempted to keep the issue off the table. MAS members of the Constituent Assembly from Chuquisaca were in a particularly vexed position, and the Inter-Institutional Committee labeled them "traitors to Chuquisaca" for not pursuing full capital status. The committee organized large demonstrations in favor of the move on March 10 and July 27, 2007, although these were dwarfed by a massive July 20 cabildo in La Paz pledging that "the seat of government shall not move."

On August 15 the Constituent Assembly moved to exclude discussion of the choice of capital from its debates, a measure that passed with a bare majority of votes. That night protesters from Sucre's civic movement launched a cascade of rockets at the wiphala that flew over the Grand Marshall Theatre and focused their rage on [Assembly President Silvia] Lazarte, whom they called an "ignorant chola."[52] Sucre's Inter-Institutional Committee called a civic strike, set up a hunger-strike picket, and held an emergency cabildo abierto. As Sucre entered a prolonged civic strike, fifty local protesters ransacked the offices of three campesino organizations. Bands of youth protesters, typically students at San Francis Xavier University or teacher-training institutes, made the streets of Sucre dangerous for constituents who were visibly indigenous, especially women dressed *de pollera*.

The debate about capital status raged on through October 24, when a multiparty agreement made Sucre the constitutional capital and promised it would house the electoral branch of government. Even this agreement did not satisfy the Inter-Institutional Committee, and the civic movement continued both mass protests and direct attacks on the Constituent Assembly. As the assembly wrapped up its deliberations in November 2007, Sucre's civic movement and visiting right-wing protesters from the eastern departments attempted to block its sessions to approve the draft constitution. The body met under guard

FIGURE 15 Poster depicting the prefect, Constituent Assembly representatives, MAS members, and the leaders of worker and campesino confederations as "traitors to Chuquisaca" during the 2007 crisis about full-capital status for Sucre.

at the Liceo Militar (military school) outside the city. The Inter-Institutional Committee held a cabildo in the central square that declared the relocated Constituent Assembly illegal, promised not to adhere to the constitution it produced, and called for Chuquisaca's autonomy from the national government.[53] Soon after, the civic movement protesters began a day-and-a-half-long push to reach the Liceo Militar. A battle of stones, burning tires, tear gas, and rubber bullets raged in the neighborhood of La Calancha. Running street confrontations took a deadly toll: two civic movement protesters—Gonzalo Durán and José Luis Cardozo—died, and about two hundred people were wounded on November 24. Inside the Liceo Militar, Lazarte was informed of the first death. The constituents proceeded to rapidly complete the day's business and abandon the city of Sucre. Leftist grassroots organizations rapidly joined this tactical retreat.[54]

Overnight, frustrated right-wing crowds burned down many of the city's police stations as well as the house of Prefect David Sánchez Heredia, who was affiliated with MAS and fled the country (he returned and eventually served as a senator). The next day civic movement crowds took over and destroyed the building of the police Transit Unit, which was still occupied. In the battle the police killed the civic protester Juan Carlos Serrudo but lost control of the building, and many police escaped only after being beaten by the crowd. The police abandoned the city for two days, until the Sucre civic movement invited them to return. The three civic protesters were hailed as martyrs of their movement, and their funerals attracted thousands of mourners.

On November 28 the National Congress authorized Lazarte to reconvene the Constituent Assembly anywhere in Bolivia, and she called for the body to meet at Oruro Technical University on December 8. Ninety opposition members boycotted the meeting. The assembly approved 411 articles in a marathon fourteen-hour session. On December 14, 2007, Lazarte and the leaders of the assembly presented the full text of the constitution to the National Congress and urged it to call a referendum.[55]

## The 2008 Political Crisis

After the constitution was ratified at the end of 2007, the opposition movement—an alliance of the five CONALDE governors and the civic movements of six departmental capitals—moved toward formal autonomy and de facto separatism by way of refusal to recognize of government power. New cabildos held on December 15, 2007, in the four Media Luna departments presented Statutes of Autonomy to these urban separatist movements. The economy of the autonomous departments was to be powered by the same resource at issue during the 2003 Gas War: the nationalized gas fields of southeastern Bolivia.

The civic movements treated the Morales government and its local indigenous supporters as pariahs and traitors to the cause of local autonomy. When the Supreme Court opened its 2008 sessions in Sucre, Morales and García Linera declined to visit the city. The justice minister who did attend the court session, Celima Torrico, faced a menacing civic movement crowd outside the building. As a U.S. State Department cable summarized, "The protesters moved a burned out vehicle—which previously served as the official car for Constituent Assembly President and MAS delegate Silvia Lazarte—to the square in front of the Supreme Court. Signs stating 'Evo Murderer' and 'Celima Your Car Awaits (referring to the burned car)' were prominently displayed."[56] Wilber Flores, a MAS member of the Chamber of Deputies, was assaulted near the central square on April 10, while Celima Torrico was attacked—along with Defense Minister Walker San Miguel—by a crowd of university students on May 6. In Flores's words, "That group of people who beat me had said, 'Finish him off! Murder him!' They repeated it the whole time they were beating me: 'Murder him! Kill that Indian!'"[57]

As the annual holiday of May 25—the anniversary of the Bolivia's first declaration of independence in 1809 in Sucre—approached, the civic movement was maintaining a de facto exclusion of Morales government officials from central spaces in the city. Civic movement violence forced supporters of the MAS-IPSP candidate for governor of Chuquisaca to campaign clandestinely.[58] When Morales made preparations to take part in official ceremonies marking the event, the Inter-Institutional Committee formally opposed his arrival.[59] Meanwhile, to celebrate the holiday, the opposition-controlled national senate prepared to have an honorary session in the Casa de la Libertad, the historic site of Bolivia's eighteenth-century declaration of independence. The honorary session was to include the formal presentation of a resolution in memory of the three men killed outside the Constituent Assembly sessions in November 2007.[60] Retreating from a more ostentatious state visit to the bicentennial commemoration, the Morales government scheduled a meeting for Morales, as head of state, to offer ambulances and land titles (a routine act of Latin American statecraft) to rural leaders in the Estadio Olímpico Patria, a sports venue away from the independence celebration. He was not welcome in the recently conceded "constitutional capital."

On the night of May 23 and the morning of May 24, civic movement protesters sought to prevent the president's visit. *Correo del Sur*, Sucre's principal paper and an ally of the civic movement, reported the protesters "swore not to let the President set foot in Sucre without 'asking forgiveness' and taking responsibility for the three fallen during Black November. They carried out their promise. With stones, dynamite charges and projectiles, they managed to throw the police and military out of the area, with the latter obliged to fall back in a humiliating manner amidst a rain of stones."[61] Morales canceled his visit, but the rural leaders had to endure a terrifying day of physical aggression, collective kidnapping, and public humiliation in Sucre's central square.[62] (Two years later, when the political tide had turned, May 24 would become Bolivia's national day against racism.)

The Media Luna departments held referenda on autonomy on three Sundays in May and June 2008. The government declared the balloting to be illegal,

FIGURE 16 Captive rural leaders, stripped to the waist, are forced by civic movement protesters to kneel in Sucre's central square. A flag or banner burns in the foreground.

and the MAS-IPSP led boycott campaigns. The autonomy statutes won more than 80 percent approval from voters, but abstention ranged from 35 percent to 65 percent of the electorate. Again, the first symbol of local autonomy was the persona non grata status of President Morales. By June, then, the president was avoiding trips to a majority of Bolivia's national territory.

Despite the polarization the Morales government and CONALDE were able to agree on a nationwide election that subjected eight prefects and President Morales to a vote of confidence. If the number of voters who rejected any of these figures was greater than those who had voted him in, he would lose his office. (Chuquisaca, where the Inter-Institutional Committee candidate Savina Cuellar had won office in June 2008, was not included in the vote.) Both sides campaigned hard before the August 10 vote, and the results offered some vindication for each. The nationwide vote gave "the process of change led by Evo Morales and Álvaro García Linera" 67.41 percent approval and destroyed the opposition narrative that support had slipped since the 2005 election; it had grown by 12 percentage points. Voters also gave Santa Cruz's Prefect Rubén Costas 66.43 percent of their vote, and likewise reaffirmed the other three Media Luna governors. However, large majorities voted out Cochabamba's Manfred Reyes Villa and La Paz's José Luis Paredes.[63] Morales's vote totals in the Media Luna departments also undermined the idea that the lowland departments rejected his rule: Morales had secured 70.9 percent support in Cochabamba; majorities in Chuquisaca and Pando; 49.8 percent in Tarija; 43.72 percent in Beni; and 40.75 percent in Santa Cruz.[64]

The separatist project now faced a now-or-never moment. The Media Luna governors had lost much of their case against the national government, which they had claimed was engaged in an undemocratic power grab. But they still had a mandate for autonomy, reinforced by their own positive showings. Rather than scale back their ambitions, the Media Luna civic movements escalated their push for regional autonomy. The five opposition prefects (including Chuquisaca's Cuellar) called for general strikes to begin on August 19, demanded funds from the government's tax on oil and gas production, and warned President Morales that he was not welcome in their territories. The Chuquisaca mobilization held only within the city of Sucre and was immediately isolated by campesino road blockades in all directions. (Among the campesinos' demands: rural officials of their choice and a full investigation of the violence on May 24.) The civic movements in the East seized or vandalized offices of the national government—including taxation, forestry, agriculture, migration, and postal offices in Santa Cruz—as well as the offices of leftist grassroots organizations and support NGOs. In response the grassroots Left organized marches on and blockades around the Media Luna capitals in September 2008, challenging their drive for independence. In Pando armed right-wing protesters (including armed employees of the departmental government) intercepted one such march. The armed employees massacred eleven pro-MAS campesinos and educators-in-training at Porvenir, outside Cobija.[65] Three additional deaths came in quick succession. On September 12 a civic movement protester and a member of the military were killed as the central government militarized Cobija and arrested the prefect for orchestrating the massacre. The next day coca growers fatally wounded a civic movement protester during clashes at a roadblock designed to block their march to Santa Cruz.

After the Porvenir massacre the Union of South American Nations (UNASUR) took a decisive stand on the side of the Morales government. At the invitation of Chile's Michelle Bachelet nine presidents stood side by side on September 15 to declare their full support for Morales and to insist that returning government buildings in the East must be a precondition of any discussions. (Without the export markets of Argentina and Brazil, a gas-exporting Camba Nation was no longer viable.) UNASUR sent investigators to Pando and a support team to Cochabamba to help mediate a left-right dialogue, which began on September 18.[66] While the opposition prefects and civic movements began a de-escalation and returned custody of government offices to the national government, leftist grassroots sectors remained mobilized. Rural movements in Cochabamba maintained an eight-point blockade surrounding and isolating the city of Santa Cruz.[67] More than three thousand Orureño campesinos and miners arrived in Cochabamba in September and began a vigil near the talks while keeping open the possibility of reinforcing the blockade in Santa Cruz. Andrés Villca, a leader of the cooperative miners, pledged, "Some 3,000 miners are ready to march in Cochabamba, and there are 12,000 miners awaiting the result of the meeting between the government and the prefects."[68] On the seventh day of the talks Cruceño peasants finally offered a truce to the Cruceño civic movement, even as they were marching to a cabildo in the city of Montero, just north of Santa Cruz.[69]

On September 27, with no agreement yet signed, progovernment forces in CONALCAM (the National Coordinadora for Change, a civil society coalition founded in 2007 to defend the Constituent Assembly) met to decide their next steps. It came down to a simple choice: surround Santa Cruz or the National Congress in La Paz. Evo Morales presided at the meeting and pushed the alliance to choose a westward march. He succeeded. "With or without dialogue," the government and its allied movements would gather forces in Caracollo on October 13 and embark on a seven-day march to surround the National Congress.[70] The talks in Cochabamba went nowhere and the arena of confrontation shifted to La Paz.

As the movements prepared their march to the National Congress, the opposition—which controlled leadership of the Senate—refused to agree to put the constitution, as written by the Constituent Assembly, to a vote. The promised *cerco*, or surrounding, of the National Congress would be the eighth since 2006 and the only one truly large enough to be worthy of the name.[71] CONALCAM and the Bolivian Workers' Central, which had signed an alliance in defense of the new constitution, gathered five thousand campesinos, indigenous people, workers, shopkeepers, and members of other movements for the two-hundred-kilometer trek. While the marchers were en route, Morales gave his vice president, Álvaro García Linera, and Minister Carlos Romero latitude to negotiate revisions to the text of the constitution. Several breakaway figures within the congressional opposition began to talk about a modest alteration of the constitution approved in Oruro, eventually drawing in members of three right-leaning opposition parties, PODEMOS (known by its acronym),

National Unity, and the MNR.[72] On October 20 Morales—who had led the first day of the march—rejoined it at Ventilla and walked the final nine hours.[73] The march arrived at the Plaza Murillo that day; the Morales government had certainly not called out the police to keep the marchers out. As many as a hundred thousand protesters surrounded the National Congress as it was called into session at 9:00 p.m.[74] An overnight session ended with 106 votes in favor calling a referendum on the constitution, just one vote over the two-thirds threshold needed. The Plaza Murillo became the site of a festival instead of a vigil.

Ninety percent of Bolivia's registered voters cast ballots in the January 25 referendum; 61.43 percent approved the new charter. The new constitution took effect on February 7, 2009, and the government formally became the Plurinational State of Bolivia. The long struggle with Media Luna separatism was essentially at an end, but the indigenizing of state spaces would go on. The government continued to incorporate indigenous symbols and practices in state spaces and to give its official imprimatur to mass gatherings of social movements. Increasingly, however, these gatherings became spaces for criticism of the government rather than the defense of a shared process of change. In the next chapter I will show how these tensions gathered under the surface and then erupted publicly in new arenas of plurinational democracy.

## CHAPTER 7

# A House Divided

*Mobilization and Countermobilization*
*Within the Plurinational State*

> *It was we, too, who initiated this process of change. And we are*
> *not going to be against our own struggle and what we ourselves*
> *have conquered. . . . [Some ministers say] we want that which is*
> *not in the [new] political constitution of the state. We know it isn't*
> *like that because we too know how to read and understand our*
> *constitution and are only demanding that our rights be fulfilled.*
> —ROSA CHAO ROCA

January 2010 promised the beginning of a new state in Bolivia. By decision of the Constituent Assembly, the square checkered rainbow flag called the wiphala, with its forty-nine squares of seven colors, carried by indigenous rebels for more than a century, had become a state symbol. The wiphala was suddenly everywhere: raised as a coequal flag at state offices, ceremonies, and military processions, and stitched onto police and military uniforms. On January 22 this banner of indigenous self-rule flew for the first time atop the National Congress, which was renamed the Plurinational Legislative Assembly. As they were sworn in for a second term, President Evo Morales and Vice President Álvaro García Linera received new medallions of office featuring the eighteenth-century Aymara rebel leaders Túpaj Katari and Bartolina Sisa alongside the creole national heroes Simón Bolívar and Antonio José de Sucre. As Morales proclaimed the formal birth of the Plurinational State of Bolivia, soldiers dressed in bright colonial red escorted the last medals of office of the Republic of Bolivia into a vault at the National Bank and thereby into history.

In the legislative chamber MAS-IPSP affiliates held a two-thirds majority in the Chamber of Deputies and nearly three-quarters of the Senate, elected in a landslide in 2009. This new chapter in Bolivian history meant a full agenda of lawmaking, with scores of laws needed to structure the new bodies of government created by the constitution and to fulfill promises around local autonomy, combating corruption, overcoming racial discrimination, and protecting Mother Earth.

Conventional stories of a revolution might end here, with a final handover of initiative from movement to state. But Bolivia's unity at the ballot box, and the indigenous-centered statecraft displayed in the birth of the Plurinational State, were deceptive. Bolivian movements did not lower their banners, bringing an end to political conflict and mass mobilization. Instead, 2010 and 2011 proved to be the most active years for protest in four decades.[1] Urban blockades, rural blockades, and marches and demonstrations all were at their peak. By the end of 2011 the MAS-IPSP's reputation as the vanguard of workers and indigenous people of anticapitalist transformation would be severely questioned. The party, which had promised a "government of social movements" in 2005, was about to be besieged by its erstwhile allies, who put forward new, and usually local, challenges to the MAS-IPSP government.

This chapter explores the new configuration of movement and state that emerged with the consolidation of the Plurinational State under the MAS-IPSP government. I first look at the party's extraordinary internal structure and how its leadership moved to transform it into a more conventional political party. In 2010 and 2011 major multiweek mobilizations by the northern La Paz town of Caranaví, the lowland indigenous movement, residents of urban and rural Potosí, people nationwide shocked by an abrupt hike in the price of fuel, striking public sector workers, and an indigenous-environmentalist coalition against a controversial highway project all would press their demands upon the government. In turn Morales and the MAS-IPSP responded by encouraging their supporters to countermobilize, just as they had against the separatist movements on the right. Suddenly the government was alleging that other leftist grassroots movements were "endangering the process of change" with their demands: indigenous peoples within the Confederation of Indigenous Peoples of Bolivia and National Council of Ayllus and Markas of Qullasuyu, striking workers in the Bolivian Workers' Central union confederation, and the militant teachers' union, as well as regional protesters who mobilized in Potosí and Caranaví. To show how the tensions within the grassroots leftist coalition played out in protest (and counterprotest), I describe the June–July 2010 indigenous march, the December 2010 Gasolinazo, the 2011 labor strike wave, and the conflict about the proposed highway through Isiboro-Sécure National Park and Indigenous Territory (TIPNIS). The power of space-claiming protest, as charted through this study, continued to be capable of reversing government decisions, but new lines of division and fracture began to appear.

## Political Instrument, Process of Change, Party-Building

The hyphenated name of Bolivia's governing party, Movement Toward Socialism–Political Instrument for the Sovereignty of the Peoples (MAS-IPSP), evokes the tension between international leftist statecraft and plural Bolivian movements' distrust of party politics at the turn of the twenty-first century. Moving an economically peripheral country toward socialism through state-led industrial investment and comprehensive redistribution programs is a well-established and -theorized tradition. Well before his 2005 election Evo Morales found mentors and allies in this process among Latin American heads of state, from Cuba's Fidel Castro to Brazil's Luiz Inácio "Lula" da Silva. On the other hand movements endorsed the creation of the MAS-IPSP as a political instrument that would return power and sovereignty to them. At the local level in places like the Villa Tunari (the municipality at the center of the Chapare), MAS-IPSP officials were expected to subordinate their decisions to those of grassroots organizations.

"At first, we said that union organizations should not involve ourselves in political life," José Santos Romero told me. "And it was our grandparents, our ancestors, who said this [as well]."[2] This rural community-leader-turned-muncipal-council-member carefully explained the steps that had led many in his generation to change their minds. For the grassroots organizations, imagining and constructing the political instrument was a carefully defined strategic choice. The goal was to intervene in the world of electoral politics—a realm of unaccountable political parties led by self-advancing, individualist politicians—without succumbing to its temptations. Like many early MAS-IPSP figures, Santos Romero was nominated as a political candidate by an organizational assembly, and he expected that it would hold him accountable.[3] The novelty of the MAS-IPSP, writes its co-founder, Filemón Escóbar, is "that all of the affiliates of the communal or union assembly, whether present or not, would then vote for the candidate that it elected."[4] Once chosen in the organizational assembly, the candidate would get near-unanimous support of union affiliates at the ballot box, giving the party powerful electoral weight, especially in the highly unionized rural areas.

While other movements focused on new forms of democratic participation, the party sought to channel popular energy into election campaigns. For Raquel Gutiérrez Aguilar, autonomy, communal control of common resources, and democracy through collective deliberation are the hallmarks of recent grassroots movements but are only dimly reflected in the alternative state project led by the MAS-IPSP.[5] In their drive to take office Morales and García Linera promised a "government of social movements." However, they did not replicate the collective accountability of (some) local MAS-IPSP communities at the national level or create a cabinet or legislature of social movements. Those organizational leaders in office "were incorporated on a personal basis, and not as representing social movements within the governmental structure," according to one study on the relationship.[6] (As discussed in chapter 6, some members of the Constituent Assembly had a more organic relationship with grassroots organizations.) Neither the ministers in the executive nor the MAS-IPSP majority in the legislature brought the multivocal turbulence of Bolivian grassroots politics to official debates about the direction of the country.

Morales's December 2005 election campaign won more than 53 percent of the vote—a figure unheard of since the 1982 restoration of multiparty democracy—but the party continued to face enormous challenges in the years that followed. Local and departmental governments and the Senate majority remained in opposition hands. As I showed in chapter 6, the MAS-IPSP navigated the 2006–2009 "catastrophic stalemate" with the right-wing opposition by judiciously countermobilizing its grassroots base. However, the national government steered these mobilizations away from extended, overt confrontation. Instead, it demobilized its allies and the police when confrontations turned deadly and redirected marchers to political targets, such as the six-day September 2008 march that ended at the National Congress, demanding authorization of a referendum on the new constitution.[7] As Jorge Komadina and Céline Geffroy's "political movement" model would predict, these grassroots pushes in the streets were paired with ballot-box contests to stock the Constituent Assembly with MAS-affiliated activists (2006), recall opposition governors in La Paz and Cochabamba (August 2008), and authorize the constitution (January 2009).[8]

While the grassroots Left was taking to the streets in defense of the Constituent Assembly, the MAS-IPSP embarked upon a major party-building effort. As it expanded rapidly to compete in four elections from 2008 to 2010, many of its new candidates and local efforts lacked the kind of organic connections to local organizations that had once defined the political instrument. The party recruited local politicians, activists, and celebrities in its effort to secure a majority in the legislature and a local presence in each of Bolivia's more than 330 municipalities. Meanwhile a substantial number of longtime, high-profile leaders and intellectuals were pushed out of, or broke with, the party and became critics of the government. Nonetheless, the campaigning and expansion efforts were enormously successful, bringing a sense of confidence and possibility to the party's leadership.

After the 2009 elections gave the party supermajorities in the Plurinational Legislative Assembly, Morales and García Linera began to publicly advocate the reorientation of the MAS-IPSP toward a model of a traditional leftist party. Lamenting the lack of a "cadre structure," the vice president observed, "Evo and I have reflected that we must reassume leadership of the MAS and bet heavily on a new wave of cadre from within the unions." The desired new cadre would have "a Bolshevik and Spartan vision," committed ideologically and resistant to corrupt influences.[9] Meanwhile they also began to label dissidents and critics of the government as "outside infiltrators" within the membership of the party and its allied organizations. These vague narratives of foreign, right-wing, or ultraleftist influence dovetailed with a general push to make party and movement members loyal to the MAS-IPSP leadership. CONALCAM, the National Coordinadora for Change, which was founded in 2007 to defend the Constituent Assembly, was reorganized as an increasingly partisan organization in September 2010. CONALCAM declared that it "recognizes and backs the leadership of brother Evo Morales Ayma" and that one of its purposes was to "impede, denounce, and sanction the infiltration of counter-revolutionary enemies within" the alliance.[10] Despite its origins as a political instrument, the MAS-IPSP began to be driven by the imperatives of party building and its leaders' desire to integrate unions in a corporatist relationship with the state.

The Bolivian government pursued bold leftist initiatives in some areas, but within a macroeconomic strategy that cooperated with international creditors and, after the rift with the eastern separatists was healed, domestic agribusiness.[11] The Bolivian government could not afford to be downgraded in international bond markets, isolated like a new Cuba, or spurned by transnational corporate investors. So the government sent clear signals to global powers about just what its brand of populism would entail. "We are not," Vice President García Linera pledged in Washington, "a populist government with easily opened pockets and cheap promises."[12] He highlighted the government's "responsible management of macroeconomics" and its willingness to say no to demands from movements that would require greater debt.

Bolivian government officials became experts at playing against type, contrasting their moderate policies with their radical reputation. They maintained small fiscal deficits, large currency reserves, and a high rate of growth in GDP. Their main antipoverty programs allocated revenues from the renationalized gas industry to cash-grant programs for senior citizens, pregnant women and new mothers, and families with small children attending school. These programs, combined with a rapidly rising minimum wage, reduced extreme poverty in Bolivia from 38.6 percent of the population to 16.8 percent in ten years.[13] However, this commitment to resource-driven redistribution drew the government ever closer to conventional capitalist industries and away from both social and communitarian economic experiments and the recognition of indigenous territorial rights.

## The 2010 National Indigenous March

In June and July 2010 hundreds of indigenous people with the Confederation of Indigenous Peoples of Bolivia (CIDOB) walked the roads of rural Beni and Santa Cruz bound for the capital, La Paz. The path stretched across this country of forests and farms, vast plains and sharp mountains. Marchers had come from the arid plain of the Chaco, from the vast Pantanal wetland, from the tropical valleys of Cochabamba and La Paz, and from the Bolivian Amazon. They hailed from seven of the country's nine departments and spanned in age from babies to grandparents, including the seasoned Mojeño leader Ernesto Noé, sixty-nine, who co-founded the Confederation of Indigenous Peoples of Beni in 1989. They marched behind a series of banners, one for each of the regional federations that make up CIDOB and one smaller banner at the front announcing that this is not the first but the Seventh Grand March of Bolivia's lowland indigenous peoples.

This time, however, they confronted new kinds of adversity, from unforgiving weather to a barrage of government hostility. A rare region-wide southern wind, a *surazo*, off the cooler Argentine plains brought storms that lashed the city of Santa Cruz and the normally tropical plains that surround it. Temperatures plummeted from the nineties to the thirties, rain fell sporadically, and everyone was unexpectedly miserable. The cold snap prompted a nationwide school closure

FIGURE 17 A farmworker from Beni gives cash support to marchers in the Seventh Grand National March of the Confederation of Indigenous Peoples of Bolivia, after praising their struggle and calling it his own.

and claimed the lives of at least twenty-one people across Bolivia. The villages that hosted the marchers each night were not prepared for these cold blasts, and a number of people fell ill and left the march, unable to carry on. Nonetheless hundreds of people, young and old, some carrying babies, continued toward Santa Cruz. In my single day's experience marching itself was the best way to keep warm, more effective than huddling around a fire or camping together in the tents, schoolhouses, and churches that provide the marchers with shelter.[14] When the rain came, the marchers pulled out white tarps or lifted their plastic banners above their heads. When it got worse, they made small virtual tents on the side of the road. And when it stopped, they went back to marching. In the late afternoon La Senda, the next community to offer hospitality for a night or two, offered them a welcome—cups filled with hot coffee and a brief speech.

The indigenous movement's cross-country marches are daily tests of commitment and solidarity. Even when the weather cooperates, the mobile community of activists must endure hardships, sustain itself, find welcoming communities to host it, and replenish its supplies with donations. As I left Santa Cruz to join the march, Maria Serabia, CIDOB's secretary, was pleading on the radio for various necessities the marchers lacked. That afternoon giant black bags of used clothes arrived at La Senda to be divided up among schoolrooms-turned-dormitories for the marchers.

CIDOB's previous marches, backing an agrarian reform law in 2006 and greater constitutional recognition of indigenous autonomy in 2007, had the support of the Morales government. This time, however, the protesters made demands directly upon the plurinational state. They wanted to modify the Framework Law on Autonomy and Decentralization, then under consideration by the Plurinational Legislative Assembly. The law was to provide a basis for indigenous territories and local governments to exercise local autonomy, taking on many of the responsibilities of municipalities. The march also sought guarantees of indigenous territorial rights, greater representation in the legislature, and participation in decision making within a variety of arenas, such as forestry and mining within their lands. One marcher, Miguel Angel Cerda Figuerero of northern La Paz, told me their demands were an extension of the 2009 constitution: "Everything should be fulfilled, it should not remain on paper, it should not end up as words but rather should end up as deed. It should be practiced. Why would we want laws that sound pretty but are not carried out?"

The legislature amended the draft of the law, but the executive branch's response was hostile. Morales, a veteran of cocalero marches to La Paz, mocked the march's pace and delay. The government insinuated that the march was a foreign-funded plot to divide the indigenous movement, that Bolivian organizations supporting it had been infiltrated by clandestine opponents and paid off by foreign money, including the U.S. Agency for International Development. The Morales administration labeled the Center for Juridical Studies and Social Investigation (CEJIS), an NGO based in Santa Cruz, a dangerous "outside influence." Combining these two allegations with a dash of old-fashioned racism, the state-funded daily *Cambio* ran an editorial cartoon depicting a stereotypical jungle savage controlled by a conniving Uncle Sam. Cocaleros in the Chapare threatened to prevent the march from passing through their region on the way to La Paz. Vice President Álvaro García Linera convened a meeting of the other members of the Pact of Unity to publicly urge CIDOB to stop the march. Pact leaders signed a manifesto denouncing CIDOB for making excessive demands, fostering division among grassroots organizations, and allegedly being financed by NGOs and right-wing opponents.

No one was more flummoxed about being labeled antigovernment conspirators than the staff of CEJIS.[15] No fewer than five former CEJIS staffers served as ministers during Morales's first term.[16] As is typical of CEJIS's history, in 1990

FIGURE 18  Editorial cartoon in the state-run daily newspaper *Cambio* shows a nefarious Uncle Sam operating a remote control (labeled CEJIS—the Center for Juridical Studies and Social Investigation) to send a stereotypical lowland savage (labeled CIDOB) to attack a tree designated as the 2009 constitution.

Ernesto Noé spent a year studying law at CEJIS, where he met its future director Carlos Romero. Providing logistical support and legal analysis to CIDOB marches was a routine part of CEJIS's work under Romero's leadership. CEJIS also supported alliances like the Pact of Unity and the political instrument that would become the MAS-IPSP. At the height of the secessionist crisis in 2008, when antigovernment crowds led by the Cruceño Youth Union (Unión Juvenil Cruceñista) took over and sacked national government buildings, CEJIS was on their hit list. After the separatists drove a Toyota Land Cruiser through the front gate, a crowd of fifty freely looted the building and built a bonfire of desks and books in the street. Less than two years later, however, CEJIS was now accused of being part of a rightist plot to disrupt the process of change. The maddening situation forced them to rethink their work: Would bringing fuel or soliciting donated clothes for the march be publicized as evidence of manipulation? If so, would they leave the indigenous movement to shiver in the cold for want of supplies?

Government and CIDOB negotiators finally began talks at the CIDOB's headquarters in Santa Cruz on Saturday, July 17. Three days in, tempers began to fray. Indigenous movement members voiced frustration that the government negotiators had neither the authority to make broad political commitments nor the skills to negotiate the text of future decrees. The vice ministers negotiating on the government's behalf, for their part, promised that lawyers and technical experts would arrive late in the week and insisted that any legislation needed broader consultation anyway. For CIDOB members, that "our brothers and sisters are suffering, that all of us are suffering the cold, as they are walking on the road," as Rosa Chao (president of CIDOB's Cochabamba regional affiliate) put it, was present in every moment of extension or delay in the talks. The difference in urgency between the two sides was palpable.[17]

In the end the talks collapsed under the weight of mutual distrust. Speaking in Cochabamba, President Morales denounced unnamed members of CIDOB as buscapegas—post seekers—corruptly seeking executive positions. Marchers gathered in a schoolhouse in San Ramón denounced the signature of Autonomy Minister Carlos Romero on the "pre-accord" that had been faxed to them, while a government negotiator ripped up a copy of the agreement in the Santa Cruz negotiating hall. Fundamental issues were left unresolved, foreshadowing further conflict.

## The Gasolinazo

On the day after Christmas 2010, Vice President Álvaro García Linera signed Supreme Decree 748 and announced that the Bolivian government would remove all subsidies on fuel, primarily gasoline and diesel, and let the prices float to international levels, a decision widely known as the Gasolinazo. Prices went up 57 to 83 percent overnight.[18] Fuel price subsidies are a costly budget item and an area where economic orthodoxy and the interests of workers directly clash.[19] For years the MAS-IPSP had railed against moves by previous governments to end price supports.[20] Now it was joining them.

Within hours transit drivers announced a national strike and moved to raise their fares, which are a basic element of family budgets.[21] Nearly every other seller of basic goods, from bread makers to peasants in the Unified Union Confederation of Rural Bolivian Workers and the National Council of Ayllus and Markas of Qullasuyu (CONAMAQ), argued that higher fuel costs would require higher prices for their products.[22] Shocked by the consequences for their pocketbooks and outraged at paying more for products considered a collective asset after the 2003 Gas War, the Bolivian public hit the streets. The El Alto Women's Federation was the first to march, banging empty casserole pans in the streets on December 27.[23] The next day representatives of thirty-eight labor unions within the Bolivian Workers' Central union confederation called for the abrogation of the decree and authorized their affiliates to participate in "surprise measures" to challenge it.[24]

In El Alto the Neighborhood Council Federation orchestrated protests on December 29 and 30. The first day's protest was planned as a public meeting to decide on how to pressure the government, but it immediately shifted into action by calling a general strike and destroying property on the highway to La Paz. The federation's message was direct, confrontational, and personal: calling for Evo Morales to resign, publicly pummeling effigies of Morales and García Linera, and burning images of both leaders in the streets. On December 30 the leadership declared itself on a "war footing," and parts of the crowd destroyed property belonging to the MAS-IPSP–controlled municipality and the national government (the Bolivian Roads tollbooth and the food supply agency). Thousands marched to downtown La Paz, joining Paceño protesters who pressed toward the Plaza Murillo on all sides. Meanwhile thousands more gathered in Oruro, Potosí, Cochabamba, Santa Cruz, Cobija, Trinidad, Sucre, and Tarija—all nine of the departmental capitals. The scene in El Alto, and the gathering wave of mobilizations nationwide, brought back collective memories of the mobilizations that had toppled presidents in 2003 and 2005, even though the numbers of participants were not yet as great.

Many of the social movements that brought the MAS-IPSP to power, such as the mine workers and neighborhood councils, did not hesitate to mobilize against the Gasolinazo. Leaders of others aligned themselves with the decree but faced criticism from their members. Members of the Six Federations of the Tropics of Cochabamba—Evo Morales's coca grower base—formed a blockade at the small town of Ivirgazama to denounce the decree. Midlevel leaders like the cocalero Eulogio Franco acknowledged, "Many people, my grassroots comrades, refuse to go along with this hike that affects us," and broke from their leadership.[25] In El Alto this break was more dramatic: protesters stoned and threw incendiary devices into the offices of the Federation of Neighborhood Councils and the mayor because of their refusal to denounce the decree. Although their leaders felt some pressure from the government, the neighborhood councils, factory workers, labor confederation, and others mobilized mass protests.

For several days the government clung to the belief that other new policies could soften the popular revulsion or that it could explain the benefits of the policy, but the streets were too angry and threatening. Daily promises that the funds used for fuel subsidies could be redirected to help those most in need seemed to only intensify the protests. Just hours before midnight on December 31 the government reversed course and returned fuel prices to their former levels. By the next day Morales was claiming that this new decision reflected his dynamic relationship with the Bolivian people: "The people listened to me and taught me, and they salute the decision that I took in defense of the poorest families."[26] The government started a nationwide advertising campaign promising to "govern by obeying the people."[27] However, officials still proposed that a renewed hike could come soon, provided that the social movements had been consulted.[28] This suggestion and the four days of price hikes set off a wave of inflation. The government had lost much of its credibility as an opponent of free-market policies. ("I think the public is realizing that it doesn't matter who is in power," Marcela Olivera told me.) On the other hand social movements had shown a dramatic ability to mobilize nearly overnight, regardless of official rhetoric and in spite of leaders more loyal to the Morales administration. Evidently the government feared giving this breach any more time to grow wider.

## 2011 Labor Mobilizations

In a series of three strike waves from February to April 2011, Bolivian workers mobilized for higher wages, stronger labor rights, and greater union involvement in economic decisions. While wages are a perennial issue for unions, the post-Gasolinazo atmosphere made the issue of pay particularly explosive. The price spiral that followed the abortive fuel price increases in December 2010 sparked street protests about the prices of fuel, sugar, local transport, and milk. For salaried workers—those represented by the unions—the best compensation for rising prices was greater take-home pay. However, the labor movement also faced internal stress: several 2010 mobilizations had collapsed when Pedro Montes, executive secretary of the Bolivian Workers' Central union confederation, negotiated agreements on pay (May 2010) and pensions (November 2010). But the more radical unions and the mobilized base of the labor movement rejected the Montes settlements. Accusations that leaders like Montes had "sold themselves to the government" had only grown louder during the Gasolinazo and the months that followed.[29]

So, rather than convening national meetings of the labor movement, its more aggressive affiliates went on strike independently, forcing the leadership to catch up to their demands. Urban and rural teachers and health-care workers took the lead in three major strike waves in late February, late March, and early April. The Morales government met some of their demands by issuing Supreme Decree 809, raising most state and all private salaries by 10 percent and increasing the minimum wage by 20 percent to Bs 815.40 (US$116) per month, retroactive to January 1, 2011. Coordinated strikes on February 18 and March 21–22 were marked by converging mass marches that culminated in sizable cabildos. This pulse of activity inspired and enabled other sectors, notably university students, airport workers, and miners at the massive San Cristóbal Mine, to advance their own demands through parallel strike campaigns.

A general strike beginning on April 4 brought out rural and urban teachers, health workers, and retirees again but also began attracting municipal, construction, and factory workers. Workers decided to concentrate their numbers on La Paz, mounting a citywide blockade on April 7. There, workers clashed with the police near the Presidential Palace and the Plaza Murillo. Soon afterward the government conceded an array of nonwage demands in an April 11 "pre-accord," including the ceremonial revocation of the 1985 Supreme Decree that inaugurated neoliberal rule, and acceding to union representation in pension and health-care reform.

As workers returned from confrontations in the capital, the labor strike wave gathered national force. Regional workers' assemblies in Oruro, Cochabamba, Beni, Chuquisaca, and Potosí decided to hold out for more than the government had offered. Blockades began in El Alto on April 12, outside the La Paz–El Alto metropolitan area on April 14, and in Potosí, near Trinidad (in Beni), and Sucre on April 15. Unlike its forerunners the April round was pulling in increasing numbers of supporters and employing the tools of a civic strike. Miners joined a convergence of labor marches in La Paz that fought for access to the Plaza Murillo. Highway blockades designed to isolate certain areas began around La Paz on April 12 and Sucre on two days later. The "blockade of a thousand corners" paralyzed central La Paz, while coordinated bridge blockades had isolated Cochabamba's downtown for much of April 14.

On the twelfth day of labor protests Cochabamba's labor movement arrived in the Plaza 14 de Septiembre for a cabildo. Large converging marches demonstrated

FIGURE 19 A speaker addresses the cabildo abierto crowd from the Fabriles building's balcony during the April 2011 labor strike.

that sympathy for the strike was spreading across organized labor, beyond the combative sectors that had been mobilizing for months. The crowd in the plaza was a rolling cacophony of sounds: chants, songs, claps, and the rattle of noisemakers made of pebble-filled soda bottles. All the bullhorn shouts and unison chants and songs that had characterized each little group during its march continued, bringing a patchwork of messages into the square. People sang threats—*It seems like he's going to fall, it seems like he's going to fall, Evo and his ministers*—pledges of commitment and fearlessness—*Rifles, machine guns, the teachers won't be silenced!*—and debating points about the availability of government funds—*They are buying airplanes* (in the next verse: *satellites*) *with the money of the people.*

The various groups had marched in behind separate banners, but a few from the largest delegations detached themselves and carried these banners to the front of the crowd, on the street in front of the Fabriles headquarters. The health and education workers, who had been pushing the effort along for two months, were joined by construction workers, the employees of the water utility

SEMAPA, departmental and municipal employees, university students and workers, postal workers, bus terminal vendors, and factory workers, all organized behind dozens of banners but melding into a single crowd. They positioned themselves wherever they could see the speakers on the balcony and covered the roadways, sidewalks, and walks within the plaza while remaining standing and focused on the rally.

With Oscar Olivera joining other labor leaders looking out over the crowd, the scene looked a lot like moments from the Water War. The third-floor balcony was a hive of activity. Each labor leader spoke to the crowd and was surrounded for the duration of his speech by a couple dozen microphones and videographers. The speakers shared words and handshakes with one another, and a few handed declarations out to the press. Their speeches rallied the crowd with news of new allies in the struggle (airport workers were joining the strike, for instance) and angry insistence on the importance of higher wages.

However, the outlook from the balcony was complicated: the government was steadfastly resisting major wage increases; the campesino federations of Cochabamba were preparing a march challenging the strike "in defense of the process of change"; and the grassroots activists in Cochabamba did not trust national labor leaders to fully press their interests. As Gustavo Sánchez, secretary general of the Urban Teachers' Union, described it in his speech, "The leaders of the Central Obrera Boliviana have one foot in the mobilization and one foot in the government." Most important, no one had breached the key social boundaries separating the rich from the working class, campesinos from the city, and unions from unorganized workers. Moors and Christians remained separate. Without a broadening base, and without rural or middle-class allies, the labor cabildo could only aspire to sovereignty. Thirty-six hours of marathon talks yielded a new government offer: a guaranteed 11 percent and perhaps 12 percent pay raise for education and health-care workers. In an April 18 general meeting the leaders of the Bolivian Workers' Central union confederation decided to end the general strike.[30]

Despite the labor–government accord on April 18, the Cochabamba departmental affiliate of CONALCAM organized three marches of campesinos, coca growers, and urban supporters "in defense of the process of change" and against the strike that had concluded the previous day. While there were no striking workers to confront in downtown Cochabamba, the marches pitted campesinos and organized labor against one another in a dramatic way. As I was passing through the square early in the morning, I encountered preparations for the march. City workers had stretched a long Bolivian tricolor garland a hundred feet along the second story of city hall, just above a similarly long banner styled after the wiphala; next they stretched out another banner, this one blue, white, and black for the MAS-IPSP. A few blocks to the east, coca growers were gathering at the Six Federations headquarters, preparing to march around Plaza Colón and into the square. Thousands had arrived from the Chapare and the Cochabamba Yungas to march in straight-line formation through the streets of central Cochabamba.

As the march rounded the Plaza Colón, I interviewed a coca grower about the falling-out with urban movements. The composite picture she painted of labor leaders involved their politicizing economic struggle into a political challenge to the government but also intimations of corruption—"He is a Trotskyist leader who sometimes is used by certain groups who pay him"; "They always mobilize by using cash [*la plata*]." In contrast "we never have mobilized [in that way, but rather] without [outside] money, each comrade on his own account goes along supporting the process of change." All around her signs (and an effigy) denounced labor leaders as opportunists, Trotskyists, and "traitors to the process of change." From the south another march, led by campesinos within the municipality, approached the plaza, marching from the Avenida Petrolera and up Ayacucho. Among them I found Christian Mamani, another heavily involved participant in the Water War of 2000. For him the labor strike was not driven by the workers at all but by "a certain handful of leaders" who put their own interests above those of the people as a whole.

Three marches converged by circling the central square. When they arrived, they paraded past the reviewing stand, which was flush with MAS government officials and senior officials from rural unions. Tucked among the thousands of campesinos were hundreds of MAS activists from within the city, who were marching behind banners saved from the last electoral campaign, and dozens of dissident health workers who proclaimed themselves "with the process of change." In the rally's final address Vice President García Linera offered an extension of earlier accusations of coup plotting, disruption, and selfishness by the strikers and their leaders. He warned the assembled crowd of thousands that destabilizing the Morales government could bring the right wing back into power.

The labor strike and the countermobilization by CONALCAM put the narrators I relied upon for this book at odds with one another. Marcelo Rojas joined his union at SEMAPA in the streets to back the strike. Oscar Olivera

was once more up on the balcony urging unity and mobilization, as well as organizing workers without a union to press for their rights. Conversely Christian
Mamani led his community into the plaza to denounce rather than support the
labor strike. María Eugenia ("Mauge") Flores Castro reflected, "I lament that
the state's co-optation of the peasant organizations is so strong . . . that it makes
their movement go against their comrades who had been allies in the struggle,
because the workers are not their enemies. And it's a shame that the state has
made this happen."[31]

## TIPNIS: Face Off over a Highway

Representatives of the Sub-Central TIPNIS, the federation of Tsimané, Yuracaré, and Mojeño-Trinitario communities living in the Isiboro-Sécure National
Park and Indigenous Territory (TIPNIS), were among the dozens of groups
presenting their struggle at the April 2010 World Peoples Summit on Climate
Change and the Rights of Mother Earth, held in Tiquipaya.[32] While left out
of the government-sponsored sessions, they were poignant voices within the
independent working group on Bolivia's internal environmental struggles.[33]
Soon thereafter sympathetic urban activists began meeting in the offices of
the Cochabamba Forum on Environment and Development, located on the
second floor of the Fabriles' building on the Plaza 14 de Septiembre. At the
Tiquipaya summit and in Cochabamba, Adolfo Moye Rosendy and Mirian
Yubanure Moye spoke passionately, even lovingly, of their territory. It was their
Loma Santa, the sacred hill sought by their Mojeño ancestors who migrated
away from colonial ranchers, and their Casa Grande, the great communal house
that provided all they needed. The proximate threat to this way of life was the
Villa Tunari–San Ignacio de Moxos highway, which would open their territory
to the colonization and deforestation that had nearly eliminated forested land
in Polygon 7, a portion of the park that was steadily occupied by coca growers
from 1986 on. The 306-kilometer road would pass through Isiboro-Sécure along
a 177-kilometer segment from Isinuta to Monte Grande, effectively dividing
the park in half. A study by the Bolivian Strategic Research Program found
the road would accelerate deforestation by increasing access to the territory for
illegal loggers as well as agricultural colonizers.[34] In May 2010 three TIPNIS
indigenous organizations held a gathering of traditional leaders and issued a
joint resolution declaring, "Opening this highway would present a threat to

our life as peoples who inhabit TIPNIS due to the loss of the natural resources and all the biodiversity upon which the Moxeños, Yuracarés, and Chimanes sustain their culture and life: a life and culture we have lived in our territory since before the creation of Bolivia and will continue to live in the future." They voted to "overwhelmingly and non-negotiably reject the construction of the Villa Tunari–San Ignacio de Moxos highway and of any highway segment that would affect our territory."[35]

In 2010 the urban Campaign in Defense of TIPNIS and the TIPNIS leaders wrestled with how best to approach the government without hostility, how to convince the government to prioritize its stated affinity for environmental protection over this road project. At a September 2010 forum jointly sponsored by the Sub-Central TIPNIS and the Campaign in Defense of TIPNIS, Adolfo Moye invoked a connection between President Morales and the territory: "When Evo Morales began his career as a leader, just in the colonized area of TIPNIS, in the Aroma union, he shared this experience of the [TIPNIS] communities. It is from then, we believe, that our president [found] what he now calls Mother Earth, because in some way he had to see a way of seeking respect for the territory, for our territory, and for the zone that is now in much danger."[36]

But the government was ignoring such calls and moving ahead with building the highway. It had crafted a preliminary design (in 2008), obtained a loan from Brazil's BNDES development bank (early 2011), and began construction of the highway in June 2011.[37] The Sub-Central TIPNIS, holder of a collective land title to the territory, was outraged that it was not consulted throughout all these stages of development, despite the government's vocal endorsement of international conventions for respecting indigenous rights.[38]

In mid-2011 the national indigenous movement, represented by both CIDOB and CONAMAQ, recognized the TIPNIS highway as a bellwether case and organized the Eighth National Indigenous March to oppose it. TIPNIS was particularly iconic as one of the four indigenous territories granted after CIDOB's first march in 1990. Once construction of the highway began, Morales explicitly denied local indigenous communities the right to choose, saying the road would be built "whether they want it or not."[39] Exasperated by the preparations for a march challenging his decision, Morales declared, "Those who oppose the exploration of oil or of gas, or finally the construction of roads, are not my indigenous brothers, whether they are from the Chaco, from Isiboro[-Sécure], or other places. How can they oppose it?"[40] Both sides recognized the dispute, then, as a key precedent affecting the right of indigenous peoples to freely consent to or reject megaprojects on their lands.

CIDOB and CONAMAQ began their cross-country march on August 15 from Trinidad, Beni, heading west this time, straight for La Paz. The government struggled to mobilize allies to block the march. In San Borja, Beni, massive efforts by march supporters outflanked a small blockade. Finally, members of the federation of agricultural colonists (Aymara and Quechua migrants in the lowlands) installed a road blockade at Yucumo, on the Beni–La Paz border. The national government interposed police troops between the march and the blockade ostensibly to prevent violence, effectively halting the march on September 15. During a ten-day delay marchers suffered food shortages and limited access to water, but a new wave of activists mobilized in solidarity. A cross-country delegation from Cochabamba, La Paz, and Santa Cruz arrived to join and supply the march.[41]

On September 24 a group of women marchers grabbed a government negotiator, Foreign Minister David Choquehuanca, and insisted he march through the police blockade with them. The government seized on this so-called kidnapping as a pretext for its plans, already underway, to break up the indigenous encampment, now located at Chaparina. That night Marcos Farfán, vice minister of Police and the Interior Regime, gathered police commanders to organize a mass arrest of the marchers. He also laid out the political stakes, saying, "If we don't produce, if we don't create industries, if we don't build highways, . . . this government will fail. Everything will be ruined."[42] Farfán later testified that "the order to intervene was taken with great reticence by the officers present [in Yucumo] who alleged it would be impossible to carry out."[43]

The next afternoon General Oscar Muñoz Colodro, a police commander, took over and coordinated a dramatic afternoon attack on the camp of indigenous marchers, beating and teargassing them, seeking out and arresting prominent leaders, and leaving behind a chaotic scene of injury, flight, and fear. Marchers, including prominent leaders, were grabbed, tackled, and handcuffed in front of network television cameras. Seventy-two to 280 protesters were injured, according to different sources.[44] Police took hundreds of marchers away in buses and vans and attempted to send them back to Trinidad, Beni. But protesters blocked the police caravan at San Borja, burned its tires in the road, and clashed with police. As police debated their next move, San Borja youth helped some marchers out of the buses and away to safety.[45] The rest were driven toward Rurrenabaque and the region's principal airport.

Members of the Tacana, Tsimane, and Mosetén peoples and Rurrenab-aque townspeople organized overnight. Hundreds had arrived at the airport by morning, attempted to provide food and water to the detainees, and became increasingly enraged at the prisoners' condition. Police prepared to put several hundred arrested marchers on planes to an unannounced destination. Unnerved by the uncertainty, the detained protesters sat on the ground, announced their refusal to board any planes, and sang the national anthem.[46] Then the Rurren-abaque protesters took the initiative. They set bonfires and torched tires on the runways and launched projectiles at the police. A Hercules C-130 military transport plane had to divert from the airport.[47] The crowds were angry and determined: one participant from the Tacana village of Tumupasa said, "If we have to die, we'll die."[48] With control of the airport slipping away, the police commander ordered the release of the protesters.

The dramatic solidarity shown by residents of San Borja and Rurrenabaque led to a groundswell of local and national actions in support of the indigenous marchers. Within the first week after the raid, street protests occurred in eight of nine departmental capitals, the Bolivian Workers' Central union confedera-tion held a twenty-four-hour general strike in solidarity, and a department-wide strike was held in Beni. The Beni Civic Committee coordinated a general strike and coordinated road blockades in the capital, Trinidad, and in Santa Rosa, San Borja, Riberalta, and Rurrenabaque. Mobilized strike rallies in La Paz and Rib-eralta each attracted more than ten thousand people. In Cochabamba teachers, university students, and municipal workers blockaded major avenues while the public transport system observed a general closure.[49]

The marchers reunited at Quiquibey, thirty-six kilometers closer to La Paz than Yucumo, and restarted the march on September 30. At Caranavi and Palos Blancos people openly welcomed them, despite predictions of confrontations with the colonos union. As the marchers climbed the steep ascent from trop-ical valleys to La Paz, the seven minority indigenous members of the Bolivian Chambers of Deputies drafted legislation to permanently protect TIPNIS from highway construction. Two of them, Pedro Nuni and Bienvenido Zacu, had been among those arrested at Chaparina.[50] A second march led by affiliates of CONAMAQ traveled from Oruro on September 26, reaching La Paz on October 10, and grew from 75 to 220 participants along the way.[51]

On Wednesday, October 19, at least twelve hundred protesters—long-term marchers and recent supporters—arrived in La Paz at the end of their five-hundred-kilometer journey (three hundred miles). On their arrival thousands

FIGURE 20 Marchers on the Eighth National Indigenous March walk uphill on a foggy road as they head toward La Paz in October 2011. (Photo by Mariella Claudio, CC-BY-NC-SA)

upon thousands of spectators lined the route or joined in the procession; the mayor presented the marchers with the keys to the city. That evening several hundred indigenous protesters set up camp in the Plaza Murillo. Winning this spot required outflanking the police; the National Police relieved Colonel Wenceslao Zea O'Phelan of his department-wide command for allowing this to happen.[52] A ring of police surrounded the plaza and isolated the encampment. The police were unwilling to attack the protesters but lobbed tear gas at supporters who arrived with food, tents, and warm clothing.

Despite clear reluctance to yield to the demands of the protesters, the Morales administration was forced to shift its position. Three kinds of events moved the government: the failure of repression, demonstrations of broadening support for the movement, and the symbolic impact of the indigenous marchers' reaching the capital, its downtown, and the Plaza Murillo. After the marchers arrived in La Paz, the government abandoned its refusal to allow the TIPNIS indigenous community to have any say about the highway being built through their lands and began detailed negotiations regarding the marchers' remaining demands. Fifteen separate agreements were signed within a week. Law 180, written by CIDOB, was enacted on October 25, 2011; it declared TIPNIS an "intangible zone" and prohibited construction of any highway across the park. Still, by the end of the mobilization the divide between the plurinational government and the ethnoecological agenda advanced by CIDOB, CONAMAQ, environmentalists, and other activists clearly was irreversible.

In late 2011, as soon as the indigenous marchers had gone home, the government sought to regain its footing and reverse the TIPNIS protection law. The Chapare cocalero movement, of which Evo Morales remains the head, and CONISUR, a confederation of indigenous communities in the colonized southern portion of TIPNIS, organized their own march in favor of the highway.[53] In both Cochabamba and La Paz, government officials were quick to promote the march and start talking about legislation. On February 10, 2012, the government enacted Law 222, which authorized a government-organized consultation on the future of the territory. When the Sub-Central TIPNIS boycotted the consultation, the government forged ahead, sending brigades of officials into the territory from July 29 to November 25, publicly bestowing gifts and development assistance implicitly or explicitly conditioned on acceptance of the highway. The official government report claims that fifty-seven communities rejected Law 180, thereby indirectly authorizing a road. However, observers sent by the Catholic church, the Permanent Assembly of Human Rights–Bolivia, and the International Federation of Human Rights, as well as by urban indigenous solidarity activists, found widespread rejection of the consultation process and of the roadway.[54] The international rights delegation found "numerous irregularities and violations of the principle of good faith, as well as of the right to free prior and informed consultation."[55] The government froze activity on the central segment of the project until 2017, when a new law and resumption of construction reactivated the conflict.

Improbably, this two-lane roadway had become the biggest symbol of division between the MAS-IPSP and parts of the Bolivian grassroots Left. While the conflict has had many twists, turns, and betrayals, the government continues to claim that it, not project opponents, is the defender of grassroots sovereignty. Where once it said the highway would be built "whether the indigenous like it or not," since November 2011 the message has been that the highway will be built precisely because the indigenous like it. More generally, the Morales government disputes what the voice of social movements is saying, and which leaders have the right to speak for those movements, but shares in the idea that the movement voice is foundational to Bolivian politics. In the years that followed, this strategy precipitated both a modest hollowing of support for the party and numerous crises within the ranks of social movement organizations.

## The Role of Space Claiming in a Turbulent Year

The events of 2010 and 2011 illustrate that politics on the street has a continuing force in Bolivia, one that is capable of overcoming the determined efforts of the national government. The Morales government had secure control of the executive and the legislature, but these tools could not legitimately overrule the people in the streets. Movements used a variety of means to make this happen, but strike waves, converging marches, cabildos, and indigenous vigils in urban centers—the forms of space claiming examined here—were the central tools. These challenges, when articulated with numbers and commitment and when they used symbolically important spaces in historically resonant ways—Alteños swarming downhill to La Paz, indigenous peoples retaking the Plaza Murillo—continued to represent "the people," whom the government must obey.

Official recognition of this political reality appeared in the text of the supreme decree that canceled the Gasolinazo, which made a nod to "civil society . . . [which] due to the impact on the popular economy that it represents, has proposed changes to the National Government by way of mobilizations."[56] It came, after 10 p.m. on New Year's Eve 2010, in the president's announcement of that decree, which promised that he would engage in "the conduct of governing by obeying the people."[57] And it showed in how Morales engaged with the pro-TIPNIS marchers camped on the Plaza Murillo in October 2011.

When challenged, the Morales government turned to its own mobilizations as a defense strategy, embraced symbols of indigenous and grassroots sovereignty, and pushed its proposals through social movement forums. While Morales and García Linera claimed a fuel price increase was essential, they repeatedly promised it would occur after consultation with social movements and their approval. During the 2011 labor mobilization the government also strove to connect its policies to the demands of social movements, both through the countermarch in Cochabamba and by positioning the government as defending an agenda of transfer payments to the poor and long-term investments in production, rather than short-term pay increases. While countermobilization has helped the government to navigate difficult moments, its use has deepened divisions among social movements.

The dueling mobilizations of 2011 soon gave way to struggles within organizations. For a brief time critics of the government took the offensive: CIDOB and CONAMAQ withdrew from the Pact of Unity, while several lowland indigenous deputies declared themselves independent of the MAS-IPSP, leaving it short of a supermajority in the Chamber of Deputies. Soon, however, the two indigenous organizations were torn apart (in 2012 and 2013) by progovernment representatives who formed parallel leaderships in the organizations, leaving both organizations with a pro- and antigovernment faction. The government refused to provide services to communities represented by the critical factions or even to meet with their representatives.[58] In the 2014 elections the government required indigenous representatives (i.e., those holding the seven Chamber of Deputies seats designated for minority indigenous communities) to affiliate with a political party, while the MAS-IPSP imposed stricter discipline on its legislators, declaring the party had no room for "free thinkers." The labor movement, which had long maintained a classist stance of independence from governments and political parties, also drew closer to the MAS-IPSP, continuing trends I observed during my fieldwork. After another contentious round of strikes in 2013, the government began offering all workers a doubling of the annual bonus (or *aguinaldo*). The leadership of the Bolivian Workers' Central union confederation formally endorsed the president and his party in the 2014 election, although the 2017 closure of some government enterprises prompted efforts within the labor movement to renounce the partnership. Government-aligned factions have also emerged in the Federation of Neighborhood Councils of La Paz and El Alto, the Permanent Assembly of Human Rights, and among health-care workers, creating schisms in longtime organizations. Nonetheless, even the rise of government-aligned social movements doesn't prevent these progovernment factions from engaging in critical mobilization, as the Gasolinazo demonstrated.

Bolivia's highly mobilized social movements did not establish a simple and unified political scene under the plurinational state. Rather they advanced disparate and conflicting claims, often in ways that directly challenged the government. While many observers have assumed that the government's close relationship to grassroots movements would defuse protest, it has continued to spark it. If anything, 2010 and 2011 cemented the role of space-claiming protest as the language of political participation in plurinational Bolivia.

# A New Way of Doing Politics

*My notion of democracy changed. . . . For me democracy had been*
*to elect a president. That was democracy, right? Every four years,*
*you go and you choose, and someone else decides for you for the next*
*four years. . . . At bottom, that was my notion of democracy, right?*
*But after the Water War, that is not democracy, you see. It's a*
*joke that must have been made up by the politicians. Democracy*
*is something else, when the people decide.*

—MARCELA OLIVERA

B y claiming space twenty-first-century mass mobilizations in Bolivia have
brought lasting changes to the country's politics. These episodes of mass
space claiming succeeded by exercising control (for brief periods of time)
over areas that would otherwise be organized and controlled by the state that
the activists challenged: small spaces with remarkable political and symbolic
weight or spaces vital for commercial flows and economic life. These partial
interruptions, and the forms of collective self-organization used by their participants, posed an alternative sovereignty and put the existing order into crisis.
Despite not being able to replace the state (or the political-economic order) as
a whole, they articulated a challenge that could not be ignored.

This elevation of a small portion of space and time as the deciding arena
for working out political conflict mirrors traditional political action. What is a
parliament if not a way of empowering a small number of human beings, operating within a single building according to a particular set of rules, to work out
the broader political conflicts of the day? Representative democracy, in essence,
requires a few hundred people to write the rules for society at large. In this sense
revolutionary upheavals expand the conversation but don't alter the principle
of using a small, visible confrontation to symbolize a society-wide conflict. A
revolution is a parliament of the oppressed.[1]

Insofar as victory in unarmed tactical struggles depends on mobilizing
greater numbers and demonstrating greater levels of commitment, it too offers

a democratic measure of society's desires. Compared with conventional politics, street politics takes place in an expanded physical arena under rules that are constantly being rewritten. When movements in the street overcome state forces in this contest, they make the street itself into the space of sovereign enunciation and add new collective tactics to the set of legitimate maneuvers.

These broad similarities between statecraft and political protest explain much that happened during Bolivia's period of grassroots upheaval. In their rituals of space claiming, protesters may walk in the footsteps of revolutionaries or don the robes of state. Sometimes both at the same time. In turn, state officials offer recognition to protest actions and the self-representations made by the movement. After weeks or months of denials officials accept the movement's claims to represent the people. They excuse or even valorize protesters' forms of fighting, adopt their symbols, and bury, mourn, or memorialize their martyrs.

In the most successful mobilizations those who occupied urban spaces defied or outlasted state attempts to quell their efforts. The tactical configuration of these mobilizations and the political constraints on repression outmatched the state's conventional tools for silencing and repressing unruly opponents. The constraints of democracy, the rule of law, human rights, and—just as important—the apparent legitimacy claimed by these mobilizations, and the presumed right to collective action through syndicalist and revolutionary means, meant that a sizable number of intermediary and elite actors could not stomach or passively accept deadly state repression. The combined physical, political, and moral aspects of these mobilizations posed an intractable problem for elites, forcing the recomposition of political life to resolve the temporary crises. At the same time the practices of disruption became part of the routines of daily life and part of a repertoire of contention that made future officeholders even less able to maneuver independent of the grassroots base. This extraparliamentary expression of grassroots sovereignty through disruptive space claiming is what I am calling the new mode of politics in Bolivia.

The mobilizations I have analyzed in this study did not just authorize a new government with a new pro-indigenous and postneoliberal political stance but also made space claiming a vital part of plurinational Bolivia's political culture. Writing elsewhere, I have proposed that over the long term Bolivian grassroots movements have become adept at intervening in politics, producing a move from disruption as authorization of political regimes to disruption as a form of participation in politics.[2] This book illustrates how meaningful political acts emerge from space-claiming protests, as protesters make use of the meanings that are inscribed in urban space. Specifically these are paralyzing strike waves (chapter 3), sovereign crowds in central plazas (chapter 4), the reversal of indigenous exclusion from central urban spaces (chapter 5), the introduction of symbols of indigenous self-rule into the state, and the protection or encirclement of legislatures (chapter 6). Each of these forms of space claiming had a role in winning an altered political order that could (and would want to) call itself a plurinational and postneoliberal Bolivia. (See table A2 in the appendix.) In the last two chapters I showed how the disruptive pattern of political action from 1999 to 2005 did not give way to a new calm but rather became the template for raising and (sometimes) resolving political conflicts. In the political culture of plurinational Bolivia disruptive space claiming continues to be recognized as the voice of the people.

As I described at the outset, scholarly and activist conceptions of revolution have three facets: revolutions are vast participatory events authorizing sudden historic change; they are shifts in the political system and in the occupants of the state; and they are changes in the economic and social structure of society brought about through the actions of the masses, the party that gains power, and the state under its leadership. In this book I have focused primarily on the first part of this definition—revolution as event—exploring just how street protests were able to reverse government decisions, overthrow presidents, change policies, and authorize changes in political and social life.

Movement-state interactions went from conventional demonstration to disruptive action and vicious fighting to formal presidential recognition of legitimacy in a matter of months or even weeks. These are brief periods of compressed historical time in which relations among preexisting and emergent social forces are renegotiated on the basis of their activity within a public domain. This book has shown how practical, space-claiming actions foster a widely held sense that political structures are vulnerable to immediate change: as Melissa Rosario characterizes it, "an embodied sense of political possibility" in which participants "unfix [i.e., transform] the future from a knowable thing to a malleable thing."[3] Within these pivotal time periods actions on the street stand in for larger social forces and, when successful, authorize widespread and enduring changes in the political or social order. Revolutionary events are peculiar configurations of illegality and legitimacy, during which movement and state actors both clash with and authorize one another.

In this conclusion I consider what the Bolivian revolution can tell us about the longer-running trend of unarmed revolutionary change and how putting it alongside the urban uprisings of 2011 illustrates the possibilities of street protest to provoke radical change. I also turn to questions related to the second and third facets of revolution: the political trajectory of the Movement Toward Socialism–Political Instrument for the Sovereignty of the Peoples (MAS-IPSP) and its relationship to the grassroots movements that began and carried out the twenty-first-century revolution in Bolivia (in many cases, these relationships have moved from profound alliances to deep ruptures); and the scale and limits of the societal transformation the MAS-IPSP led from the state. To do so I share some of the grassroots voices that began to separate themselves from the party and state during the years of my fieldwork. I argue that the creation of a mechanism for questioning and revoking policies from the streets is itself a potent shift in any political system, one that should be included, alongside political and economic changes, in any evaluation of the difference made by a revolutionary period. Doing so forces us to reexamine the conventional narrative of revolution in ways that decenter the political party and the state.

## No Longer "the Government of Social Movements"

How has the party founded as a political instrument, run by and subordinate to social movements, become such a powerful force within and often against them? This is the most unavoidable, personal, and painful question for many in Bolivian grassroots politics. Privately or on the record, many of those I met, interviewed, and collaborated with have expressed deep feelings of disappointment and betrayal. I leave it to them to articulate their feelings when and how they choose but invite the reader to consider the experience of the indigenous movement and its grassroots allies gathered at Chaparina during the 2011 march in defense of TIPNIS. Celso Padilla, president of the Guaraní People's Assembly, suffered multiple hematomas from the police assault. Eight months later he publicly lamented the loss of "that Evo Morales" in whom indigenous people had put their hopes, the one who would defend the rights of Mother Earth and of all Bolivians. "He simply used us to sit in the [presidential] chair and convert himself into one more executioner."[4] When Morales stood before Padilla and the other marchers in the Plaza Murillo, he repeated his "thousand apologies" for the Chaparina crackdown. But he also pleaded with them: "As for what happened in Yucumo, I could never have ordered . . . what happened to you. I have been victim so many times of that kind of damage."[5] It was as if he could not crack his own presidential persona, "that Evo Morales" who symbolically represents the arrival of the indigenous, the humble, and the protester within the walls of the government.

While individual leaders—and moments of rupture like the Chaparina raid—have played a role, I believe that much of the blame for the deepening divide lies with the structural imperatives of party building and maintaining and using state power. The Morales government has found a winning combination of new and old elements, of indigenous participation but limited territorial rights, of social democratic redistribution and macroeconomic stability, of nationalized resource revenues and large-scale capitalism. State policy is motivated by the need to constantly maintain both sources of revenue and relationships with economically powerful actors like the large agricultural exporters and private businesses. As a consequence the state rebuffed grassroots demands for local control of resource extraction and the redistribution of large productive estates. It navigated the nationalization of gas in ways that kept existing

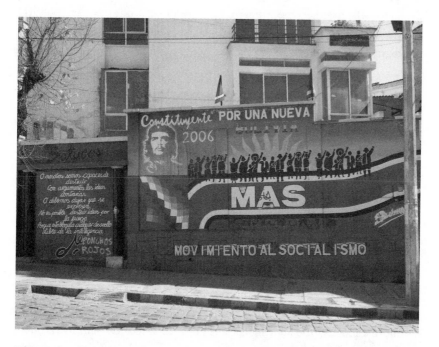

FIGURE 21  A campaign mural in the La Paz neighborhood of Sopocachi celebrates the Movement Toward Socialism, associating it with Che Guevara and the indigenous wiphala. The mural is by the pro-MAS artist collective Satucos.

foreign investors in the country as the de facto operators of its facilities. Fears about the confidence of international lenders and the memory of hyperinflation encouraged the government to make cautious budgetary choices, putting off large wage increases and investment in favor of income-redistributing cash-transfer programs.

In August 2018 Evo Morales surpassed Víctor Paz Estenssoro's record to become Bolivia's longest-serving president. Rather than groom a successor, the party and its closest movement allies were preparing to put him forward for a fourth term. This required breaking earlier promises and the term limits stated in the 2009 constitution. A February 2016 referendum to amend that term limit failed narrowly, with 51.3 percent opposed. The no vote was the first national electoral defeat for the MAS-IPSP in its twelve-year rule. Undeterred, the government challenged the provision before the Plurinational Constitutional Tribunal, which in December 2017 struck down term limits as a violation of the president's civil and political rights. The question of Morales's fourth term brought together dissident indigenous and civic movements, numerous leftist dissidents who have become critical of the government's direction, and political parties on the left and right. However, there was no sign of a shared ballot line or program that would unite these forces during national elections in late 2019.

## The Critics' Position: Retaking Leadership of the Process of Change

While the government and its defenders pushed toward blaming what they called counterrevolutionary leaders within grassroots movements for conflict within the country, those critical of the government developed a different perspective. If those in progovernment countermobilizations described themselves as "defending the process of change," critics on the grassroots Left asserted that the process had run off the rails and must be restored. They articulated their demands and theories of the political situation around a failure of the government to carry forward the process in the desired manner and a need for movements to retake the initiative for its direction.

The discussion at the Fourth National Forum of Social Organizations offers a window into the critics' perspective. On November 27, 2010, I sat in a crowded room in the center of Cochabamba's Martadero, a former slaughterhouse remade into a community space for arts and culture. It had more than a casual resemblance to the scores of convergence spaces in which I had sat in meetings of the North American global justice movement from the 1999 disruption of the Seattle World Trade Organization meetings through the protests at the 2004 Republican National Convention. The setting was so familiar—white drywall and brick, butcher paper recording the views of participants, who were tightly packed and filling a room with a low murmur of chatter and the scent of sweaty, unshowered bodies—that the differences stood out even more clearly. The men and women in the room were older, most of clearly indigenous ancestry, and poor. More clutched plastic bags of coca leaves than held cell phones, although a laptop and projector were set up to record the plenary session's demands.

This forum was a weekend-long showcase of the discontent within Bolivian popular movements just a year after Morales was elected to his second term. Leaders and rank-and-file participants in grassroots movements took part in a joint process: first, thematic workshops to discuss the current situation and then gatherings organized by region of the country to compile lists of their proposals. I attended the most general workshop, on participatory democracy. A particular attentiveness was given to delegates from Potosí Department, a region that gave more than 80 percent of its votes to the Movement Toward Socialism but had recently held a nineteen-day general strike that won promises of industrialization and infrastructure investment from the government. (The mobilization—which brought 150,000 people into the streets and motivated 500 people to go on hunger strike—had been fueled by pervasive poverty, historical grievances, and a sense of neglect by the government.) A catchphrase emerged from the room: "It's up to the social movements to retake the leadership of the process of change" back from the government.[6]

In their challenges these activists used the same rhetoric that the government uses to show its grassroots legitimacy. "We, the social movements, are the central actors," said one participant, articulating a widely held view. An organizer from Potosí defined the regional strikers as "in the process of change" and its demands as advancing "the October agenda" from the overthrow of President Gonzalo Sánchez de Lozada in 2003. Carlos Macha of the Federation of Neighborhood Councils of La Paz observed, "We made the constitution . . . if we want to keep moving forward, we will do so." Celestino Condori, the leader of the Potosí Civic Committee, insisted, "We believe that change is what the organizations, persons, and the public in general do. It is not accomplished by a minister or a vice president." A member of the neighborhood federation in Plan Tres Mil (a poor section of urban Santa Cruz) said, "The government needs to come down and consult with the grassroots," and then defined an uncritical allegiance to the state as a new form of colonialism, saying, "We need to decolonize ourselves and demand this from them." His metaphor—removing the colonial "chip," sort of a political version of mobile phone SIM cards—bounced around the conversation among enthusiastic speakers eager to validate their frustrations.

Half a year later the TIPNIS mobilization provided a new opportunity for leftist grassroots critiques of the government. Even before the march began, solidarity efforts became a reason for diverse critical movements and their intellectual allies to collaborate. In June 2011 leading grassroots organizers, including Oscar Olivera, the former lands minister Alejandro Almaraz, intellectuals, and activists signed a manifesto titled "For the Recuperation of the Process of Change by and for the People." The document, which charged that "the great majority of our people find themselves in the same situation of poverty, precariousness, and anguish that they have always been in," struck out at the limits of nationalization and debt-led development. It reserved its strongest critique, however, for the "strong authoritarian turn" of the government, alleging that it had reduced spaces for discussion and participation to "insignificant protocol-laded simulacra" and responded to "legitimate demands and mobilizations" with "calumnious disqualification, systematic intimidation, or violent and brutal repression." Moreover, with the TIPNIS conflict as a prime example, it charged the government with favoring a destructive extractivism and "obstructing, distorting, postponing, or abandoning" the construction of a truly plurinational state.[7]

The government could not and did not ignore this critique, issuing a book-length counterargument by Álvaro García Linera entitled *NGOism: Infantile Disease of Rightism*, which was circulated by the state-owned daily *Cambio*. The critics responded with a book titled *The MASquerade of Power*. As the years have passed, this debate has only deepened, a crisis of intellectual and political legitimacy that clouds the Bolivian Left, and resurfaces as movements with unmet demands forge alliances critical of the state. Yet this skeptical Left has not coalesced into a single electoral project. In the 2014 election the independent leftist parties—the Without Fear Movement (MSM) led by Juan del Granado, and the Green Party, which put the TIPNIS indigenous leader Fernando Vargas atop its ticket—split the small but visible protest vote. These two forces failed to unify, dooming both to disqualification as they narrowly missed the 3 percent threshold to hold congressional seats or contest the next election.

On the other hand, Bolivian political radicalism, made yet more skeptical of parties and caudillos during the Morales years, continues to see movements rather than the state as the prime mover. As Pablo Solón reflects:

> Generally, in the initial moments of a process of change, the new government promotes reform or transformation of the old state power structures by way of constitutional processes or insurrection. Those changes, while radical, will never be sufficient to prevent the new governing forces from being co-opted by the logic of power. . . . The only way to avoid this lies outside of the state, in the strength, independence of the government, self-determination and creative mobilization of the social organizations, movements and various social actors that gave birth to those transformations.[8]

Moreover, mass mobilization continues to emerge behind demands and visions, old and new. As Eliana Quiñones Guzmán, the Cochabamba feminist and third-generation activist, observed, "The debates have begun to surge again, so that the people again say what they think. Because we can be sure that at some moment, we are going to achieve everything."[9] Is their dynamism and dispersion any less powerful now than it was between 2000 to 2003? Does a new point of convergence by them lurk ahead? Only the future will tell.

## Beyond Bolivia: People Power Movements and the 2011 Uprisings

One scholarly purpose of this book has been to explain the mechanism of a contemporary form of revolutionary change. This contemporary form is what Doug McAdam and William Sewell call "people power" revolutions, which date to the 1986 overthrow of Ferdinand Marcos in the Philippines, the 1989 upheaval in Eastern Europe, and the unsuccessful prodemocracy protests in Burma (1988–90) and China (1989).[10] At the its core people power is expressed in "relatively nonviolent demonstrations in which hundreds of thousands simply showed their disgust, lack of fear, and unwillingness to cooperate with the old regime in massive demonstrations in urban public spaces."[11]

Some scholars have proposed that rigorous nonviolence is the linchpin of people power's success.[12] The Bolivian experience and other recent revolutionary upheavals, which combined nonviolence with street confrontations and destruction of property, throw that premise into question. Where protest movements have won, their victories have been practical as well as moral. As Kurt Schock argues in a comparative study, "Successful unarmed insurrections remained resilient in the face of repression, mobilized the withdrawal of support from the state, and generated sufficient leverage against the state to tip the balance of power in their favor."[13]

Antineoliberal movements in Latin America, and most successful uprisings of 2011 and beyond, combined mass nonviolent demonstrations with street confrontations, prolonged road blockades, property destruction, and building occupations. These unarmed militant tactics enable crowds to hold significant urban spaces in defiance of state repression and to directly interrupt commerce and mobility. They both generate prolonged "prefigurative moments" for "alternative forms of community, authority and collectivity," as Yarimar Bonilla found in Guadeloupe, and turn "urban (im)mobility" into "a tool of political mobilization," as Claudio Sopranzetti observed regarding recent Thai protests.[14] Militant tactics were essential to the Arab Spring protests in 2011, particularly in Egypt. In 2019 vast crowds in Hong Kong and Puerto Rico challenged unpopular regional governments. In both cases mass mobilizations dovetailed with direct confrontation, reversing unpopular extradition legislation in Hong Kong and unseating Puerto Rico's governor. In all these cases practical control of streets and cities combined with the democratic legitimacy of mass demonstrations to justify major shifts in power and the resignation of sitting heads of state.

One vital thing this book contributes to studies of the 2011 uprisings is recognition of these tools. In some ways the democratic drama on the square has been too attractive to scholars trying to make sense of what are sometimes called plaza uprisings. Yes, the plaza is a place for demonstrating political legitimacy, for sharing visions of transformation, and for experimenting with collective control of people's own living space and the direction of the mobilization. But scholars and strategists cannot overlook the other components of political power examined in this study: applying sustained economic pressure, bringing marginalized people to the center of the society, and successful physical contests for symbolically vital spaces. As I argue in chapter 2, demonstrating popular legitimacy and putting effective pressure on the government are the two legs that allow a movement to walk forward. Not just in Bolivia but in France (in 2006), Oaxaca (in 2006–2007), and Egypt (in 2011), mass movements interspersed pressure campaigns with massive rallies to demonstrate the public support.

Moreover, tactical victories matter in these movements. As in the February 2000 battle of the Water War, protesters' mass seizure of Tahrir Square in Cairo changed history. It was accomplished not by chance and not by social media persuasion[15] but by gathering scores of small crowds in residential neighborhoods, strategically misdirecting the police with false plans, and gathering numbers en route, "so that by the time demonstrators reach the announced locations, they would be large crowds that security couldn't corral."[16] Further tactical innovations would be required to outlast the government's various efforts to attack the movement. Ultimately the uprisings' success was not just a matter of communicating a vision but offering a claim to sovereignty. When most successful, as in the overthrow of Hosni Mubarak in Egypt, uprisings were (as I outline in chapter 4) not only numerous and committed but also diverse, widespread, irrepressible, and in control.

## Rethinking the Story and Time Line of Revolution

Histories of revolutionary periods are usually written in a way that focuses on the political party (or other force) that takes state power. This creates a certain kind of time line in which the masses in the streets make a neat handoff to the leaders in the palace and legislature. With the modern template of revolution now in its third century, we often find stories that have been told before: narratives of the rise and fall of protest, of the substitution of reformist policies for revolutionary demands, of disappointments and betrayals, and of formerly revolutionary governments disarming the movements that made them possible. The Bolivian story has elements of some of these narratives, but close engagement with the country has left me skeptical of applying these frameworks too quickly, without paying attention to what actually happened. Above all, scholars should hesitate before describing the Morales government as an inherently demobilizing force, when its interaction with grassroots mobilization has been more complicated—and both collaborative and conflictive.

Studies of disruptive protest in Bolivia have tended to describe 2005 as a sharp turning point, a singular revolutionary moment that marked the end of the time of rebellion against an existing system and the beginning of a new period of diminished activity. This book, with its vantage point on the street during protest, shows greater continuities across that watershed year. Regional and sectoral protests, of which the Cochabamba Water War was an emblematic example, were initially not connected to a drive to overthrow the neoliberal state (an effort that hadn't really started in 2000). Before 2003 these efforts did not cohere into a direct challenge to the national government. After 2005 protesters continued to mobilize, blockade, and intrude upon symbolic spaces of power to carry forward their demands every year, sometimes as part of a national wave of activity and sometimes fracturing the presumed unity of the grassroots Left and the MAS-IPSP. Disruptive space claiming has become a conventional means of staking claims in plurinational Bolivia.

Equally important is that the powerful symbolism of sovereignty from the streets, and from grassroots movements, remains an ongoing part of politics in Bolivia. The postrevolutionary period as commonly understood—marked by demobilization and the criminalization of disruptive tactics—seems to be repeatedly postponed. As chapters 4 and 6 show, Evo Morales and the MAS-IPSP sought their legitimacy in gatherings of social movements and symbols of indigenous self-rule that were conferred by mass organizations (as well as by indigenous spiritual practitioners). In turn grassroots movements have used their place within the Constituent Assembly and the government's popular diplomacy to advance their claims. The government also turned to mass mobilization of its base and allies rather than the tools of state in its 2006–2009 face-off with right-wing civic movements in the East and in the center of the country. These movements too, while not the subject of this book, used cabildos, blockades, and the rhetoric of autonomy as part of their claims to political legitimacy. Finally, regional and sectoral mobilizations on the left, from the Gasolinazo to the Potosí strike waves of 2010 and 2015, pair policy demands with claims to sovereign power. When a set of tools, practices, and rhetoric acquires such widespread currency among disparate political actors, it must be regarded as a feature of the political culture rather than a phase that interrupts conventional politics.

If the time line of revolution is different than expected, then scholars must also alter the ways they think about and evaluate revolutionary change. The presumption of many theories of revolution is that a revolutionary period constitutes a brief interregnum between stable orders. The new order is charged with vital mandates from the interrupting forces, and it can be judged according to its fidelity to these mandates. This approach judges the new regime's leaders as either faithful torchbearers or deceitful betrayers of the revolution.

The perspective I take in this study, which focuses on disruption as a continuing form of participation in politics, sees a different time line for revolutions. It takes the fierce independence of Bolivian movements, expressed through the idea that the "process of change is not a person, not a political party," but something more that belongs to everyone, as a source of theoretical insight. It shifts the focus from the successor government after the upheaval to the relations among movement(s), society, and state. It turns to a focus on political culture, of which the contentious repertoire and shared beliefs about the nature of revolution are crucial parts. By keeping my eyes on the streets, I have written a study of the creation and persistence of new forms of participation through grassroots upheaval. While I intend this account to stand on its own, I also offer it as a complement to policy-focused readings of revolutionary upheaval. With this shift in focus we can look beyond the state, its policies and structures, statements and inconsistencies, for evidence of the effectiveness of revolutionary upheavals.

While changes in material situation, symbolic esteem, and structures of participation in national decisions are crucial goals of revolutionary movements, they achieve these goals by throwing the stability and legitimacy of the existing order into question.[17] A government that emerges through a revolutionary situation can and should be judged by how well it achieves these goals. However, so long as it remains dependent upon mobilization to achieve its goals (as in the catastrophic stalemate) or vulnerable to renewed mobilization (as in the current period), the element of dynamism that shook the old order remains. This suggests that weaker postrevolutionary states, or ones facing ongoing challenges that require mass mobilization to overcome, may have more profound and dynamic revolutions. Failures of a new government to achieve the ambitious visions that animated the upheaval that brought it to power, or to reconcile the contradictions among these visions, can and should be challenged, corrected, and guided from below.

Revolutionary events produce not only a new regime but also a new familiarity among its participants with the practice of making politics and with the possibility of becoming the source of sovereignty. These capacities provide a new context in which those elevated to government office make their decisions; these capacities also provide a new flexibility in imagining how society can be remade. As they define what their country will become through struggle, Bolivians now have an expanded set of tools and models. The future of their struggle relies on the continued ability of people to agree on, articulate, and defend common visions. While these visions have not been fulfilled, and are not embodied in a single organization, Bolivians still have openings for further transformation by taking over the street.

## The Role of Lasting Political Dynamism in Evaluating Revolutions

For Bolivians the transformation promised by the early twenty-first-century revolts is incomplete. The profound shifts in values proposed on the streets and echoed in the Constituent Assembly do not yet orient the society. Many material demands of the movements that animated the grassroots upsurge have not been achieved. While vast shifts in priorities have been accomplished, water, gas, and land are not managed to benefit all. Many in the country's urban peripheries in particular still lack access to the basic necessities for which they organized locally and rebelled collectively. And on many fronts—water service in Cochabamba is a paradigmatic case—progress is neither evident nor even on the horizon. The reconceptualization of the democratic process around indigenous sovereignty and mass participation, and of the economy around the collective control of resources and respect for Mother Earth, remains to be clearly articulated, much less carried out.

Thirteen years into Evo Morales's presidency, the promise of a "government of social movements" has been replaced by a government that struggles to manage or defuse the demands of still active but divided social movements. The grassroots base cannot readily alter governmental priorities around resource extraction, developmentalism, and limited wage growth. These are matters for Bolivians to work through as they define, through struggle and vision, what plurinational Bolivia will become. This study has examined the means by which these matters are worked out on the ground, through movement. Social movement alliances and waves of grassroots mobilization (when they achieve broad adherence) remain the touchstones of democratic legitimacy. The media and ordinary people recognize such events as legitimate expressions of popular will, much like voting. Despite its wishes and its institutional advantages the government cannot afford to ignore either of these forms of popular democracy.

The events described in this study confirm that space-claiming protest has become part of Bolivian political culture in ways that seem destined to endure.

Mass mobilization now stands as a source of political legitimacy comparable to armed force in past revolutions and electoral victories in liberal democracies. Movements continue to participate in politics by disrupting everyday life. Protesters, politicians, and the media now claim that the people have spoken through mass mobilization. As chapters 2 through 5 show, the voice of these mobilizations acquires significance, and dares to aspire to sovereignty, when it controls and claims urban spaces. Potosinos, those protesting the Gasolinazo in 2010, and the defenders of TIPNIS in 2011 retraced this pathway and confirmed its significance. Plurinational Bolivia was created and continues to be defined through acts that use and reconfigure the relation of these spaces, the bodies within them, and political and racial power.

Depending on one's perspective, the current political moment in Bolivia could be understood in very different ways. One school of thought sees the MAS-IPSP–led state in the process of consolidating its power, by dividing and weakening its adversaries while remaining a potent electoral force. This view emphasizes the dangers of an increasingly authoritarian state aloof from popular demands. Another perspective views the government as in a repeated state of uncertainty, unable to consistently impose its mandates and periodically forced to react to critical mass mobilizations. This view remembers its progressive policy shifts and sees how street responses constrain government. There is truth in both perspectives, but perhaps the purpose of political analyses is not only to find the truth. Perhaps instead the goal of analyzing is (as its etymology suggests) to break down the current political situation into its parts and to make possible the formation of new realities tomorrow.

When one sees the MAS-IPSP in dynamic equilibrium with the continued "creative tensions" of the grassroots movements that brought it to power, the key strategic questions involve how to make policy catch up with the needs and demands of the Bolivian people. These are meaningful questions in the halls of the Plurinational State, and outsiders who would too readily dismiss the achievements of the past decade would do well to examine the substantive changes there.[18]

But there are reasons that I rarely heard this kind of at-a-distance perspective from the people who filled the streets to demand a different Bolivia. From their vantage point the continuities of rule are what are most clear. They see where the Plurinational State echoes the economic choices of the neoliberal era, the divide-and-rule tactics of the MNR, and the modernizing and civilizing impulses of the colonial state. The long memories and critical stance of radical political movements not only motivate continued demands for transformative change. They make accepting anything less a betrayal.

If the goal is not to observe history but to make it, you cannot start by putting yourself in the government's shoes. Instead you take a stand from within the reality you can envision and see how the government stacks up from there. Or you take those demands to the street and force the government to show you how it will react. And when you climb to the balcony to stand before the crowd, you will see the distance between the current political reality and the world as it could be. If done right, the process of mobilization will make that gap visible to everyone else.

# APPENDIX

TABLE A1  Regime transitions and their relation to social movement disruptions

| Regime | Year | Change in leader/state | Disruptive action justifying political change | Constituency represented | Symbolic handover |
|---|---|---|---|---|---|
| Military socialism | 1936 | David Toro presidency through Germán Busch coup | April–May strike wave | Organized labor | 1938 national convention |
| | 1945 | Villarroel decrees of May 1945 abolish rural servitude | Strikes and rural unrest in late 1930s, early 1940s | Indian campesinos | National Indigenous Congress in La Paz, May 10–15, 1945 |
| National revolution | 1952 | MNR assumes power | "Cycle of rebellion," 1947–52; popular insurrection, April 1952 | Organized labor, campesinos | Worker and party militias parade through La Paz |
| | 1952 | Tin mining nationalized | Miners' assistance in April insurrection | Organized labor | Decree-signing ceremony in Catavi Siglo XX complex |
| | 1953 | Agrarian reform | Wave of land takeovers; armed presence of campesinos in Cochabamba | Campesinos | Reform law signed August 2, 1953, in Ucureña, Cochabamba. |
| Popular Assembly | 1970 | Labor and leftist parties proposed co-government | October 7 general strike in defense of military populism | Organized labor, leftist parties | Left agreed to co-government with conditions; offer was rescinded. |
| | 1971 | Popular Assembly | Defense against right-wing coup, October 1970 and January 1971 | Organized labor, leftist parties, independent campesinos | Assembly held in National Congress building, June–July 1970 |

| | Year | Event | Mobilization | Social actors | Ceremony / location |
|---|---|---|---|---|---|
| Transition to democracy | 1978 | Political prisoners released, elections held | Hunger-strike campaign supported by rural blockades | Miners' wives, miners, campesinos | — |
| | 1979 | Natusch Busch coup reversed; Lidia Gueiler becomes president | General strike; urban and rural road blockades | Organized labor, campesinos, urban middle class | Gueiller's inauguration in Presidential Palace |
| | 1982 | Restoration of democratic rule; Democratic and Popular Union takes office | Peasant strikes, labor strikes | Organized labor, peasants | Postinaugural address in Plaza San Francisco |
| Plurinational State | 2003 | Vice President Carlos Mesa assumes presidency | Gas War: general strikes, urban and rural road blockades, wave of hunger strikes | Organized labor, Indigenous campesinos, urban masses | Mesa attends El Alto memorial and campesino gathering in Plaza San Francisco |
| | 2005 | Supreme Court head Eduardo Rodriguez becomes interim president | May–June crisis: general strikes, urban and rural road blockades. | Organized labor, Indigenous campesinos, urban masses | — |
| | 2006 | Evo Morales becomes president | Previous disruptions plus December 2005 electoral mandate | Organized labor, Indigenous campesinos, urban masses, electoral majority | Three-part presidential inauguration at Tiwanaku, Congress, Plaza San Francisco |
| | 2008–9 | Plurinational State affirmed through new constitution | September 2008 crisis; march on National Congress | Indigenous, campesinos, urban masses | Congress surrounded; Plaza Murillo proclamation |

TABLE A2 Forms of space claiming described in this book

| | Form of space claiming | Tactic | Element(s) of geography |
|---|---|---|---|
| Ch. 3 | Civic strike | Road blockade | Infrastructural spaces: rural highways, bridges, arterial roads |
| | | "Mobilized strike": abstaining from work and marching | Central urban roadways |
| | Strike wave | Same tactics in multiple locations simultaneously | |
| Ch. 4 | Converging marches | Multiple mass mobilizations, sometimes street battles to enter and converge into central spaces | Protests originated in spaces linked to grassroots constituencies, ended in downtown centers and symbolically important central plazas |
| | Distributed hunger strikes | Hunger-strike "pickets" | Government offices, social movement headquarters, churches, neighborhood centers |
| | Sovereign crowd | Large public gathering | Symbolically important central plazas |
| | Cabildo abierto | Large public gathering with open decision making between those on stage and in crowd | Symbolically important central plazas; other locations |
| Ch. 5 | Indigenous march | Extended, multiday march | From rural or indigenous spaces, through daily stops in supportive locations, into central cities |
| | "Being indigenous in public space" | Overt performance of indigenous identity, use of indigenous symbols of rule | Spaces marked by a history of racial exclusion |
| Ch. 6 | Indigenizing state spaces | Use of indigenous symbols of rule, performance of indigenous/popular identity, religious ceremony | Spaces owned by the government, public plazas |
| | Defensive vigil | Protecting space around event | Area surrounding state spaces |
| | Encirclement of legislature | Large public gathering | Area surrounding legislature |

# NOTES

## Introduction

1. Supreme Decree 173 of June 17, 2009. In the decree the government also recognizes the Guaraní celebration of Yasitata Guasú. It will later combine these holidays into an Andean-Amazonian New Year.

2. Katari and Sisa's role in the Age of Andean Insurrection is detailed by Sinclair Thomson (2002, 180–232).

3. Galeano (1973, 237).

4. The three firms co-owned the Pacific LNG consortium that was organizing the project, including a pipeline out of Bolivia, a gas liquefaction plant in a Chilean port, and a regasification plant in Mexico. They also were the operators of the Margarita gas field in Tarija, where the gas would be extracted (Juan Forero, "Lingering Feud with Chile Threatens Bolivia's Pipeline Plan," *New York Times*, July 8, 2002).

5. For a detailed description of the corporate beneficiaries of the privatization, see Villegas Quiroga (2004, 90–112).

6. Summaries of protest activity appear in Ramos Andrade (2004, 159–81).

7. Seligson, Moreno Morales, and Schwarz Blum (2004, 78).

8. Bolivia has very few Afro-descendant people: most of the twenty to thirty thousand self-described Afro-Bolivians live in the rural Yungas region of La Paz. Afro-Bolivians have also migrated to cities, including La Paz and Cochabamba. Since I lack any locally recognizable markers of Yungas culture or rural labor, my African phenotype was readily recognized as foreign, outside the local hierarchy, though I was as often assumed to be Ecuadorian or Brazilian as North American.

9. Mesa Gisbert's speech of October 17, 2003, was reprinted by the Bolivian news agency Bolpress, under the headline "Discurso de posesión de Carlos Diego Mesa

Gisbert como presidente de la República," http://www.bolpress.net/art.php?Cod= 2002073644. Unless otherwise noted, I translated all quotations in this book from Spanish to English.

10. "El presidente Carlos Mesa promete justicia en El Alto," *El Diario*, October 19, 2003, http://www.eldiario.net/noticias/2003/2003_10/nt031019/5_00nal.html. Roberto de la Cruz is paraphrased in Ornelas (2004, 193).

11. Anderson (1991).

12. These details are from Duran Chuquimia (2006); "La Plaza de los Muertes Fue la de los Heroes" (*Página 12 Anuario 2006*, 51).

13. AP Archive (2017).

14. Wood (2012, 36–37).

15. Wood (2012).

16. The Goldman Environmental Prize is one of the most prestigious international environmental awards. Endowed by Richard and Rhoda Goldman, it honors six recipients each year for grassroots environmental accomplishments.

17. Goldman Environmental Prize (2013). Because he was then in the midst of a protest march, Olivera sent his remarks to be delivered by a comrade in 2001, and he attended the ceremony in 2002.

18. Paz Miño Cepeda (2002).

19. Colectivo Situaciones (2011).

20. The programming of Indymedia Bolivia, which operated from 2002 to 2007, is archived at http://archivos.bolivia.indymedia.org/. On the formation of Independent Media Centers, see Juris (2005).

21. On the Miami model, see FTAA Miami Independent Media Center Video (2004); Gibson (2008); Vitale (2007).

22. The ten countries were Brazil (2002 and 2010), Argentina (2003); Uruguay (2004); Bolivia (2005); Chile, Nicaragua, Ecuador, and Venezuela (2006); Paraguay (2008); and Uruguay (2009) (Coronil 2011, 240–41).

23. Prevost (2012).

24. Gilly (2007); Hylton and Thomson (2007); Dunkerley (2007). See also Gilly, "Bolivia, una revolución del siglo XXI," *La Jornada*, March 2, 2004, https://www.jornada.com.mx/2004/03/02/per-bolivia.html.

25. In Spanish the name of the party is Movimiento al Socialismo–Instrumento Político por la Soberanía de los Pueblos.

26. "Movilización Impide Visita de Evo," *Correo del Sur*, May 25, 2008.

27. Defensoría del Pueblo (2009, 17).

28. As noted, for example, by Lee Baker (2010) with reference to U.S. anthropology.

29. For more about the Kataristas, see chap. 1.

30. María Eugenia Flores Castro, interview by author, December 15, 2010, Cochabamba.

31. Literate men of all races were permitted to vote in the 1940 and 1951 elections. However, Indian literacy was registered at just 15.9 percent of adults in the 1950 Census (Presidencia de la República 1962, 79).

32. Guenther (2006, 17).

33. The *ayllu* is the basic structure of Andean highland rural communities. It refers to the community's encompassing its living and ancestral members and the landscape itself.

34. Other cocaleros live in the Yungas region of northern La Paz Department and the Yungas of Vandiola in Cochabamba Department.

35. Felix Ticona Quispe, interview by author, March 20, 2010, La Paz.

36. Ortiz (1953, 18).

37. Ortiz, while a liberal advocate of freeing the Indian from servitude, remained an insistent believer of biological difference in crude terms. She insists that "the cholo carries white blood in his veins and this fact can do no less than be reflected in his psychology. He is no longer the submissive and oppressed being, now speaks Spanish and acts with the mentality of a free man for better and for worse" (Ortiz 1953, 18).

38. The racial question was eliminated in the 2012 census, making LAPOP's stratified-sample survey the best available source of data on this question. There was considerable public debate about including mestizo on the list of peoples in 2012, but this option was ultimately rejected by the National Statistical Institute.

39. LAPOP (2012, 241).

40. Both relative demographic factors (indigenous birthrates are higher) and increased social acceptability of indigeneity may be driving this shift (LAPOP 2012, 242).

41. In the definitive study by Ramiro Molina Barrios (2005) the total indigenous population was 65.8 percent of Bolivians older than fifteen in 2001 (younger Bolivians were not asked the relevant questions in the Census).

42. Castells (2015, 60, 61, 10–11).

43. Marcela Olivera, interview by author, April 5, 2011, Cochabamba.

44. Tufekci (2017, xxiv).

45. Tufekci (2017, 117–34).

46. Davis (2004, 10).

47. Holston (2009, 249).

48. Lazar (2008); Albro (2010); Goldstein (2004); Achi Chiritèle and Delgado (2007).

49. On levels of protest participation, see Dunning et al. (2011); Moseley and Moreno (2010); and Moseley (2015). Polling by the Latin American Public Opinion Project in 2004 found that 36 percent of Bolivian adults said they had participated in protest. This lifetime participation rate equals or exceeds that recorded in 29 of 31 countries surveyed in the Pew Research Center's Spring 2014 Global Attitudes Survey; only Bangladesh (37 percent) and Egypt (47 percent) reported a higher share (Seligson, Moreno Morales, and Schwarz Blum 2004).

50. "Reciprocity: US Citizens Need Visas to Visit Bolivia," *MercoPress*, August 15, 2007, http://en.mercopress.com/2007/08/15/reciprocity-us-citizens-need-visas-to-visit-bolivia.

51. *La Prensa* had summarized the organizers' announcement as follows: "The markets . . . will be closed until nightfall, the neighborhood shops and businesses will

not attend the public, because control brigades will watch over them ensuring the fulfillment of this civic measure" ("La policía evitará que se registren incidentes contra la Embajada de Estados Unidos," *La Prensa*, June 9, 2008).

52. "Violenta marcha Alteña intenta tomar La Embajada de EEUU," *La Razón*, June 10, 2008.

53. See page 103.

54. The crucial exception is Raquel Gutiérrez Aguilar's *The Rhythms of Pachakuti* (2008a, 2014), which emphasizes Cochabamba as well as the Altiplano and provides a national overview.

55. See, for example, Zibechi (2006); Mamani Ramírez (2004); Patzi (2003).

56. Gluckman (1940); Van Velsen (1967); Garbett (1970).

57. Michael Burawoy (1998, 18, 17) argues that the extended-case method provides insight by "compiling situational knowledge into an account of social process" and observing how "a social order reveals itself in the way it responds to pressure."

58. For impressive recent examples of tracking a community or organization in Bolivia, see Gustafson (2009) and Lazar (2008).

59. Tilly (1978, 232). I owe my interest in this approach to Pablo Mamani Ramírez's *El Rugir de las Multitudes* (2004).

60. Tarrow (1995).

61. Several research groups have kept quantitative records of Bolivian protests, including Fundación UNIR Bolivia's project on Governability, the Defensoría del Pueblo, and private academics, but the Center for Studies of Economic and Social Reality offers the longest-running dataset.

62. Laserna, Villarroel Nikitenko, and Centro de Estudios de la Realidad Económica y Social (2008, 23, 18, 56–68).

63. Some observers see this incorporation as a problem. "Bolivian society lives in a state of permanent agitation," writes César Rojas Ríos (2015, 21). "Not on a single day, for 43 years has the country had peace or quiet." Rojas Ríos is only the latest writer to view protest in Bolivia as a social and economic problem rather than a form of political participation. This book, it should be clear by now, takes a different view.

64. Bjork-James (2018).

65. On writing eventful accounts of societal change, see Sewell (2005, 100–11).

## Chapter 1

From the author's interview of Marcela Olivera, April 5, 2011, Cochabamba.

1. Giulino (2009, 89–100).

2. Giulino (2009, 106).

3. Gotkowitz (2007); Lagos (1994); Olivera and Lewis (2004).

4. For a detailed look at the role of the Club Social in formation of Cochabamba's elite, see Gordillo, Rivera Pizarro, and Sulcata Guzmán (2007, 30–62).

5. Interview by author, July 4, 2008, Cochabamba.

6. Goldstein (2004, 54–75).

7. Ledo García (2002, 196).

8. Goldstein (2004, 55).

9. Biblioteca Virtual Carlos D. Mesa Gisbert, October 20, 2003, https://www.you tube.com/watch?v=QFBH_1yWH2o.

10. Trotsky ([1920]1980, 17).

11. This distinction between political and social revolutions is articulated by John Foran (1993, 8–17), who accepts Theda Skocpol's definition of social revolution.

12. McAdam and Sewell (2001, 103).

13. For a theory of this spread and waves of synchronous revolutions like those in 1968 (and 2011), see Katsiaficas (1987).

14. Mamani Ramírez (2017, 68, 69).

15. For Raquel Gutiérrez Aguilar (2008a, 2014), this divergence was an inevitable consequence of the state-centered project led by the MAS-IPSP that supplanted the initiative of grassroots mobilization. She sees a point of inflection between the two in 2004.

16. I offer a detailed take on the accomplishments and limits of the Morales government's project in these three areas, as well as the government's motivations in Bjork-James (2020).

17. Jeffrey Webber (2016) has analogized this process to the "passive revolutions" that Antonio Gramsci saw taking place when nationalists come to power in the economic periphery. Raquel Gutiérrez (2008a, 2014) presciently identified a disconnect between the alternative political and ethical order envisioned by many grassroots movements and the alternative state project led by the Movement Toward Socialism—Political Instrument for the Sovereignty of the Peoples (MAS-IPSP).

18. The quote appears in numerous sources, some of which link it to Mao Zedong, but it is often described as a response to a question from a visiting Henry Kissinger. Strobe Talbott (2003, 2) claims he heard this directly from Kissinger during his return flight from China.

19. Since the 1980s a transnational movement has aligned indigenous identity with ecological responsibility, cultural preservation, spirituality, and a political agenda that challenged "states, markets, and modernity" while demanding "self-determination, land rights, and cultural survival" (Brysk 2000, 59). Bolivian indigenous politicization stands both within and beyond this tradition.

20. Eliana Quiñones Guzmán, interview by author, April 29, 2011, Cochabamba.

21. Ayni refers to "a symmetrical exchange of delayed reciprocity between equals, usually manifest in labor exchanges," and is often translated as mutual aid (Allen 1981, 165).

22. Ángel Hurtado, interview by author and Carmen Medeiros, March 28, 2011, Cochabamba. For more on Hurtado's ethical perspective, see Bjork-James (2018).

23. Quiñones Guzmán, interview.

24. There was no successful handoff between the 1969–71 movement, which convened a popular assembly in the National Congress building, and the sympathetic government of General Juan José Torres.

25. See Albro (2010, 144–49).
26. Quiñones Guzmán, interview.
27. Lazar (2008, 174; 2006).
28. Lazar (2004, 188–89).
29. Throughout this text I use the politically constructed *campesino* in place of the English term *peasant*. *Campesino* and other terms that denote "rural worker" cross the boundaries between landless workers and small tenants and have acquired an active political meaning that differs from the English term.
30. Serulnikov (2003, 154).
31. See Hylton et al. (2003).
32. On the role of these figures in contemporary protest, see Dangl (2019).
33. Michael Löwy (1981) describes at length the theory of permanent revolution, under which the working class takes on the modernizing and democratizing tasks accomplished by bourgeois revolutions in countries like France and the United States. June Nash (1979, 310–34) offers an explanation of why miners in particular assumed a directing role in Bolivian class struggle.
34. From the Tesis de Colquiri (Colquiri Thesis), reprinted in Zavaleta Mercado (2011, 763–64).
35. Hylton and Thomson (2007); Larson (2004); Gotkowitz (2007).
36. Rivera Cusicanqui (1990, 163–64).
37. "Manifiesto de Tiahuanaco," July 30, 1973, https://www.slideshare.net/wilmichu/manifiesto-de-tiahuanaco-revisado.
38. Albó (1987).
39. On "popular anarchism" in Latin America, see Yuen (2005).
40. María Josefina Saldaña-Portillo (2003) discusses a longer trajectory of this rethinking in Mexico, Central America, and the Caribbean.
41. Gutiérrez Aguilar (2006, 140–41).
42. Gutiérrez Aguilar describes her experiences and the lessons she drew from them in *¡A desordenar!* (2006). A third-party account of the insurgency appears in Quispe Quispe (2005).
43. Gutiérrez Aguilar 2006, 139.
44. Escóbar recounts his political trajectory in a 2008 memoir, *De la revolución al Pachakuti* (From the Revolution to Pachakuti).
45. For more on this ideal, see Bjork-James (2018) and Escóbar (2008).
46. Thomassen (2012, 681–82).
47. Nash (1979).
48. Durkheim (1915, 210–11).
49. Turner (1969, 1974); Alexander (1991, 27–43).
50. Turner (2012, 84–141).
51. Nash (2001).
52. Zolberg (1972, 183, 206).
53. McAdam and Sewell (2001, 102).

54. A noted turning point in this process is Max Gluckman's 1940 article "Analysis of a Social Situation in Modern Zululand," which makes just this leap, acknowledging that describing colonial power relations is critical to understanding contemporary life in traditional societies.

55. Sahlins (1985, 138).

56. Sewell (2005).

57. Thomassen (2012, 684).

58. Marcela Olivera, interview by author, April 5, 2011, Cochabamba.

59. Tilly (2000).

60. On the dynamics of this unarmed militancy, see Bjork-James (forthcoming).

61. On "a new type of insurrection," see Colectivo Situaciones (2001). On direct-action protest, see Epstein (1991), Graeber (2009).

62. Massey (1994, 265).

63. Massey (1994, 259).

64. Latour (2005, 175–83).

65. Ruddick (1996, 140).

66. Ruddick (1996, 135).

67. Rama (1996, 18).

68. Fanon (2004, 3, 4, 15). On parallels between Fanon's anticolonialism and that of Bolivian indigenous movements, see Lucero (2008).

69. Among the last are Mamani Ramírez (2005) and Soruco Sologuren (2011).

70. Tilly (2000, 137).

71. Smith (1996)

72. Sewell (2005).

73. McAdam and Sewell (2001, 103)

74. Raquel Gutiérrez Aguilar orients her study (2008a; Gutiérrez 2012) of Bolivian movements around "horizons of desire"; the concept also animates Forrest Hylton and Sinclair Thomson's (2005, 2007) work.

# Chapter 2

1. Banzer and Paz Estenssoro's parties collaborated in drafting the economic package (Jeffrey Sachs, *Commanding Heights*, June 15, 2000, interview produced by WGBH for PBS, https://www.pbs.org/wgbh/commandingheights/shared/minitext/int_jeffreysachs.html).

2. Conaghan and Malloy (1994, 129). Machiavelli's original advice was, "The injuries should be done all together so that, because they are tasted less, they will cause less resentment; [then] benefits should be given one by one, so that they will be savoured more" (*The Prince*, chap. 8).

3. Sachs (1994, 268). In the next decade Sachs would serve as economic adviser to Poland, Yugoslavia, Slovenia, Russia, Estonia, Mongolia, Kyrgyzstan, as well as intergovernmental efforts through the World Bank and United Nations.

4.  Sachs (1987); Kohl and Farthing (2006).
5.  The summary of what happened to wages and food and fuel prices comes from Conaghan and Malloy (1994, 140). See Kohl and Farthing (2006) and Vos et al. (1998) on the drop in wages and their eight-year stagnation.
6.  Ángel Hurtado, interview by author and Carmen Medeiros, March 28, 2011. This interview is the source of all quotations attributed to Hurtado in this chapter.
7.  Guardia B and Mercado B (1995); Ledo García (2002).
8.  Christian Mamani, interview by author, April 4, 2010, Cochabamba.
9.  For a parallel interpretation of the role of miners in El Alto's mass mobilizations, also based on oral histories, see Arbona (2008).
10. Mamani, interview.
11. Olivera (2004, 45).
12. *Assemblies* refers to meetings of an organization's membership, whereas *cabildos* are mass meetings that include the entire movement (or that part of the movement currently engaged in a strike) and are held in the plaza to decide direction.
13. Mamani, interview.
14. For a chronology of the antiglobalization movement in this period that leans toward the global North, see Juris (2008, 48–51). For one focused on the global South, see the World Development Movement's *States of Unrest* reports: Ellis-Jones and Hardstaff (2003); Woodroffe and Ellis-Jones (2000).
15. The privately held San Francisco–based Bechtel Holdings, Inc., was the sole share-holder in International Water (Aguas del Tunari) Limited, a Cayman Islands–based corporation that was the lead (55 percent) investor in Aguas del Tunari when the contract was signed on September 3, 1999 (International Centre for Settlement of Investment Disputes 2005, 471). The Italian energy corporation Edison S.p.A. bought a 50 percent stake in International Water in November 1999. See Bechtel Corporation, "Bechtel and Edison Reach Agreement on Edison's Acquisition of a 50% Stake in International Water Limited," news release, 1999, https://www.bechtel.com/newsroom/releases/1999/11/bechtel-edison-reach-agreement-edisons-acq/.
16. Spronk (2007, 13).
17. The Defense Committee sometimes designated itself the Defense Committee of Water and the Popular Economy as well.
18. Kruse (2005, 146).
19. Assies (2001, 12).
20. Orellana Aillón (2004, 515).
21. Gutiérrez Aguilar (2008a, 75).
22. Gutiérrez Aguilar (2004, 57).
23. A chronology, available online at https://woborders.blog/water-war-chronology, analyzes the major events of the Water War as part of these two moments.
24. The position of Oscar Olivera, Gonzalo Maldonado, and Gabriel Herbas was reported in "Insisten en que la toma será pacífica," *Los Tiempos*, January 31, 2000.
25. In the original Spanish text, each of these "takes" is the verb *tomar*.

26. "No se descarta un estado de sitio" and "Cívicos piden no 'tomar la ciudad,'" *Los Tiempos*, February 6, 2000.

27. "Cochabamba decidió continuar protestas," *Los Tiempos*, February 5, 2000, p. A8.

28. Kruse (2005, 147).

29. The exercise echoed similar efforts undertaken by Mexico's Zapatistas.

30. Assies (2001, 15).

31. Communiqué No. 20 is reproduced in Olivera et al. (2008, 178–79); capitalization original.

32. Bolivia Cámara de Diputados (2001, 56). Twenty-one protesters had bullet wounds, according the Permanent Assembly of Human Rights ("DD.HH.: En la Llajta de 32 heridos, 21 recibieron impactos de bala," *La Razón*, April 14, 2000).

33. Bjork-James (forthcoming).

34. "Como en la dictadura," *Los Tiempos*, February 2, 2000.

35. Olivera et al. (2008, 169).

36. "DD.HH.: En La Llajta de 32 heridos, 21 recibieron impactos de bala," *La Razón*, April 14, 2000.

37. The civic committees are broadly representative of regional elites. The Santa Cruz Civic Committee, an institution of the local oligarchy, is the oldest of these organizations. Other civic committees were formed in the 1960s and 1970s, with Cochabamba's and Potosí's the most politically progressive. The committees backed democratization during the repression of the 1970s (from which they were largely spared) but have taken divergent stances since 2000, embracing the separatist Right in the eastern Media Luna (half moon) departments (Pando, Beni, Santa Cruz, and Tarija) and Chuquisaca while incorporating unions and grassroots organizations in Potosí. See Kohl and Farthing (2006, 49–53).

38. Salazar Ortuño (2011, 103). The term *desconocer* is used when grassroots organizations withdraw their consent for confederations or leaders to negotiate on their behalf.

39. "Reyes Villa, Montaño y otros aprobaron tarifazo," *Los Tiempos*, January 23, 2000.

40. "El tarifazo también molesta a los pudientes," *Los Tiempos*, January 20, 2000; "El tarifazo pone en alerta a la Cámara de Industria," *Los Tiempos*, January 23, 2000; "Iglesia: El tarifazo del agua es una medida injusta y antipopular," *Los Tiempos*, January 31, 2000.

41. Ann Mische and Philippa Pattison (2000) document a similar process of forming a broad-based coalition behind the impeachment of Brazilian president Fernando Collor de Melo in 1992. While I have not replicated their social network analysis, my attention to the breadth of the mobilization in the Water War owes a debt to their careful documentation of the Brazilian case.

42. Ceceña (2004, 84).

43. Both Raúl Zibechi (2010) and Pablo Mamani Ramírez (2005) offer readings of grassroots power based on the activities of recent civic strikes. For Zibechi "times in which there is an intensely creative outpouring—during which social groups release huge amounts of energy—act like a bolt of lightning capable of illuminating

subterranean molecular cooperation. . . . During the uprising, shadowed areas (that is, the margins in the eyes of the state) are illumined, albeit. fleetingly. The insurgency is a moment of rupture in which subjects display their capacities, their power as a capacity to do, and deploy them, revealing aspects hidden in moments of repose, when there is little collective activity" (2010, 11).

44. "Bolivia: A diez años de La 'Guerra del Agua,' la lucha continúa," *Cambio*, April 12, 2010.

45. García Linera (2011, 12).

46. The coverage of water service by local organizations was estimated at 20 percent of the population, compared with 49 percent coverage by SEMAPA, in figures presented by the academic Roberto Prada at the Foro Metropolitano de Agua y Saneamiento on March 22, 2011.

47. Hurtado, interview.

48. An array of community activists, SEMAPA managers and engineers, and academics attested to all three failings at a public panel I attended on April 15, 2010, at the Universidad Mayor de San Simón.

49. Hurtado, interview.

50. Mamani, interview.

## Chapter 3

From the author's interview of Lubia Vargas Padilla at a teachers' union barricade, April 14, 2011, Cochabamba.

1. Escuela del Pueblo Primero de Mayo (2002).

2. Escuela del Pueblo Primero de Mayo (2002, 7).

3. On the third day of the strike, May 3, two Chicago workers were killed by police. The next day a rally in Haymarket Square was met by a detachment of police. A homemade bomb was thrown at the police, ultimately killing seven officers. The police fired on the crowd, leaving at least four dead and dozens wounded. Eight anarchist labor activists were put on trial for the bombing; four of them were executed in 1887.

4. An exchange on the streets between Oscar Olivera and Evo Morales in the 1990s saw them dispute this literal vanguard position. See Komadina and Geffroy (2007, 43).

5. Gutiérrez Aguilar (2008b).

6. Wanderley (2009, 50, Gráfico 4). Labor laws apply only to formal employment, not including short-term contracts. Widespread subcontracting and informalization have shrunk the reach of official labor protections to just 18 to 20 percent of the national workforce ("Más derechos laborales cada año, pero menos personas que los gozan," *La Razón*, April 28, 2013).

7. Marcela Olivera, interview by author, April 5, 2011.

8. Olivera and Lewis (2004, 47); Olivera et al. (2008, 50).

9. Olivera credits himself, Gutiérrez Aguilar, and García Linera in Olivera and Lewis (2004, 128).

10. Gutiérrez Aguilar (2004, 100, 102).
11. Gutiérrez Aguilar (2004, 103). For Gutiérrez Aguilar (2008a), finding and interpreting this kind of "political horizon" is essential to understand the significance of these processes of revolt. For García Linera (2001b), the emphasis instead seems to be on identifying new protagonists of revolt, the "plebian" and the "multitude," drawing on the Marxist tradition of Bolivian theorist René Zavaleta Mercado.
12. Gill (2016, 73-76).
13. Olivera and Lewis (2004, 47).
14. For a compendium of theoretical writings in this tradition, see Lotringer, Marazzi, and Power (2008). On the concept of the multitude, see Virno (2004).
15. While the other names of events listed here affirm the power of the grassroots, Black October (*Octubre Negro*) describes the deadly repression used against the 2003 protests. No one with whom I spoke called the 2005 events "the Second Gas War," as many secondary sources do.
16. *La Razón,* June 1, 2008.
17. Critical Mass—a monthly protest happening that originated in San Francisco—gathers dozens, hundreds, or thousands of cyclists to defend their right to be on the road and to promote a alternative ecological vision for the city. At the time of my fieldwork a Cochabamba environmentalist had organized a small version of the protest at twilight on Fridays.
18. "La protesta de ayer impidió la salida de buses a los Yungas: Vecinos del noreste bloquean por seguridad y agua potable," *La Prensa,* June 24, 2008.
19. This and succeeding quotes from Christian Mamani come from Christian Mamani, interview by author, April 4, 2010, Cochabamba.
20. Lubia Vargas Padilla, interview by author, April 14, 2011.
21. Vargas Padilla, interview.
22. The Cochabamba delegation to these national protests included a man who suffered a traumatic eye injury.
23. Raúl Zibechi (2006), Luis Gómez (2004), Sian Lazar (2008), and Pablo Mamani Ramírez (2005) all have documented the role of El Alto's neighborhood committees in revolts from 2000 to 2005, which meant mobilizing practical organizations for new political ends.
24. Achi Chiritèle and Delgado (2007).
25. Lazar (2006, 194); Zibechi (2010, 11-32).
26. Orellana Aillón (2004, 506).
27. Orellana Aillón (2004, 505-7). "The Regantes" refers to the Cochabamba Departmental Federation of Irrigation Users (*Federación Departamental Cochabambina de Regantes*).
28. Olivera et al. (2008, 161).
29. Olivera et al. (2008, 161); "Forman 14 comités para defender el agua," *Los Tiempos,* January 23, 2000.
30. Communiqué No. 20, reproduced in Olivera et al. (2008).
31. Escuela del Pueblo Primero de Mayo (2002, 23).

32.  Virilio and Lotringer (1983, 35).

33.  Evia, Laserna, and Skaperdas (2008, 36–37).

34.  Evia, Laserna, and Skaperdas (2008, 49).

35.  Evia, Laserna, and Skaperdas (2008, 37). The study does not extend past 2005, so it is not possible to see whether this economic impact peaked during 2000–2005 relative to the years of the Evo Morales presidency (2006–present).

36.  Gallup, Gaviria, and Lora (2003, 85); Calderon and Servén (2004, 10–11, 22–23).

37.  Olivera et al. (2008, 178).

38.  Marcelo Rojas, interview by author, December 7, 2010.

39.  Kohl and Farthing (2006, 168). The rural workers' union is the Unified Union Confederation of Rural Bolivian Workers (Confederación Sindical Única de Trabajadores Campesinos de Bolivia), and the coca growers are united as the Six Federations of the Tropic of Cochabamba.

40.  The Quechua term *mita* (sometimes *mit'a*), which dates to the Inca era, designates rotating labor responsibilities. In that period it covered "labor for communal tasks, for the fields of the local lords and for the lands of the idols, and as support for local kuraka [hereditary leaders]" and the Inca state. Colonial governments adapted the state labor obligation to funnel workers into the mines (Rostworowski and Morris 1999, 822). When used, as here, within communities, it refers to a horizontal obligatory system of labor for collective ends. *Ayni* refers to "a symmetrical exchange of delayed reciprocity between equals, usually manifest in labor exchanges," and is often translated as "mutual aid" (Allen 1981, 165).

41.  Quispe Huanca (2001, 171).

42.  Patzi (2003, 218). Pablo Zárate Willka led the Aymara forces who allied with the La Paz–centered Liberal Party in the federal revolution of 1899. As with many other indigenous military ventures, Willka's effort combined local rebellion with taking sides in an internal conflict in dominant society. After the war Willka and thirty-one other Indian military leaders were executed in retaliation for the Mohoza massacre, itself an Indian reprisal for Liberal attacks on Indian communities.

43.  Patzi (2003, 218).

44.  Carlos Mesa Gisbert, "Mensaje de Carlos Mesa anunciando su renuncia," March 6, 2005, https://www.bolivia.com/noticias/autonoticias/DetalleNoticia25357.asp.

45.  Patzi (2003, 263–64).

46.  Larkin (2013, 333).

47.  Escuela del Pueblo Primero de Mayo (2002, 5).

48.  Mesa Gisbert (2005).

49.  Despite shutdowns of airports in 2005 and 2010, foreign airlines continued to add flights to Bolivia's international airports.

50.  Rojas, interview.

51.  Olivera, interview.

52.  "Los vecinos bloquearon todo, no pasarano ni las bicicletas," *La Razón*, April 8, 2000.

53. García Linera (2001a).
54. Foucault (2007, 105–8, 325).
55. Scott (2009, 10–11).
56. This happened, for example, when La Paz drivers arranged blockades to oppose a new law increasing penalties for drunk driving ("Paro de choferes culmina con dos enfrentamientos," *El Diario*, March 5, 2010).
57. On blockades, see Miguel E. Gómez Balboa, "El dilema del fuero," *La Prensa*, August 29, 2004.

## Chapter 4

1. Marcelo Rojas, interview by author, December 7, 2010, Cochabamba.
2. "Gral. Pérez: Policía sólo gastó 10 mil balines y 7 mil gases," *Opinión*, February 9, 2000.
3. "Retornó la calma, Gobierno cedió a presión," *El Deber*, February 6, 2000.
4. Bellah (1967, 2).
5. Honorary sessions of the National Congress are a Bolivian civic tradition—the legislature meets in a departmental capital rather than in La Paz's Legislative Palace, often to celebrate a region's history or contribution to the country as a whole.
6. Olivera et al. (2008, 169).
7. Rojas, interview.
8. Goodwin, Jasper, and Polletta (2004, 418–19).
9. Durkheim (1915, 427).
10. Durkheim (1915, 210–11).
11. V. Turner (1969, 10). "Togetherness itself" is one definition of *communitas* offered by Edith Turner (2012, 11).
12. Juris (2008, 126).
13. A parallel interpretation comes from James Jasper: "Groups seem to be strengthened when they share reflex emotions in response to events and when they share affective loyalties to one another" (2011, 294).
14. Trotsky ([1920]1980, chap. 11).
15. Tilly (2000, 137).
16. Tilly (2000, 137–38).
17. This happened, for example, on October 15, 2010, when federations of disabled people, pensioners, and campesinos all rallied in the plaza.
18. One rare exception was a November 12, 2010, march by urban teachers challenging the national labor confederation's stance on a proposed pension law.
19. Eliana Quiñones Guzmán, interview by author, April 29, 2011, Cochabamba.
20. Christian Mamani, interview by author, April 4, 2010, Cochabamba.
21. Remarkably, they did so even after the divisive events of January 2007, which I discuss in chap. 6.
22. Herbas (2002, 102).
23. Mamani, interview.
24. Olivera and Lewis (2004, 47).

25. Marcela Olivera, interview by author, April 5, 2011, Cochabamba.
26. At least twenty men, one sixty-five-year-old woman, and six minors (one of them female) were hit with live ammunition, according to Fernando Salazar Ortuño (2011, 217–19). Injuries may not be a representative sample of those most engaged in confrontation because women sometimes successfully shamed the police (nearly all men) sent to attack them (Bustamante, Peredo, and Udaeta 2005).
27. Tom Kruse's photo appears in Shultz and Draper (2009, 8).
28. Bustamante, Peredo, and Udaeta (2005, 82).
29. Bustamante, Peredo, and Udaeta (2005, 80).
30. Rojas, interview.
31. Ángel Hurtado, interview by author and Carmen Medeiros, March 28, 2011, Cochabamba.
32. Quiñones Guzmán, interview.
33. Turner (2012, 4).
34. "Como en la dictadura," *Los Tiempos*, February 5, 2000.
35. "Cochabamba decidió continuar protestas," *Los Tiempos*, February 5, 2000.
36. "La 'Guerra del Agua,' 12 años después," *Los Tiempos*, April 8, 2012.
37. "Multitud pidió elecciones: Cochabamba cabildeó, ayer," *Gente*, June 10, 2005.
38. My linguistic analysis here expands on Sewell's comments (2005, 246–47) on *le peuple* in the context of the French Revolution. In the local Spanish-language press, the word *llajta* (Quechua for "town") is used as a synonym for the city of Cochabamba and is deployed in several of these ways.
39. Cabildos abiertos allowed for public election of municipal officials and decisions on major issues such as "the fight against epidemics, the founding and moving of cities, defense of those cities against the Indians, fulfillment of religious obligations, payment of tithes, and the suppression or addition of festivals to the calendar" (Tapia 1969, 59, 61). See also Barnadas (2002).
40. Tapia (1969, 62, 63).
41. Marcela Olivera, interview.
42. Plaza Sebastián Pagador, Oruro, honors Sebastián Pagador of Oruro, a creole who issued a call to arms against peninsular Spaniards on February 10, 1781. May 25 Plaza, Sucre, is where creoles gathered at the Universidad San Francisco Xavier to proclaim independence on May 25, 1809. Plaza Murillo, La Paz, is named for Pedro Murillo, the lead conspirator in La Paz's July 16, 1809, uprising. Plaza 14 de Septiembre, Cochabamba, is named for the date in 1810 when Francisco del Rivero, Esteban Arze, and Melchor Villa Guzmán led a force of a thousand men to seize Cochabamba's main institutions. Plaza 24 de Septiembre, Santa Cruz, marks the day of the first battle in the 1810 uprising fomented by Santa Cruz rebels. Plaza 6 de Agosto, Potosí, commemorates Simón Bolívar's pivotal victory at Junin on August 6, 1824, and Bolivia's declaration of its independence one year later.
43. The Movimiento Nacionalista Revolucionario called a cabildo in February 1952, before its revolution. Student protesters responded to the 1967 massacre of miners by convening cabildos abiertos in La Paz and Cochabamba (Lora 1997).

44. Herbas (2002, 102).
45. For a fuller exploration of organic grassroots ethics and its constraints on leaders, see Bjork-James (2018).
46. Herbas (2002, 110) called this horizontalism. Marina Sitrin (2006, 2012) describes the parallel emergence of horizontalism as a political ethic in Argentina during and after the 2001 economic collapse.
47. Quiñones Guzmán, interview.
48. Herbas (2002, 103).
49. Achbar and Abbott (2003).
50. "Dolor en el adios a Víctor Hugo," *Opinión*, April 10, 2000.
51. Achbar and Abbott (2003).
52. Aside from practical issues, Oscar Olivera speaks of a political reason that organizers sought to prioritize the Coordinadora assembly's decisions over those made in cabildos. By letting the Zona Sur–led assembly set the agenda for cabildos, the Coordinadora ended up with the rich "march[ing] behind the slogans of the poor, instead of the other way around" (Olivera and Lewis 2004, 47).
53. I explore these dynamics in Bjork-James (2018).
54. Transcribed from field recording, February 18, 2011.
55. The full text of the resolution was published in the Partido Obrero Revolucionario's newsletter *Masas*, March 18, 2011.
56. Hurtado, interview.
57. The Fabriles financed construction of the eight-story building from regular contributions from all their members (Cerruto 1972, 131).
58. Fights over the plaza took place in 1809, 1811, 1814, 1862, 1865, 1871, 1898, 1946, 1952, and 2002; see Gerl and Chávez (2012, 6; pages not numbered). President Gualberto Villarroel was overthrown and hung from a lamppost in the plaza in 1946, while the Revolutionary Nationalist Movement and militias were there when they proclaimed victory in the April 1952 Revolution.
59. The Citizen Security Law (Law 2494) promulgated on August 4, 2003, imposed severe criminal penalties—multiple years in prison—on those who blocked a road, river, or air transportation. "Ley 'antibloqueo' tiene plena vigencia en el país," *Correo del Sur*, August 12, 2003.
60. Ramos Andrade (2004).
61. Alex Contreras Baspineiro, "La 'Guerra del Gas' comienza en Bolivia," *BolPress*, September 18, 2003. The National Committee for the Defense and Recovery of Gas had been formed a year earlier, in mid-2002 ("Manifiesto de creación del Comité del Gas," AGP: Archivos de los Protestos Globales, August 2, 2002, https://www.nadir.org/nadir/initiativ/agp/free/imf/bolivia/txt/2002/0802comite_del_gas.htm). Oscar Olivera describes an earlier founding of the gas coordinadora in April 2003 (Gutiérrez Aguilar 2008a, 209).
62. Gutiérrez Aguilar (2008a, 211).
63. "Preludio de la tormenta," *Correo del Sur*, October 17, 2004.
64. "Preludio de la protesta," *La Prensa*, September 18, 2003.

65. Kohl and Farthing (2006, 173–75).
66. Lazar (2004, 184).
67. Marcela Olivera, interview.
68. Hugo Torres, interview by author, April 14, 2010, La Paz.
69. Rivero (2006, 74–75). Romero de Campero served as Bolivia's human rights ombudswoman (Defensoría del Pueblo) from 1998 to 2003.
70. Cities with pickets included La Paz, Oruro, Cochabamba, Santa Cruz, Sucre, Tarija, Trinidad, Potosí, Riberalta, Camiri, Bermejo, Tupiza, Yacuiba, and Llallagua. There were more than one hundred hunger strikers at sixteen sites in the city of Cochabamba, including the municipal council chambers, departmental labor federation headquarters, Jesuit church, and Chamber of Exporters building ("Se sentó un precedente contra el abuso de poder," *Opinión,* October 18, 2003, "Informe Sucesión" sec., p. 10).
71. Rivero (2006, 80).
72. Rivero (2006, 83).
73. Radio Erbol, quoted in Rivero (2006, 228).
74. "Los últimos días," *La Prensa,* October 26, 2003, Sunday sec., p. 5. Quintana later served as Evo Morales's minister of the presidency.
75. Rivero (2006, 84).
76. "Masiva marcha termina en violencia," *La Prensa,* October 17, 2003, archived at https://www.nadir.org/nadir/initiativ/agp/free/imf/bolivia/txt/2003/1017massiva _marcha.htm.
77. A careful account appears in Komadina and Geffroy (2007, 62–69). For Raquel Gutiérrez Aguilar (2008a, 2014), this marked the point of inflection between the pursuit of autonomous power by social movements up to 2003 and the increasing prominence of a state-based project afterward.
78. "Hubo riguroso control policial y militar: Alteños hicieron toma simbólica de planta de YPFB en Senkata," *El Diario,* May 3, 2005.
79. "Queremos que el presidente (Carlos Mesa) cumpla su compromiso del 18 de Octubre. Prometió ni olvido ni perdón, también dijo que el gas se iba a nacionalizar e industrializar, que no iba a traicionar a la ciudad de El Alto" ("Bolivia se encuentra en un callejón sin salida," *Los Tiempos,* May 17, 2005).
80. Hylton (2005).
81. Hylton (2005); Hylton and Thomson (2007, 125).
82. Mesa Gisbert (2008, 290).
83. Mesa Gisbert (2008, 296).
84. Mesa Gisbert (2008, 297). The embassy evidently preferred Vaca Díez's succession to the presidency rather than his resignation, according to both Mesa and its own cables. "Mesa Offers to Resign; Bolivia Paralyzed by Blockades as Congress Seeks to Deliberate," sensitive cable no. La Paz 001753, U.S. Embassy, La Paz, to State Department Headquarters, June 7, 2005, obtained by Keith Yearman under the Freedom of Information Act, http://www.cod.edu/people/faculty/yearman/bolivia /La_Paz_001753_07June2005.pdf (accessed November 7, 2009).

85. Mesa Gisbert (2008, 297, 294–96).
86. Mesa Gisbert (2008, 301); "Una amenaza despertó a Vaca Díez del sueño presidencial," *La Razón*, June 24, 2005.
87. From Cortés's account, published in Mesa Gisbert (2008, 301–6).
88. "Los piquetes de huelga se levantan paulatinamente," *La Razón*, June 10, 2005.
89. Mesa Gisbert (2008, 301); Hylton (2005).
90. "Desmayos, lágrimas, acrobacias; los legisladores entraron en pánico," *La Razón*, June 24, 2005.
91. "Following Pitched Battle, Congress Selects Eduardo Rodriguez as President," sensitive cable no. La Paz 001785, U.S. Embassy, La Paz, to State Department headquarters, June 10, 2005, obtained by Keith Yearman under the Freedom of Information Act, http://www.cod.edu/people/faculty/yearman/bolivia/La_Paz _001785_10June2005.pdf (accessed November 7, 2009).
92. Mesa Gisbert (2008, 187–90) perceived Morales as the hidden coordinator of the entire effort, but Raquel Gutiérrez Aguilar (2008a, 290–95) argues persuasively that Morales was committed to using an election to determine succession and hung back from the Second Gas War. Martin Sivak (2010, 145) quotes David Choquehuanca's description of Morales in May 2005: "Evo has decided to be president."
93. Felipe Quispe Huanca was likewise threatened. Agencia de Prensa Alteña, "Trabajadores alteños someterán a justicia comunitaria a Evo y al Mallku si traicionan," *BolPress*, March 15, 2005, archived at http://www.bolpress.com/art.php?Cod =2002085819.
94. Sivak (2010, 154).
95. Mamani, interview.
96. Durkheim (1915, 213).
97. Tilly (1999, 2004).
98. It creates a situation of "dual power" in Trotsky's formulation or exercises "constituent power" in Antonio Negri's.

## Chapter 5

1. Marcelo Guzman, public speech, January 25, 2011, recording in the author's personal files.
2. Farthing and Kohl (2010, 200).
3. Grisaffi (2010).
4. Evo Morales Ayma, "Discurso de Asunción," January 22, 2006, La Paz. His address is available online at https://www.bivica.org/file/view/id/3836, but the pages of the pdf are not numbered.
5. Waskar Ari (2014, 81–91) provides an overview of racial segregation in independent Bolivia.
6. Sivak (2010:161).
7. "No more than ten" indigenous people served as deputies in the cohort elected in 1997, reports Donna Lee Van Cott (2003, 752), summarizing several sources.

8. Sivak (2010, 81–82) details these experiences in a lengthy list that includes the following: "They accused him of . . . being the dictator of El Chapare, being the king of El Chapare. . . . They made fun of him publicly, saying he didn't know how to add. They mocked the way he spoke and what he said when he did speak. They gave him—through the president of private businesses—a Bible and a constitution to civilize him."

9. Ruddick (1996, 136–37). She also cites Elijah Anderson, Philomena Essed, Grace Halsell, bell hooks, Achille Mbembe, and Cornel West as making the link between public racialization and personal subjectivity.

10. Ruddick (1996, 136).

11. Indigenous women used these phrases to describe their experiences of discrimination in a 2015 poll (Coordinadora de la Mujer 2015, 38).

12. Guardia Crespo (1997, 190).

13. Forrest Hylton (2003, 176) gives Rivera Cusicanqui (2001, 100) as the source of this claim. She argues that this pushed women to be the primary presenters of Indian tradition in La Paz.

14. Goodrich (1971, 19).

15. Goodrich (1971, 19).

16. Ortíz and her daughter then shared tears of their own. She tried but failed to follow, and later tried to locate the man she had taken advantage of, but her guilt was a different side of this story (Ortiz 1953, 27–28).

17. On Tlacotalpan, see Staples (1994, 121); on Chiapas, see Kovic (2005, 123); on apartheid South Africa, see Nightingale (2012, 269); on the American North, specifically Albany, New York, see Holsaert (2010, 102); and on the American South, see Loukaitou-Sideris and Ehrenfeucht (2009, 87–89) and Coker (2007, 169–71).

18. Butrón Mendoza (1992, 70).

19. According to C. Esteva Fabregat's data ("Poblacion mestizaje en les ciudades de iberoamericana: Siglo XVIII," in F. de Solano, ed., *Estudios sobre la ciudad iberoamericana* [Madrid, 1975], 599), which are quoted in Morse (1984, 89), 35.6 percent of urban residents in the late eighteenth century were whites and 14.1 percent were mestizos. The urban Indian population of 1.73 million accounted for 36.8 percent of the total urban population, with the remainder made up of Afro-descendant groups: Mulattos (8.9 percent) and Negroes (4.6 percent).

20. Puwar (2004, 42)

21. Puwar (2004, 33, 48–52).

22. Canessa (2006).

23. Zibechi (2008); Achi Chiritèle and Delgado (2007).

24. Lazar (2006, 186–92).

25. Christian Mamani, interview by author, April 4, 2010, Cochabamba.

26. The two Quechua words mean, respectively, "water" and "land" or "place."

27. Coordinadora de la Mujer 2015.

28. Steve Boggan, "Coca Is a Way of Life," *Guardian*, February 9, 2006.

29. María Eugenia ("Mauge") Flores Castro, interview by author, December 15, 2010, Cochabamba.

30. Flores Castro, interview.

31. Villarroel's Government Ministry issued a communiqué to all departments and municipalities certifying that the constitution prohibited any such restriction. As La Calle celebrated, "The free passage of indigenous people through the streets and plazas of the national territory is now guaranteed" (Rivera Cusicanqui 1985, 166; Antezana Ergueta and Romero Bedregal 1973, 97).

32. Butrón Mendoza (1992, 69).

33. Goodrich (1971, 19–20).

34. Presidencia de la República (1962).

35. Ortiz (1953, 27).

36. This information comes from newspaper accounts cited by Tórrez Rubín de Celis, Carrasco, and Cámara (2010, 134–36) and Mendieta (2008, 223–25).

37. Malloy (1971, 125).

38. Butrón Mendoza (1992, 69).

39. Canedo Vásquez (2011, 98).

40. The estimate is from García Linera, Chávez León, and Costas Monje (2004, 218), citing Z. Lehm Arcaya, *Milenarismo y movimientos sociales en la amazonia boliviana* (1999).

41. Angel Torres, "Mucha euforia pero no violencia habrá en marcha indígena del 12 de Octubre," *Los Tiempos*, October 10, 1992.

42. *Hoy*, October 12, 1992.

43. Fabricant (2008–10, 128; 2012, 212n1).

44. This was not the first time the cocaleros had seized Cochabamba's central plaza in a show of coca-chewing defiance. The January–February 2002 "Coca War" extended from the Chapare through the coca leaf market in Sacaba, a town east of Cochabamba, and eventually into the Plaza 14 de Septiembre, where cocaleros attempted to achieve a mass public act of coca chewing (Gutiérrez Aguilar 2008a, 176–85).

45. Nicole Fabricant describes how the 2006 indigenous march "infused the main square [of Cochabamba] with dynamic highland Andean cultural forms and practices," reinforcing indigenous claims to citizenship (2008–10, 138–39).

46. "The Regantes" refers to the Cochabamba Departmental Federation of Irrigation Users (*Federación Departamental Cochabambina de Regantes*).

47. Albro (2006, 403).

48. Quijano (2000, 2008).

# Chapter 6

1. Sucre's 1778 population is cited in Serulnikov (2009, 443). Potosí's 1610 population is cited in Stavig (2000, 533).

2. The university's extensive title—which is literally translated as Higher, Royal, and Pontifical University of Saint Francis Xavier of Chuquisaca—neatly encapsulates the union of intellectual, governmental, and ecclesiastical power in the lettered city.

3. On events in Sucre during the 1780s, see Serulnikov (2009).

4. Bolivia, Dirección General de Estadístico y Estudios Geográficos (1920, 30).

5. Malloy and Thorn (1971, 41).

6. As I discussed in chapter 4, miners and campesinos focused their blockades at a greater distance from the plaza, but together with other protesters, they blocked the city's four exits and its airport.

7. Albó (2008, 60).

8. De la Fuente Jeria (2008, 93–94).

9. Valcarce (2008, 42).

10. Ortiz (1953, 107).

11. De la Fuente Jeria (2008, 93).

12. Juan Forero and Larry Rohter, "Bolivia's Leader Solidifies Region's Leftward Tilt," *New York Times*, January 22, 2006. Modern Bolivian nationalists claim Tiwanaku as their ancient cultural precursor, much as Peruvians claim the Inca culture and Mexicans claim the Aztecs.

13. De Munter and Salman (2009, 433–34).

14. "Bolivia: Primer indígena canciller y primera mujer encargada de la seguridad. 2006," *Agence France Presse*, January 23, 2006, http://www.aporrea.org/interna cionales/n72120.html.

15. Government insiders describe how this process was undertaken with caution. Raúl Prada Alcoreza (2010, 104, 105), for instance, recalled in an interview, "The decision had been made to go forward haltingly, not to replace the public functionaries radically; I believe there was a fear that we would be overcome and would put ourselves on the path to chaos, since when we came to government power, we had neither the tradition nor the custom of handling the public apparatus. The experience was lacking." (His description focuses on the Ministry of Economy and Finance.) Yet this caution came within "a structural transformation of the Ministry and of the state" in accordance with the new constitution.

16. Lidia Mamani, "Los empleos en empresas públicas crecieron 23 veces en una década," *Página Siete*, May 1, 2016.

17. Soruco Sologuren 2016.

18. Ángel Hurtado, interview by author and Carmen Medeiros, March 28, 2011, Cochabamba.

19. Electoral participation also rose substantially, with 89.26 percent of eligible voters going to the polls, the highest level in the democratic era (Servicio Intercultural de Fortalecimiento Democrático 2013).

20. Hurtado, interview.

21. The pact's exact membership has varied, but its core has been five national organizations: the Unified Union Confederation of Rural Bolivian Workers, National Confederation of Peasant and Indigenous Women of Bolivia–Bartolina Sisa,

Union Confederation of Intercultural Communities of Bolivia, Confederation of Indigenous Peoples of Bolivia (CIDOB), and the National Council of Ayllus and Markas of Qullasuyu.

22. For CIDOB's perspective see Zacu Mborobainchi and Ontiveros (2006). For the Cochabamba Coordinadora's see Herbas (2002, 113).

23. Eliana Quiñones Guzmán, interview by author, April 29, 2011, Cochabamba.

24. Gutiérrez Aguilar (2014, 121).

25. Ley especial de convocatoria a la Asamblea Constituyente, Law 3364, March 6, 2006.

26. During the Coyuntura y Modelos de Desarrollo en Bolivia session organized by the Bolivia Section of the Latin American Studies Association and held May 27, 2012, in San Francisco, Oskar Vega argued that the Pact of Unity faced the choice in early 2006 of renouncing a partisan structure for the constituent assembly or imposing a constituent structure upon it; the pact chose the latter option.

27. Programa NINA and Garcés (2010, 50).

28. For more on the role of organic members of the Constituent Assembly and their political position, see Prada Alcoreza (2010).

29. Programa NINA and Garcés (2010, 84); Schavelzon (2012).

30. Programa NINA and Garcés (2010, 136 [appendix 6]).

31. Despite the pledges, this relationship was difficult to maintain. Over time inter-party negotiations outside the Constituent Assembly, between the MAS-IPSP and its right-wing opponents, became a more influential force in directing the assembly and later in revising the text before it was put to a national vote.

32. Muruchi Escobar and Calla Cárdenas (2008, 41).

33. Muruchi Escobar and Calla Cárdenas (2008, 44).

34. Muruchi Escobar and Calla Cárdenas (2008, 41). Organizers of the assembly had arranged simultaneous translation, so this was not a practical objection. Martín Balcázar Martínez, "Las sesiones serán multilingüe," *Correo del Sur*, August 10, 2008.

35. José Santos Romero, interview by author, April 20, 2011, Sucre.

36. The Guaraní word Camba had originally referred to lowland indigenous groups but became a geographic descriptor.

37. This summary is from Dory (2009, 139).

38. Albó (2008, table 16).

39. Maria Eugenia Flores Castro, interview by author, December 15, 2010, Cochabamba.

40. Flores Castro, interview.

41. Reprinted by Asamblea Permanente de Derechos Humanos de Cochabamba (2008, appendix 2, 115).

42. Asamblea Permanente de Derechos Humanos de Cochabamba (2008, 64).

43. Asamblea Permanente de Derechos Humanos de Cochabamba (2008, 68–74).

44. Flores Castro, interview.

45. Harasic Rojas's letter is available online at http://culpinak.blogspot.com/2007/01/era-tan-solo-un-joven.html, among numerous other locations.

46. In Sucre this cultural identification became a visceral hostility to the elite's campesino neighbors during the catastrophic stalemate period (Sánchez C 2008, 41–44).

47. Instituto Nacional de Estadistica (2005, 47). The population grew to 261,201 by the 2012 Census (around 239,000 of them in the urban areas of the municipality), per Instituto Nacional de Estadistica (2012).

48. Sánchez C (2008, 70). The figures combine the municipalities of Sucre, Oropeza, and Yamaparez; another 2.5 percent of urban residents identified as Aymara.

49. "Capitalía, principal demanda," *Correo del Sur*, August 6, 2006.

50. "Chuquisaca radicaliza medidas y decide n paro de 24 horas," *Correo del Sur*, August 30, 2006.

51. "Chuquisaca mantiene vigente las medidas de protesta," *Correo del Sur*, August 31, 2006.

52. De la Fuente Jeria (2008).

53. Defensoría del Pueblo (2009, 15).

54. Carasco Alurralde and Albó (2008).

55. Carasco Alurralde and Albó (2008).

56. U.S. Embassy La Paz, "Evo Avoids Sucre, Justice Minister Unwelcome Too," cable (no. 08LAPAZ24) leaked by Wikileaks and dated January 4, 2008. The cable is archived by the Bolivian government at http://wikileaks.vicepresidencia.gob.bo /EVO-AVOIDS-SUCRE-JUSTICE-MINISTER.

57. "Un diputado Masista fue golpeado cerca de la Plaza Central de Sucre," *Correo del Sur,* April 11, 2008.

58. See pages 15–18 in the introduction.

59. "Marcha inicia medidas de protesta," *Correo del Sur*, May 21, 2008.

60. "Senado celebrará session de honor con los caídos de la Calancha," *Correo del Sur*, May 21, 2008.

61. "Movilización impide visita de Evo," *Correo del Sur*, May 25, 2008.

62. For more about what happened, see Observatorio del Racismo (2008); Defensoría del Pueblo (2009).

63. In both cases an overwhelmingly rural vote combined with nearly half of voters in the capital cities to defeat candidates of urban origins (Bolivia, Tribunal Supremo Electoral and Programa de las Naciones Unidas para el Desarrollo 2012, 185–90).

64. Bolivia, Tribunal Supremo Electoral and Programa de las Naciones Unidas para el Desarrollo (2012, 160).

65. The death of departmental employee Pedro Oshiro the same day occurred under disputed circumstances. César Brie makes a convincing case that Oshiro was killed in a confrontation with armed campesinos that was separate from the main massacre. César Brie, "Apuntes sobre la masacre de Porvenir y los periodistas," *Nueva Crónica y Buen Gobierno*, October 2014, http://www.nuevacronica.com/politica /apuntes-sobre-la-masacre-de-porvenir-y-los-periodistas-/.

66. "Unasur decide enviar misión para dialogar," *Los Tiempos*, September 18, 2008; "Hoy inician diálogo; sectores presionan," *Los Tiempos*, September 18, 2008.

67.   "Pese a diálogo y devolución de oficinas, sigue bloqueo Masista," *Los Tiempos*, September 19, 2008.
68.   "Campesinos y mineros listos para reforzar las presiones," *Los Tiempos*, September 19, 2008.
69.   "Cerco a Santa Cruz termina con un cabildo en Montero," *Los Tiempos*, September 25, 2008.
70.   "Seguidores del MAS se alista para presionar," *Los Tiempos*, September 27, 2008.
71.   Seven earlier *cercos* are described in Gisela Alcócer Caero, "Reanudan diálogo con la presión de un cerco," *Los Tiempos*, October 13, 2008.
72.   Romero Bonifaz, Böhrt Irahola, and Peñaranda Undurraga (2009, 60–61).
73.   Romero Bonifaz, Böhrt Irahola, and Peñaranda Undurraga (2009, 196).
74.   Crowd estimate by *La Jornada* of Mexico, quoted in Romero Bonifaz, Böhrt Irahola, and Peñaranda Undurraga (2009, 185).

## Chapter 7

1.   The CERES Conflict Observatory counted 884 "conflictive events" in 2011, the highest level of any year in its dataset (1970–2012) (Laserna and Centro de Estudios de la Realidad Económica y Social 2013, 81).
2.   José Santos Romero, interview by author, April 20, 2011.
3.   In his case the organization was the Chaunaca Subcentral campesino union.
4.   Escóbar (2008, 260).
5.   Gutiérrez Aguilar (2008a, 2014).
6.   Zegada, Tórrez, and Cámara (2008, 55).
7.   Among the deadly clashes were those in January 2007 in Cochabamba, and the November 2007 and May 2008 events in Sucre.
8.   Komadina and Geffroy (2007).
9.   "El gobierno de Morales quiere que el estado controle el 35 por ciento de la economía," *EFE*, December 2, 2009; "García Linera: 'El proceso de cambio no es una taza de leche,'" *Los Tiempos*, August 6, 2010.
10.   Under its centralist regulations Conalcam's member organizations are obliged to "defend and make respected the leadership of the President" and to respect Conalcam decisions.
11.   For more on the government's economic strategy, see Bjork-James (forthcoming).
12.   This and following quotes come from my transcription and translation of Álvaro García Linera's speech at the Center for Strategic and International Studies, July 21, 2006, https://www.csis.org/events/%C3%A1lvaro-garc%C3%ADa-linera-vice-president-bolivia.
13.   The figures for 2005 and 2015 appear in Morales Ayma (2017, 100).
14.   I also interviewed march participants on site, attended a march supporters' meeting, observed negotiations with the government in Santa Cruz, and interviewed Rosa Chao of the Cochabamba indigenous confederation shortly afterward.

15. "Usaid y Fobomade Promueven movilizaciones contra el gobierno," *La Jornada*, June 10, 2010.

16. Former CEJIS staffers included Alfredo Rada (minister of government), Carlos Romero (minister of autonomies, of government, and of the presidency), Susana Rivero (minister of rural development), Hugo Salvatierra (minister of rural development), René Orellana (minister of water and environment), and Alejandro Almaraz (vice minister of lands).

17. Chao Roca, interview.

18. "DS748 suben gasolina y diesel, datos y cifras," *Somos Sur*, December 26, 2010, https://somossur.net/economia/hidrocarburos-y-energia/545-261210-ds748-suben -gasolina-y-diesel-datos-y-cifras.html.

19. Cancellation of these subsidies has sparked protests from Venezuela to India to Nigeria to Haiti.

20. This was despite the MAS-IPSP's opposition to the move when previous governments proposed removing fuel price supports. For a historical review of previous price hikes and attempted price hikes, see Gandarillas G (2011).

21. Transit fares are set by agreement between drivers and the government and may not be raised unilaterally.

22. Observatorio Social de América Latina (2011, 11).

23. Observatorio Social de América Latina (2011, 11).

24. "Ampliado de la COB exige abrogar gasolinazo y aprueba movilizaciones," *EA Bolivia*, December 28, 2010, https://www.eabolivia.com/2010/5720-ampliado-de -la-cob-exige-abrogar-gasolinazo-y-aprueba-movilizaciones.html.

25. "Duro rechazo a 'Gasolinazo' se hizo sentir en todo el país," *Correo del Sur*, December 31, 2010.

26. Sandra Arias, "Evo abre debate sobre crisis de hidrocarburos," *Los Tiempos*, January 2, 2011.

27. The phrase is a Zapatista slogan.

28. Vague references to an economic summit eventually materialized as the Plurinational Encounter to Deepen the Change (in January 2012), but the government did not try to cut fuel subsidies again.

29. María Elena Soria Galvarro, executive secretary of the Trotskyist-led urban teachers' union, charged in May 2010 that Montes "has made himself a spokesperson for and agent of the government" and "has sold himself body and soul to the governing party" ("Ejecutivo de la COB 'Pedro Montes se vendió en cuerpo y alma al gobierno,'" *La Patria*, May 3, 2010). By January 2011 Montes was taking public offense at the characterization and trying to refute it literally: "To accuse Pedro of being sold out, as if I had ever received anything from the government. Not one boliviano and not one cent, and this I can say with all my honor and with my head held high. I will never do that" ("Gobierno busca traidores. Organizaciones identifican responsables," *EJU.TV*, January 4, 2011, http://eju.tv/2011/01/gobierno -busca-traidores-organizaciones-identifican-responsables/).

30. Nonetheless teachers, health workers, and the regional labor federation in Santa Cruz publicly held to the goal of a 15 percent raise and vowed future mobilizations.

31. María Eugenia Flores Castro, interview by author, April 14, 2011, Cochabamba.

32. Isiboro-Sécure was established as a national park on November 22, 1965. It spans 1,372,180 hectares (5,298 square miles; about the size of Connecticut) and straddles the undemarcated border between the Cochabamba and Beni departments in Bolivia.

33. The session, titled Mesa 18 because the official summit had seventeen tracks called *mesas* (literally, tables, or working groups), was held two blocks outside the summit, separate and apart from the official sessions. CONAMAQ, four smaller indigenous organizations, one campesino federation, the Landless Workers' Movement, environmentalists, and academics sponsored the Mesa 18.

34. The study projected deforestation of 64 percent of the park by 2030 if the road was built, a major increase from the already worrisome projection of 43 percent loss without the road (Programa de Investigación Estratégica 2011).

35. Resolution No. 0001/2010 of the 29th Extraordinary Meeting of Corregidores of the Autonomous Isiboro-Securé Indigenous Territory and National Park from the Moxeño, Yuracaré, and Chimane Indigenous Peoples, May 18, 2010.

36. Sub-Central TIPNIS and Campaña en Defensa del Tipnis (2010, 33). My translation.

37. The publicly owned National Bank for Economic and Social Development (Banco Nacional de Desenvolvimento Econômico e Social) typically provides overseas loans for projects constructed by Brazilian construction firms.

38. ILO Convention 169 and the UN Declaration on the Rights of Indigenous Peoples require such consultation, and the latter requires "free, prior, and informed consent." The declaration was incorporated in Bolivian law on November 7, 2007, by means of Law No. 3760, but its provisions are not effective. The government contends guarantees for consultation in the 2009 constitution are restricted to hydrocarbon extraction.

39. In Morales's words, "Whether they want it or not, we are going to build this road and we are going to deliver under [my] current administration the Cochabamba–Beni/Villa Tunari–San Ignacio de Moxos road" (*Página Siete,* June 30, 2011).

40. "Evo observa a quienes se oponen a la exploración en áreas protegidas como El TIPNIS," *Erbol Digital,* July 14, 2011.

41. Participants also included Gustavo Guzmán (former Bolivian ambassador to the United States), Lino Villca (former MAS senator), Omar Fernández (former irrigators' union leader in Cochabamba), Moisés Torres and Vladimir Machicado (Movimiento Sin Tierra, or the landless movement), feminists, university students, and El Alto community leaders ("Cerca de 50 personas parten de La Paz a reforzar la marcha," *Página Siete,* September 21, 2011).

42. The vice minister's comments were video-recorded and leaked to the press in 2017; they are archived online at https://www.youtube.com/watch?v=eC7tD4fyEAI. My

transcription and translation are available at https://woborders.blog/2017/08/06/marcos-farfan-2011/.

43. This quotation appears in Farfán's report, published online by *Erbol* at https://www.slideshare.net/weberbol/20111115esp.

44. A Prosecutor's Office report in September referred to 74 wounded (*Página Siete*, October 6, 2011); a legal complaint presented by the marchers asserts 280 were injured (*Erbol Digital*, October 15, 2011). The most severe cases included Celso Padilla, leader of the Assembly of the Guaraní People, who was hospitalized with multiple hematomas from his beating but rejoined the march, and Wilson Melgar, a grandfather and Sirionó indigenous marcher, who suffered an embolism and who could remain paraplegic from the incident (*Página Siete*, October 6, 2011).

45. Defensoría del Pueblo (2011, 37).

46. "Liberación de los Indígenas," *Correo del Sur*, September 27, 2011.

47. Defensoría del Pueblo (2011, 109–110).

48. Defensoría del Pueblo (2011, witness P-5, 40).

49. "Masivas movilizaciones en 9 regiones repudian violencia policial contra Indígenas," *Erbol Digital*, September 28, 2011, http://www.erbol.com.bo/noticia.php?identificador=2147483950162.

50. In January 2012 Nuni, Zacu, and Julio Cortez distanced themselves from the MAS-IPSP and formed an independent indigenous bloc in the Chamber of Deputies. Before the 2014 national election the MAS-IPSP reorganized the election of special indigenous representatives, and its own party rules, to avoid future defections.

51. "Marcha del CONAMAQ llega a La Paz y este martes se suma a La Caminta por el TIPNIS," *Erbol Comunicaciones*, October 10, 2011, http://www.erbol.com.bo/noticia.php?identificador=2147483950572.

52. "Destituyen a jefe policial por permitir la vigilia indígena en Plaza Murillo," *Bolpress*, November 20, 2011, http://www.bolpress.com/art.php?Cod=2011102006.

53. Albó (2012, 19–20, 46–48).

54. Asamblea Permanente de Derechos Humanos de Bolivia (2013); Sub-Central TIPNIS and Comisión Recorrido (2012).

55. Asamblea Permanente de Derechos Humanos de Bolivia and Federación Internacional de Derechos Humanos (2013, 13). These concerns are reaffirmed in Defensoría del Pueblo (2016, 137–40).

56. Decreto Supremo No. 759, December 31, 2010.

57. "Evo Morales abroga Decreto 748 que disponía el alza de precios de diesel y gasolina," *Bolivia TV*, December 31, 2010, https://www.youtube.com/watch?v=8XECln2mvRM.

58. Sectoral organizations, by long-standing tradition and under the 1994 Law of Popular Participation, are supposed to channel community demands for government services and receive government support.

## Conclusion

1. Not just, as Lenin would have it, a festival of the oppressed that must be guided by a wiser political party (Lenin 1963, chap. 13).

2. Bjork-James (2013, 55–99).

3. Rosario (2014).

4. Pablo Ortiz, "Indígenas lloran a sus mártires en Chaparina; esperan a Evo para dialogar," *El Deber*, May 26, 2012.

5. "Evo Morales saludó a contingente indígena," *teleSUR tv*, October 21, 2011, https://www.youtube.com/watch?v=zvkyfeA0uqs.

6. This phrasing is from the activist intellectual Raúl Prada, who served in the Constituent Assembly of 2006–2007 and spoke at the forum. However, the phrase *reconducir el proceso de cambio* (redirect the process of change) was used repeatedly in the conference and among grassroots activists throughout 2010 and 2011.

7. Coordinadora Plurinacional de la Reconducción, "Por la recuperación del proceso de cambio para el pueblo y con el pueblo," *VientoSur*, June 26, 2011, http://viento sur.info/spip.php?article5583.

8. Pablo Solón, "Some Thoughts, Self-Criticisms and Proposals Concerning the Process of Change in Bolivia," *Systemic Alternatives* (blog), March 26, 2017, https://systemicalternatives.org/2017/03/26/some-thoughts-self-criticisms-and-proposals-concerning-the-process-of-change-in-bolivia/. Solón is an environmentalist who served as Bolivia's ambassador to the United Nations in Morales's first term.

9. Eliana Quiñones Guzmán, interview by author, April 29, 2011, Cochabamba.

10. McAdam and Sewell (2001, 115–16).

11. McAdam and Sewell (2001, 115).

12. Nepstad (2011); Lakey (2012).

13. Schock (2005, 147–48).

14. Bonilla (2010, 127); Sopranzetti (2014, 122).

15. Contra the narrative of Manuel Castells (2015, 81–82) that "the revolution happened, without warning and strategy."

16. The activist Ziad al-'Ulaymi, quoted in El-Ghobashy (2012, 28).

17. This list briefly rephrases Nancy Fraser's (1997, 2005) theory of redistribution, recognition, and representation as distinct forms of justice.

18. For reviews of the substantive changes and their limits, see Bjork-James (2020) and Farthing (2017).

# REFERENCES

Achbar, Mark, and Jennifer Abbott, dirs. 2003. *The Corporation*. Documentary based on the book by Joel Bakan.

Achi Chiritèle, Amonah, and Marcelo Delgado. 2007. *A la conquista de un lote: Estrategias populares de acceso a la tierra urbana*. La Paz, Bol.: Fundación PIEB.

Albó, Xavier. 1987. "From MNRistas to Kataristas to Katari." In *Resistance, Rebellion, and Consciousness in the Andean Peasant World, 18th to 20th Centuries*, edited by S. J. Stern, 379–419. Madison: University of Wisconsin Press.

Albó, Xavier. 2008. "Datos de una encuesta: El perfil de los constituyentes." *T'inkazos: Revista Boliviana de ciencias sociales* 11, no. 23–24:49–64.

Albó, Xavier. 2012. "Una mirada profunda del TIPNIS." In *Coraje: Memorias de la octava marcha indígena por la defensa del TIPNIS*, edited by A. Contreras Baspineiro, 12–40. Cochabamba, Bol.: Industria Gráfica "J.V." Editora. Available at http://www.plataformademocratica.org/Publicacoes/21580.pdf.

Albro, Robert. 2006. "The Culture of Democracy and Bolivia's Indigenous Movements." *Critique of Anthropology* 26, no. 4:387–410.

Albro, Robert. 2010. *Roosters at Midnight: Indigenous Signs and Stigma in Local Bolivian Politics*. Santa Fe, N.Mex.: School for Advanced Research.

Alexander, Bobby. 1991. *Victor Turner Revisited: Ritual as Social Change*. Atlanta: Scholars Press.

Allen, Catherine J. 1981. "To Be Quechua: The Symbolism of Coca Chewing in Highland Peru." *American Ethnologist* 8, no. 1:157–71.

Anderson, Benedict R. O'G. 1991. *Imagined Communities: Reflections on the Origin and Spread of Nationalism*. Rev. and extended ed. London: Verso.

Antezana Ergueta, Luis, and Hugo Romero Bedregal. 1973. *Historia de los sindicatos campesinos: Un proceso de integración nacional en Bolivia*. La Paz, Bol.: Consejo Nacional de Reforma Agraria, Departamento de Investigaciones Sociales.

AP Archive. 2017. "Evo Morales Takes Office—2006." *Today in History*, January 22. https://www.youtube.com/watch?v=s8s8WGkmVYw.

Arbona, Juan Manuel. 2008. "Histories and Memories in the Organisation and Struggles of the Santiago II Neighbourhood of El Alto, Bolivia." *Bulletin of Latin American Research* 27, no. 1:24–42.

Ari, Waskar. 2014. *Earth Politics: Religion, Decolonization, and Bolivia's Indigenous Intellectuals*. Durham, N.C.: Duke University Press.

Asamblea Permanente de Derechos Humanos de Cochabamba. 2008. *El 11 de enero: Desde la visión de los derechos humanos*. Cochabamba, Bol.: UNITAS and Editorial Verbo Divino.

Asamblea Permanente de Derechos Humanos de Bolivia, and Federación Internacional de Derechos Humanos. 2013. *Informe de verificación de la consulta realizada en el territorio indígena Parque Nacional Isiboro Sécure (TIPNIS)*. https://www.fidh.org/IMG/pdf/bolivia609esp2013.pdf.

Assies, W. 2001. "David vs. Goliath en Cochabamba: Los derechos del agua, el neoliberalismo y la renovación de la protesta social en Bolivia." *T'inkazos: Revista Boliviana de ciencias sociales* 4, no. 8:106–34.

Baker, Lee D. 2010. *Anthropology and the Racial Politics of Culture*. Durham, N.C.: Duke University Press.

Barnadas, Josep M. 2002. "Cabildo abierto." In *Diccionario histórico de Bolivia*, edited by J. M. Barnadas, G. Calvo, J. Ticlla, and Grupo de Estudios Históricos, 391–92. Sucre, Bol.: Grupo de Estudios Históricos.

Bellah, Robert N. 1967. "Civil Religion in America." *Daedalus*, 1–21.

Bjork-James, Carwil. 2013. "Claiming Space, Redefining Politics: Urban Protest and Grassroots Power in Bolivia." Ph.D. diss., anthropology, City University of New York, New York.

Bjork-James, Carwil. 2018. "Binding Leaders to the Community: The Ethics of Bolivia's Organic Grassroots." *Journal of Latin American and Caribbean Anthropology* 23, no. 2:363–82.

Bjork-James, Carwil. 2020. "Left Populism in the Heart of South America: From Plurinational Promise to a Renewed Extractive Nationalism." In *Beyond Populism: Angry Politics and the Twilight of Neoliberalism*, edited by Sophie Bjork-James and Jeff Maskovsky. Morgantown: West Virginia University Press.

Bjork-James, Carwil. Forthcoming. "Unarmed Militancy: Tactical Victories, Subjectivity, and Legitimacy in Bolivian Street Protest." *American Anthropologist*.

Bolivia. Cámara de Diputados. 2001. *Informed de actividades, Comisión de Derechos Humanos, Legislatura 2000–2001*. La Paz, Bol.: Cámara de Diputados.

Bolivia. Dirección General de Estadístico y Estudios Geográficos. 1920. *Anuario geográfico y estadístico de la Republica de Bolivia 1919*. La Paz, Bol.: Artistica.

Bolivia. Tribunal Supremo Electoral and Programa de las Naciones Unidas para el Desarrollo. 2012. *Atlas electoral de Bolivia*. Vol. 2: *Referendums 2004–2009*. La Paz, Bol.: TSE, PNUD.

Bonilla, Yarimar. 2010. "Guadeloupe Is Ours: The Prefigurative Politics of the Mass Strike in the French Antilles." *Interventions* 12, no. 1:125–37.

Brysk, Alison. 2000. *From Tribal Village to Global Village: Indian Rights and International Relations in Latin America*. Stanford, Calif.: Stanford University Press.

Burawoy, Michael. 1998. "The Extended Case Method." *Sociological Theory* 16, no. 1:4–33.

Bustamante, Rocío, Elizabeth Peredo, and María Esther Udaeta. 2005. "Women in the 'Water War' in the Cochabamba Valleys." In *Opposing Currents: The Politics of Water and Gender in Latin America*, edited by V. Bennett, S. Dávila-Poblete, and N. Rico, 72–90. Pittsburgh: University of Pittsburgh Press.

Butrón Mendoza, Julio. 1992. *Eran solo unos Indios: Pasajes de la cara india de una revolución*. Bolivia: Weinberg.

Calderon, Cesar A., and Luis Servén. 2004. *Trends in Infrastructure in Latin America, 1980–2001*. Policy, Research Working Paper WSP 3401. Washington, D.C.: World Bank.

Canedo Vásquez, Gabriela. 2011. *La Loma Santa una utopía cercada: Territorio, cultura y estado en la Amazonía Boliviana*. La Paz, Bol.: Plural Editores.

Canessa, Andrew. 2006. "Todos somos indígenas: Towards a New Language of National Political Identity." *Bulletin of Latin American Research* 25, no. 2:241–63.

Carasco Alurralde, Inés Valeria, and Xavier Albó. 2008. "Cronología de la Asamblea Constituyente." *T'inkazos: Revista Boliviana de ciencias sociales* 11, no. 23–24:101–23.

Castells, Manuel. 2015. *Networks of Outrage and Hope: Social Movements in the Internet Age*. Malden, Mass.: Polity Press.

Ceceña, Ana Esther. 2004. *Cochabamba: Una experiencia de construcción comunitaria frente al neoliberalismo y al Banco Mundial*. Cochabamba, Bol.: Coordinadora de Defensa del Agua y de la Vida.

Cerruto, Waldo. 1972. "Informe del prefecto de La Paz, Sr. Waldo Cerruto." Paper presented at Primera Conferencia Nacional de Prefectos y Alcaldes, April 22–25, La Paz, Bolivia.

Coker, Joe L. 2007. *Liquor in the Land of the Lost Cause: Southern White Evangelicals and the Prohibition Movement*. Lexington: University Press of Kentucky.

Colectivo Situaciones. 2001. "Cuarta declaración del Colectivo Situaciones (sobre la insurrección Argentina de los días 19 y 20)." http://www.nodo50.org/colectivosituaciones/declaraciones_04.html.

Colectivo Situaciones. 2011. *19 & 20: Notes for a New Social Protagonism*. Translated by Nate Holdren and Sebastián Touza. New York: Minor Compositions and Common Notions.

Conaghan, Catherine, and James M. Malloy. 1994. *Unsettling Statecraft: Democracy and Neoliberalism in the Central Andes*. Pittsburgh: University of Pittsburgh Press.

Coordinadora de la Mujer. 2015. *Exclusión y discriminación: Informe de análisis de la "Encuesta Nacional Sobre Exclusión y Discriminación desde la Percepción de las Mujeres."* La Paz, Bol.: Coordinadora de la Mujer.

Coronil, Fernando. 2011. "The Future in Question: History and Utopia in Latin America (1989–2010)." In *Business as Usual: The Roots of the Global Financial Meltdown*, edited by C. J. Calhoun and G. M. Derluguian, 231–92. New York: New York University Press.

Dangl, Benjamin. 2019. *The Five Hundred Year Rebellion: Indigenous Movements and the Decolonization of History in Bolivia*. Chico, Calif.: AK Press.

Davis, Mike. 2004. "Planet of Slums: Urban Involution and the Informal Proletariat." *New Left Review* 26:5–34.

Defensoría del Pueblo. 2009. *Informe defensorial sobre los acontecimientos suscitados en la ciudad de Sucre el 24 de mayo de 2008.* La Paz, Bol.: Defensoría del Pueblo.

Defensoría del Pueblo. 2011. *Informe defensorial respecto a la violación de los derechos humanos en la Marcha Indígena.* La Paz, Bol.: Defensoría del Pueblo.

Defensoría del Pueblo. 2016. *Sin los pueblos indígenas no hay estado plurinacional: Situación de los derechos de los pueblos indígena originario campesinos en el Estado Plurinacional de Bolivia.* La Paz, Bol.: Defensoría del Pueblo.

de la Fuente Jeria, José. 2008. "Los alrededores de la Asamblea Constituyente." *T'inkazos: Revista Boliviana de ciencias sociales* 11, no. 23–24:85–100.

De Munter, Koen, and Ton Salman. 2009. "Extending Political Participation and Citizenship: Pluricultural Civil Practices in Contemporary Bolivia." *Journal of Latin American and Caribbean Anthropology* 14, no. 2:432–56.

Dory, Daniel. 2009. *Las raíces históricas de la autonomía Cruceña: Una interpretación política.* Santa Cruz, Bol.: Gobierno Departamental Autónomo.

Dunkerley, James. 2007. "Evo Morales, the 'Two Bolivias' and the Third Bolivian Revolution." *Journal of Latin American Studies* 39. no. 1:133–66.

Dunning, Thad, Fabiana Machado, Carlos Scartascini, and Mariano Tommasi. 2011. "Political Institutions and Street Protests in Latin America." *Journal of Conflict Resolution* 55, no. 3:340–65.

Duran Chuquimia, Mario Ronald. 2006. "El poder popular." *América Latina en movimiento,* January 22. https://www.alainet.org/es/active/10516.

Durkheim, Émile. 1915. *The Elementary Forms of the Religious Life.* Translated by J. W. Swain. Edited by M. S. Cladis. London: George Allen & Unwin.

El-Ghobashy, Mona. 2012. "The Praxis of the Egyptian Revolution." In *The Journey to Tahrir: Revolution, Protest, and Social Change in Egypt,* edited by J. L. Sowers and C. J. Toensing, 21–40. London: Verso.

Ellis-Jones, Mark, and Peter Hardstaff. 2003. *States of Unrest III: Resistance to IMF and World Bank Policies in Poor Countries.* London: World Development Movement.

Epstein, Barbara. 1991. *Political Protest and Cultural Revolution: Nonviolent Direct Action in the 1970s and 1980s.* Berkeley: University of California Press.

Escóbar, Filemón. 2008. *De la Revolución al Pachakuti: El aprendizaje del respeto reciproco entre blancos e indianos.* La Paz, Bol.: Garza Azul.

Escuela del Pueblo "Primero de Mayo." 2002. *Métodos de lucha.* Cochabamba, Bol.: Federación de Trabajadores Fabriles, Ediciones Primero de Mayo.

Evia, José Luis, Roberto Laserna, and Stergios Skaperdas. 2008. *Conflicto social y crecimiento económico en Bolivia (1970–2005).* Cochabamba, Bol.: Centro de Estudios de la Realidad Económica y Social (CERES), COSUDE, and Instituto para la Democracia.

Fabricant, Nicole. 2008–10. "Mapping a New Geography of Space and Power." *Bolivian Studies Journal* 15–17:114–49.

Fabricant, Nicole. 2012. *Mobilizing Bolivia's Displaced: Indigenous Politics & the Struggle over Land.* Chapel Hill: University of North Carolina Press.

Fanon, Frantz. 2004. *The Wretched of the Earth*. Translated by R. Philcox. New York: Grove Press.

Farthing, Linda. 2017. "Evo's Bolivia: The Limits of Change." The Next System Project, August 17. https://thenextsystem.org/learn/stories/evos-bolivia-limits-change.

Farthing, Linda, and Benjamin Kohl. 2010. "Social Control: Bolivia's New Approach to Coca Reduction." *Latin American Perspectives* 37, no. 4:197–213.

Foran, John. 1993. "Theories of Revolution Revisited: Toward a Fourth Generation?" *Sociological Theory* 11, no. 1:1–20.

Foucault, Michel. 2007. *Security, Territory, Population: Lectures at the Collège de France, 1977–78*. Translated by G. Burchell. Edited by M. Senellart. New York: Palgrave Macmillan.

Fraser, Nancy. 1997. *Justice Interruptus: Critical Reflections on the "Postsocialist" Condition*. London: Routledge.

Fraser, Nancy. 2005. "Re-Framing Justice in a Globalizing World." *New Left Review* 36. https://newleftreview.org/issues/II36/articles/nancy-fraser-reframing-justice-in -a-globalizing-world.

FTAA Miami Independent Media Center Video Group. 2004. *The Miami Model*. Available at http://archive.org/details/miamimodel.

Galeano, Eduardo. 1973. *Open Veins of Latin America: Five Centuries of the Pillage of a Continent*. New York: Monthly Review Press.

Gallup, John Luke, Alejandro Gaviria, and Eduardo Lora. 2003. *Is Geography Destiny?: Lessons from Latin America*. Washington, D.C.: Inter-American Development Bank.

Gandarillas G, Marco. 2011. "Gasolinazos: Columna vertebral del neoliberalismo en Bolivia." *PetroPress*, March special edition.

Garbett, G. Kingsley. 1970. "The Analysis of Social Situations." *Man* 5, no. 2:214–27.

García Linera, Álvaro. 2001a. "Multitud y comunidad: La insurgencia social en Bolivia." *Chiapas* 11:7–16.

García Linera, Álvaro. 2001b. "Sindicato, multitud y comunidad: Movimientos sociales y formas de autonomía política en Bolivia." In García Linera, Quispe, Gutiérrez, Prada, and Tapia, *Tiempos de rebelión*, 9–79.

García Linera, Álvaro. 2011. *Las tensiones creativas de la revolución: La quinta fase del proceso de cambio*. La Paz, Bol.: Vicepresidencia del Estado.

García Linera, Álvaro, Felipe Quispe, Raquel Gutiérrez, Raúl Prada, and Luis Tapia. 2001. *Tiempos de rebelión*. La Paz, Bol.: Muela del Diablo Editores.

García Linera, Álvaro, Marxa Chávez León, and Patricia Costas Monje. 2004. *Sociología de los movimientos sociales en Bolivia: Estructuras de movilización, repertorios culturales y acción política*. La Paz, Bol.: DIAKONIA, Accion Ecuménica Sueca.

Gerl, Carlos, and Randy Chávez. 2012. *Plaza Murillo*. Edited by P. Susz Khol. La Paz, Bol.: Gobierno Autónomo Municipal de La Paz.

Gibson, John. 2008. "A Model for Homeland Defense? The Policing of Alterglobalist Protests and the Contingency of Power Relations." *Alternatives: Global, Local, Political* 33, no. 4:435–60.

Gill, Lesley. 2016. *A Century of Violence in a Red City: Popular Struggle, Counterinsurgency, and Human Rights in Colombia.* Durham, N.C.: Duke University Press.

Gilly, Adolfo. 2007. "The Spirit of Revolt: Bolivia's Ongoing Revolutions." Prologue in *Revolutionary Horizons: Past and Present in Bolivian Politics*, by F. Hylton and S. Thomson, xiii–xx. London: Verso.

Giulino, Meghan Elizabeth. 2009. "Taking Democracy to the Streets: Contentious Politics and the Rise of Anti-Neoliberalism in Bolivia." Ph.D. diss., government, Georgetown University. https://repository.library.georgetown.edu/bitstream/handle/10822/553082/giulinoMeghan.pdf.

Gluckman, Max. 1940. "Analysis of a Social Situation in Modern Zululand." *Bantu Studies* 14:1–30, 147–74.

Goldman Environmental Prize. 2013. *2001 Goldman Environmental Prize Ceremony: Oscar Olivera.* https://www.youtube.com/watch?v=Lb-vIbcOL4M.

Goldstein, Daniel M. 2004. *The Spectacular City: Violence and Performance in Urban Bolivia.* Durham, N.C.: Duke University Press.

Gómez, Luis A. 2004. *El Alto de pie: Una insurrección Aymara en Bolivia.* La Paz, Bol.: HdP, Comuna, and Indymedia Bolivia.

Goodrich, Carter. 1971. "Bolivia in the Time of Revolution." In *Beyond the Revolution: Bolivia Since 1952*, edited by J. M. Malloy and R. S. Thorn, 3–24. Pittsburgh: University of Pittsburgh Press.

Goodwin, Jeff, James M. Jasper, and Francesca Polletta. 2004. "Emotional Dimensions of Social Movements." In *The Blackwell Companion to Social Movements*, edited by D. A. Snow and S. A. Soule, 413–32. Malden, Mass.: Blackwell.

Gordillo, José M., Alberto Rivera Pizarro, and Ana Evi Sulcata Guzmán. 2007. *¿Pitaq kaypi kamachiq?: Las estructuras de poder en Cochabamba, 1940–2006.* La Paz, Bol.: CESU, DICYT-UMSS, and Fundación PIEB.

Gotkowitz, Laura. 2007. *A Revolution for Our Rights: Indigenous Struggles for Land and Justice in Bolivia, 1880–1952.* Durham, N.C.: Duke University Press.

Graeber, David. 2009. *Direct Action: An Ethnography.* Oakland, Calif.: AK Press.

Grisaffi, Thomas. 2010. "We Are Originarios . . . 'We Just Aren't from Here': Coca Leaf and Identity Politics in the Chapare, Bolivia." *Bulletin of Latin American Research* 29, no. 4:425–39.

Guardia B, Fernando, and David R. Mercado B. 1995. *Procesos históricos de conformación de la red urbana del valle alto de Cochabamba: Asentamientos rurales, villas coloniales, ciudades republicanas.* [Cochabamba, Bol.]: Colegio de Arquitectos de Cochabamba, Fondo Nacional de Vivienda Social.

Guardia Crespo, Marcelo. 1997. "Música popular Boliviana." In *En defensa del patrimonio cultural Boliviano*, edited by M. A. Rojas Boyán. La Paz, Bol.: Ediciones Fondo Editorial FIA, SEMILLA, CEBIAE.

Guenther, Mathias. 2006. "Discussion: The Concept of Indigeneity." *Social Anthropology* 14, no. 1:17–32.

Gustafson, Bret Darin. 2009. *New Languages of the State: Indigenous Resurgence and the Politics of Knowledge in Bolivia.* Durham, N.C.: Duke University Press.

Gutiérrez Aguilar, Raquel. 2004. "The Coordinadora." In Olivera and Lewis, *Cochabamba!: Water War in Bolivia*, 53–64.

Gutiérrez Aguilar, Raquel. 2006. *¡A desordenar!: Por una historia abierta de la lucha social*. Mexico City: Tinta Limón Ediciones.

Gutiérrez Aguilar, Raquel. 2008a. *Los ritmos del Pachakuti: Movimiento y levantamiento indígena-popular en Bolivia*. La Paz, Bol.: Ediciones Yachaywasi/Textos Rebeldes.

Gutiérrez Aguilar, Raquel. 2008b. "¿Qué hemos aprendido?: El nuevo mundo del trabajo." In Oscar Olivera, *Nosotros somos la Coordinadora*. La Paz, Bol.: Fundación Abril & Textos Rebeldes.

Gutiérrez Aguilar, Raquel. 2014. *Rhythms of the Pachakuti: Indigenous Uprising and State Power in Bolivia*. Translated by S. A. D. Skar. Durham, N.C.: Duke University Press.

Gutiérrez, Raquel. 2012. "The Rhythms of the Pachakuti: Brief Reflections Regarding How We Have Come to Know Emancipatory Struggles and the Significance of the Term Social Emancipation." *South Atlantic Quarterly* 111, no. 1:51–64.

Herbas, Gabriel. 2002. "La Guerra del Agua en Cochabamba." Interview by A. E. Ceceña. *Chiapas* 14:97–114.

Holsaert, Faith S. 2010. *Hands on the Freedom Plow: Personal Accounts by Women in SNCC*. Urbana: University of Illinois Press.

Holston, James. 2009. "Insurgent Citizenship in an Era of Global Urban Peripheries." *City & Society* 21, no. 2:245–67.

Hylton, Forrest. 2005. "Stalemate in Bolivia, Agony Postponed?" *CounterPunch*, June 14.

Hylton, Forrest, and Sinclair Thomson. 2005. "The Chequered Rainbow." *New Left Review* 35:41–64.

Hylton, Forrest, and Sinclair Thomson. 2007. *Revolutionary Horizons: Past and Present in Bolivian Politics*. London: Verso.

Hylton, Forrest, Felix Patzi, Sergio Serulnikov, and Sinclair Thomson. 2003. *Ya es otro tiempo el presente: Cuatro momentos de insurgencia indígena*. La Paz, Bol.: Muela del Diablo Editores.

Instituto Nacional de Estadistica. 2005. *Chuquisaca: Indicadores sociodemográficos por provincia y secciones de provincia 1992–2001*. La Paz: INE.

Instituto Nacional de Estadistica. 2012. *Resultados Censo Nacional de Población y Vivienda 2012*. La Paz: INE.

International Centre for Settlement of Investment Disputes. 2005. "Aguas del Tunari, S. A. V. Republic of Bolivia: Decision on Respondent's Objections to Jurisdiction." *ICSID Review: Foreign Investment Law Journal* 20, no. 2:450–580.

Jasper, James M. 2011. "Emotions and Social Movements: Twenty Years of Theory and Research." *Annual Review of Sociology* 37:285–303.

Juris, Jeffrey S. 2005. "The New Digital Media and Activist Networking Within Anti-Corporate Globalization Movements." *Annals of the American Academy of Political and Social Science* 597, no. 1:189–208.

Juris, Jeffrey S. 2008. *Networking Futures: The Movements Against Corporate Globalization*. Durham, N.C.: Duke University Press.

Katsiaficas, George. 1987. *The Imagination of the New Left: A Global Analysis of 1968.* Boston, Mass.: South End Press.

Kohl, Benjamin H., and Linda C. Farthing. 2006. *Impasse in Bolivia: Neoliberal Hegemony and Popular Resistance.* London: Zed Books.

Komadina, Jorge, and Céline Geffroy. 2007. *El poder del movimiento político: Estrategia, tramas organizativas e identidad del mas en Cochabamba (1999–2005).* La Paz, Bol.: Fundación PIEB.

Kovic, Christine Marie. 2005. *Mayan Voices for Human Rights: Displaced Catholics in Highland Chiapas.* Austin: University of Texas Press.

Kruse, Thomas. 2005. "La 'Guerra del Agua' en Cochabamba, Bolivia: Terrenos complejos, convergencias nuevas." In *Sindicatos y nuevos movimientos sociales en América Latina,* edited by E. de la Garza Toledo, 121–61. Buenos Aires: CLACSO. Available at http://bibliotecavirtual.clacso.org.ar/ar/libros/grupos/sindi/kruse.pdf.

"La Plaza de Los Muertes Fue la de los Heroes." 2006. In *Página 12 Anuario 2006.* Bolivia: Página 12.

Lagos, Maria L. 1994. *Autonomy and Power: The Dynamics of Class and Culture in Rural Bolivia.* Philadelphia: University of Pennsylvania Press.

Lakey, George. 2012. "The More Violence, the Less Revolution." *Waging Nonviolence: People Powered News & Analysis,* March 6. https://wagingnonviolence.org/feature/the-more-violence-the-less-revolution/.

LAPOP. 2012. *Cultura política de la democracia en Bolivia, 2012: Hacia la igualdad de oportunidades.* Cochabamba, Bol.: Ciudadanía, Comunidad de Estudios Sociales y Acción Pública and Proyecto de Opinión Pública en América Latina.

Larkin, Brian. 2013. "The Politics and Poetics of Infrastructure." *Annual Review of Anthropology* 42:327–43.

Larson, Brooke. 2004. *Trials of Nation Making: Liberalism, Race, and Ethnicity in the Andes, 1810–1910.* New York: Cambridge University Press.

Laserna, Roberto, and Centro de Estudios de la Realidad Económica y Social. 2013. *43 años de conflictos sociales en Bolivia: Enero de 1970–diciembre de 2012: Descripción general y por periodos gubernamentales.* Cochabamba, Bol.: Centro de Estudios de la Realidad Económica y Social.

Laserna, Roberto, Miguel Villarroel Nikitenko, and Centro de Estudios de la Realidad Económica y Social. 2008. *38 años de conflictos sociales en Bolivia: Enero de 1970–Enero de 2008: Descripción general y por periodos gubernamentales.* Cochabamba, Bol.: Centro de Estudios de la Realidad Económica y Social.

Latour, Bruno. 2005. *Reassembling the Social: An Introduction to Actor-Network-Theory.* New York: Oxford University Press.

Lazar, Sian. 2004. "Personalist Politics, Clientelism and Citizenship: Local Elections in El Alto, Bolivia." *Bulletin of Latin American Research* 23, no. 2:228–43.

Lazar, Sian. 2006. "El Alto, Ciudad Rebelde: Organisational Bases for Revolt." *Bulletin of Latin American Research* 25, no. 2:183–99.

Lazar, Sian. 2008. *El Alto, Rebel City: Self and Citizenship in Andean Bolivia.* Durham, N.C.: Duke University Press.

Ledo García, Carmen. 2002. *Urbanisation and Poverty in the Cities of the National Economic Corridor in Bolivia: Case Study, Cochabamba.* Delft, Nld.: DUP Science.

Lenin, Vladimir Ilich. 1963. *Two Tactics of Social-Democracy in the Democratic Revolution.* New York: International.

Lora, Guillermo. 1997. *Obras completas.* Vol. 23 of 69 vols. La Paz, Bol.: Ediciones Masas.

Lotringer, Sylvère, Christian Marazzi, and Nina Power. 2008. *Autonomia: Post-Political Politics.* Cambridge, Mass.: MIT Press.

Loukaitou-Sideris, Anastasia, and Renia Ehrenfeucht. 2009. *Sidewalks: Conflict and Negotiation over Public Space.* Cambridge, Mass.: MIT Press.

Löwy, Michael. 1981. *The Politics of Combined and Uneven Development: The Theory of Permanent Revolution.* London: NLB.

Lucero, José Antonio. 2008. "Fanon in the Andes: Fausto Reinaga, Indianismo, and the Black Atlantic." *International Journal of Critical Indigenous Studies* 1, no. 1:13–22.

Malloy, James M. 1971. "Revolutionary Politics." In Malloy and Thorn, *Beyond the Revolution*, 111–56.

Malloy, James M., and Richard S. Thorn, eds. 1971. *Beyond the Revolution: Bolivia Since 1952.* Pittsburgh: University of Pittsburgh Press.

Mamani Ramírez, Pablo. 2004. *El rugir de las multitudes: La fuerza de los levantamientos indígenas en Bolivia/Qullasuyu.* La Paz, Bol.: Aruwiyiri.

Mamani Ramírez, Pablo. 2005. *Microgobiernos barriales: Levantamiento de la Ciudad de El Alto (Octubre 2003).* El Alto, Bol.: CADES, IDIS–UMSA.

Mamani Ramírez, Pablo. 2017. "'Estado plurinacional' autoritario del siglo XXI." *Religación* 2, no. 6:68–95.

Massey, Doreen. 1994. *Space, Place, and Gender.* Minneapolis: University of Minnesota Press.

McAdam, Doug, and William H. Sewell Jr. 2001. "It's About Time: Temporality in the Study of Social Movements and Revolutions." In Ronald R. Aminzade, Jack A. Goldstone, Doug McAdams, Elizabeth J. Perry, William H. Sewell Jr., Sidney Tarrow, and Charles Tilly, *Silence and Voice in the Study of Contentious Politics*, 89–125. Cambridge: Cambridge University Press.

Mendieta, Pilar. 2008. *Indígenas en política: Una mirada desde la historia.* La Paz, Bol.: Instituto de Estudios Bolivianos.

Mesa Gisbert, Carlos D. 2008. *Presidencia sitiada: Memorias de mi gobierno.* La Paz, Bol.: Fundación Comunidad/Plural Editores.

Mische, Ann, and Philippa Pattison. 2000. "Composing a Civic Arena: Publics, Projects, and Social Settings." *Poetics* 27, no. 2–3:163–94.

Molina Barrios, Ramiro. 2005. *Los pueblos indígenas de Bolivia: Diagnóstico sociodemográfico a partir del censo de 2001.* Santiago, Chl.: Naciones Unidas, Comisión Económica para América Latina y el Caribe.

Morales Ayma, Evo. 2017. "Informe de Gestión 2016." January 22. https://bolivian embassy.ca/wp-content/uploads/2017/01/Informe_anual_del_Presidente_a_la_Asamblea_2016.pdf.

Morse, Richard M. 1984. "The Urban Development of Colonial Spanish America." In *The Cambridge History of Latin America*. Vol. 2: *Colonial Latin America*, edited by Roberto González Echeverría and Enrique Pupo-Walker, 67–104. Cambridge: Cambridge University Press.

Moseley, Mason Wallace. 2015. "Contentious Engagement: Understanding Protest Participation in Latin American Democracies." *Journal of Politics in Latin America* 7, no. 3:3–48.

Moseley, Mason, and Daniel Moreno. 2010. "The Normalization of Protest in Latin America." *AmericasBarometer Insights* 42:1–7.

Muruchi Escobar, Khantuta, and Andrés W. Calla Cárdenas. 2008. "Transgresiones y racismo." In *Observando el racismo: Racismo y regionalismo en el proceso constituyente*, 38–54. La Paz, Bol.: Defensor del Pueblo y Universidad de la Cordillera.

Nash, June C. 1979. *We Eat the Mines and the Mines Eat Us: Dependency and Exploitation in Bolivian Tin Mines*. New York: Columbia University Press.

Nash, June. 2001. *Mayan Visions: The Quest for Autonomy in an Age of Globalization*. New York: Routledge.

Nepstad, Sharon Erickson. 2011. *Nonviolent Revolutions: Civil Resistance in the Late 20th Century*. New York: Oxford University Press.

Nightingale, Carl Husemoller. 2012. *Segregation: A Global History of Divided Cities*. Chicago: University of Chicago Press.

Observatorio del Racismo. 2008. "¿Cómo entender el 24 de Mayo en Sucre?" In *Observando el racismo: Racismos y regionalismos en el proceso autonómico hacia una perspectiva de clase*. La Paz, Bol.: Defensor del Pueblo y Universidad Cordillera.

Observatorio Social de América Latina. 2011. *Cronología del conflicto social: Bolivia, diciembre de 2010*. Quito, Ecu.: Consejo Latinoamericano de Ciencías Sociales.

Olivera, Oscar, and Tom Lewis. 2004. *¡Cochabamba!: Water War in Bolivia*. Cambridge, Mass.: South End.

Olivera, Oscar, Raquel Gutiérrez Aguilar, Marcela Olivera, and Tom Lewis. 2008. *Nosotros somos la coordinadora*. [La Paz, Bol.]: Fundación Abril & Textos Rebeldes.

Orellana Aillón, Lorgio. 2004. "El proceso insurreccional de Abril: Estructuras materiales y superestructuras organizativas de los Campesinos regantes en el Valle Central Cochabambino." In *Ruralidades Latinoamericanas: Identidades y luchas sociales*, edited by N. Giarracca, B. Levy, and B. L. Cordero Díaz, 477–550. Buenos Aires: CLACSO. Available from http://biblioteca.clacso.edu.ar/ar/libros/ruralidad/Orellana.pdf.

Ornelas, Raúl. 2004. "La Guerra del Gas: Cuarenta y cinco días de resistencia y triunfo popular." *Chiapas* 16:185–96.

Ortiz, Alicia. 1953. *Amanecer en Bolivia*. Buenos Aires: Hemisferio.

Patzi, Felix. 2003. "Rebelión indígena contra la colonialidad y la transnacionalización de la economía: Triunfos y vicisitudes del movimiento indígena desde 2000 a 2003." In *Ya es otro tiempo el presente: Cuatro momentos de insurgencia indígena*, edited by F. Hylton, F. Patzi, S. Serulnikov, and S. Thomson, 199–279. La Paz, Bol.: Muela del Diablo.

Paz Miño Cepeda, Juan José. 2002. *Golpe y contragolpe: La "Rebelión de Quito" del 21 de enero de 2000*. Quito, Ecu.: Ediciones Abya–Yala.

Prada Alcoreza, Raúl. 2010. "Raúl Prada: Dentro de la Asamblea Constituyente." In *Balance y perspectivas: Intelectuales en el primer gobierno de Evo Morales*, edited by P. Stefanoni, B. Fornillo, and M. Svampa, 37–76. La Paz, Bol.: Le Monde Diplomatique.

Presidencia de la República. 1962. *Bolivia: 10 años de revolución (1952–1962)*. [La Paz, Bol.]: Dirección Nacional de Informaciones.

Prevost, Gary. 2012. "Argentina's Social Movements: Confrontation and Co-Optation." In *Social Movements and Leftist Governments in Latin America: Confrontation or Co-Optation?*, edited by Carlos Oliva Campos, Gary Prevost, and Harry E. Vanden, 22–33. London: Zed Books.

Programa de Investigación Estratégica en Bolivia. Programa de Investigación Ambiental. 2011. *Viabilidad economica para el desarrollo de iniciativa que reduzcan la deforestacion en el TIPNIS*. La Paz, Bolivia: PIEB. https://www.scribd.com/document/68630238/Investigacion-TIPNIS-PIEB.

Programa NINA and Fernando Garcés. 2010. *El pacto de unidad y el proceso de construcción de una propuesta de constitución política del estado: Sistematización de la experiencia*. La Paz, Bol.: Unitas.

Puwar, Nirmal. 2004. *Space Invaders: Race, Gender and Bodies out of Place*. New York: Berg.

Quijano, Aníbal. 2000. "Coloniality of Power, Eurocentrism, and Latin America." *Nepantla: Views from South* 1, no. 3:533–80.

Quijano, Aníbal. 2008. "Coloniality of Power, Eurocentrism, and Social Classification." In *Coloniality at Large: Latin America and the Postcolonial Debate*, edited by M. Moraña, E. D. Dussel, and C. A. Jáuregui, 181–224. Durham, N.C.: Duke University Press.

Quispe, Felipe. 2001. "Organización y proyecto político de la rebelión indígena Aymara-Quechua." In García Linera, Quispe, Gutiérrez, Prada, and Tapia, *Tiempos de rebelión*, 163–89.

Quispe Quispe, Ayar. 2005. *Los Tupakataristas revolucionarios*. La Paz, Bol.: Editorial Willka.

Rama, Angel. 1996. *The Lettered City*. Translated by J. C. Chasteen. Durham, N.C.: Duke University Press.

Ramos Andrade, Edgar. 2004. *Agonía y rebelión social: 543 motivos de justicia urgente*. La Paz, Bol.: Capítulo Boliviano de Derechos Humanos, Democracia y Desarrollo, Plataforma Interamericana de Derechos Humanos, Democracia y Desarrollo, and Comunidad de Derechos Humanos.

Rivera Cusicanqui, Silvia. 1985. "Apuntes para una historica de las luchas campesinas en Bolivia." In *Historia política de los campesinos Latinoamericanos*, edited by G. C. Pablo, 3:146–207. Madrid: Siglo XXI de España Editores. Available from http://dialnet.unirioja.es/servlet/libro?codigo=9863.

Rivera Cusicanqui, Silvia. 1990. "Liberal Democracy and Ayllu Democracy in Bolivia: The Case of Northern Potosí." *Journal of Development Studies* 26, no. 4:97.

Rivera Cusicanqui, Silvia. 2001. *Bircholas. Trabajo de mujeres: Explotación capitalista y opresión colonial entre las migrantes aymaras de La Paz y El Alto.* La Paz: Mama Huaco.

Rivero, María del Carmen. 2006. *El poder de las luchas sociales. 2003: Quiebre del discurso neoliberal.* La Paz, Bol.: Centro de Estudios para el Desarrollo Laboral y Agrario (CEDLA).

Rojas Ríos, Cesar. 2015. *Conflictividad en Bolivia (2000–2014): ¿Cómo revertir la normalización de la presión social?* La Paz, Bol.: Friedrich Ebert Stiftung-Bolivia.

Romero Bonifaz, Carlos, Carlos Böhrt Irahola, and Raúl Peñaranda Undurraga. 2009. *Del conflicto al diálogo: Memorias del acuerdo constitucional.* La Paz, Bol.: Fundación Boliviana para la Democracia Multipartidaria.

Rosario, Melissa. 2014. "Revolutionary Time: First Thoughts on a Concept." *Savage Minds* (blog), December 17, 2014. http://savageminds.org/2014/12/17/revolutionary-time-first-thoughts-on-a-concept/.

Rostworowski, María, and Craig Morris. 1999. "The Fourfold Domain: Inka Power and Its Social Foundations." In *The Cambridge History of the Native Peoples of the Americas*, edited by F. Salomon and S. B. Schwartz, vol. 3, pt. 1, 864–903. Cambridge: Cambridge University Press.

Ruddick, Susan. 1996. "Constructing Difference in Public Spaces: Race, Class, and Gender as Interlocking Systems." *Urban Geography* 17, no. 2:132–51.

Sachs, Jeffrey. 1987. "The Bolivian Hyperinflation and Stabilization." *American Economic Review* 77, no. 2:279–83.

Sachs, Jeffrey. 1994. "Shock Therapy in Poland: Perspectives of Five Years." The Tanner Lectures on Human Values, April 6 and 7, University of Utah.

Sachs, Jeffrey. 2000. *Commanding Heights*, June 15. Interview produced by WGBH for PBS. https://www.pbs.org/wgbh/commandingheights/shared/minitext/int_jeffrey sachs.html.

Sahlins, Marshall. 1985. *Islands of History.* Chicago: University of Chicago Press.

Salazar Ortuño, Fernando. 2011. *Movimientos sociales en torno al agua en Bolivia: Privatización e insurrección social en la Guerra del Agua en Cochabamba.* Cochabamba, Bol.: ASDI.

Saldaña-Portillo, María Josefina. 2003. *The Revolutionary Imagination in the Americas and the Age of Development.* Durham, N.C.: Duke University Press.

Sánchez C, Wálter, Alejandra Ramírez S., Gretel Lambertín, Franz Flores, Carlos Vacaflores, and Pilar Lizárraga. 2008. *Narrativas y políticas de la identidad en los Valles de Cochabamba, Chuquisaca y Tarija.* La Paz, Bol.: Fundación UNIR Bolivia.

Schavelzon, Salvador. 2012. *El nacimiento del estado plurinacional de Bolivia: Etnografía de una Asamblea Constituyente.* La Paz, Bol.: Plural.

Schock, Kurt. 2005. *Unarmed Insurrections: People Power Movements in Nondemocracies.* Minneapolis: University of Minnesota Press.

Scott, James C. 2009. *The Art of Not Being Governed: An Anarchist History of Upland Southeast Asia.* New Haven, Conn.: Yale University Press.

Seligson, Mitchell A., Daniel Moreno Morales, and Vivian Schwarz Blum. 2004. "Democracy Audit: Bolivia 2004 Report." LAPOP–Latin American Public Opinion Project, USAID. https://www.vanderbilt.edu/lapop/bolivia/2004-audit.pdf.

Serulnikov, Sergio. 2003. *Subverting Colonial Authority: Challenges to Spanish Rule in Eighteenth-Century Southern Andes*. Durham, N.C.: Duke University Press.

Serulnikov, Sergio. 2009. "Crisis de una sociedad colonial. Identidades colectivas y representación política en la ciudad de Charcas (Siglo XVIII)." *Desarrollo económico* 48, no. 192:439–69.

Servicio Intercultural de Fortalecimiento Democrático. 2013. *Democracia representativa en cifras de participación ciudadana*. La Paz, Bol.: Tribunal Supremo Electoral.

Sewell, William H., Jr. 2005. *Logics of History: Social Theory and Social Transformation*. Chicago: University of Chicago Press.

Shultz, Jim, and Melissa Draper. 2009. *Dignity and Defiance: Stories from Bolivia's Challenge to Globalization*. Berkeley, Calif.: University of California Press.

Sitrin, Marina. 2006. *Horizontalism: Voices of Popular Power in Argentina*. Oakland, Calif.: AK Press.

Sitrin, Marina. 2012. *Everyday Revolutions: Horizontalism and Autonomy in Argentina*. London: Zed Books.

Sivak, Martín. 2010. *Evo Morales: The Extraordinary Rise of the First Indigenous President of Bolivia*. New York: Palgrave Macmillan.

Smith, Neil. 1996. "Spaces of Vulnerability: The Space of Flows and the Politics of Scale." *Critique of Anthropology* 16, no. 1:63–77.

Sopranzetti, Claudio. 2014. "Owners of the Map: Mobility and Mobilization Among Motorcycle Taxi Drivers in Bangkok." *City & Society* 26, no. 1:120–43.

Soruco Sologuren, Ximena. 2011. "El Porvenir, the Future That Is No Longer Possible: Conquest and Autonomy in the Bolivian Oriente." In *Remapping Bolivia: Resources, Territory, and Indigeneity in a Plurinational State*, edited by N. Fabricant and B. Gustafson, 73–95. Santa Fe, N.Mex.: School for Advanced Research Press.

Soruco Sologuren, Ximena. 2016. "La nueva burocracia plurinacional en Bolivia." *L'Âge d'or. Images dans le monde ibérique et ibéricoaméricain*, no. 9. https://journals.open edition.org/agedor/1177.

Spronk, Susan. 2007. "Roots of Resistance to Urban Water Privatization in Bolivia: The 'New Working Class,' the Crisis of Neoliberalism, and Public Services." *International Labor and Working-Class History* 71, no. 1:8–28.

Staples, Anne. 1994. "Policia y Buen Gobierno: Municipal Efforts to Regulate Public Behavior, 1821–1857." In *Rituals of Rule, Rituals of Resistance: Public Celebrations and Popular Culture in Mexico*, edited by W. H. Beezley, C. E. Martin, and W. E. French, 115–26. Wilmington, Del.: SR Books.

Stavig, Ward. 2000. "Continuing the Bleeding of These Pueblos Will Shortly Make Them Cadavers: The Potosi Mita, Cultural Identity, and Communal Survival in Colonial Peru." *The Americas* 56, no. 4:529–62.

Sub-Central TIPNIS and Campaña en Defensa del Tipnis. 2010. *Memoria: Foro departamental: Territorio indígena y Parque Nacional Isiboro Sécure (Cochabamba, 23 de Septiembre de 2010)*. Cochabamba, Bol.: CENDA.

Sub-Central TIPNIS and Comisión Recorrido. 2012. *Informe del recorrido realizado por las comunidades del TIPNIS: El proceso de consulta propio y la visión de desarrollo para el territorio indígena*. Edited by Iván Bascopé Sanjinés and Ramiro Orías Arredondo. La Paz, Bol.: Red Jurídica Amazónica and Fundación Construir.

Talbott, Strobe. 2003. "U.S.-China Relations in a Changing World." In *U.S.-China Relations in the Twenty-First Century*, edited by C. Marsh and J. T. Dreyer, 1–12. Lanham, Md.: Lexington Books.

Tapia, Francisco X. 1969. "Algunas notas sobre el cabildo abierto en Hispanoamerica." *Journal of Inter-American Studies* 11, no. 1:58–65.

Tarrow, Sidney G. 1995. "Cycles of Collective Action: Between Moments of Madness and the Repertoire of Contention." In *Repertoires and Cycles of Collective Action*, edited by M. Traugott, 89–115. Durham, N.C.: Duke University Press.

Thomassen, Bjørn. 2012. "Notes Towards an Anthropology of Political Revolutions." *Comparative Studies in Society and History* 54, no. 3:679–706.

Thomson, Sinclair. 2002. *We Alone Will Rule: Native Andean Politics in the Age of Insurgency*. Madison: University of Wisconsin Press.

Tilly, Charles. 1978. *From Mobilization to Revolution*. New York: McGraw-Hill.

Tilly, Charles. 1999. "From Interactions to Outcomes in Social Movements." In *How Social Movements Matter*, edited by Marco Guigni, Doug McAdam, and Charles Tilly, 253–70. Minneapolis: University of Minnesota Press.

Tilly, Charles. 2000. "Spaces of Contention." *Mobilization: An International Quarterly* 5, no. 2:135–59.

Tilly, Charles. 2004. *Social Movements, 1768–2004*. Boulder, Colo.: Paradigm.

Tórrez Rubín de Celis, Yuri, Daniela Carrasco, and Gloria Cámara. 2010. *El Indio en la prensa: Representación racial de la prensa Boliviana con respecto a los levantamientos indígenas/campesinos (1899–2003)*. Cochabamba, Bol.: Centro Cuarto Intermedio.

Trotsky, Leon. (1920) 1980. *The History of the Russian Revolution*. Translated by M. Eastman. New York: Pathfinder.

Tufekci, Zeynep. 2017. *Twitter and Tear Gas: The Power and Fragility of Networked Protest*. New Haven, Conn.: Yale University Press.

Turner, Edith. 2012. *Communitas: The Anthropology of Collective Joy*. New York: Palgrave Macmillan.

Turner, Victor. 1969. *The Ritual Process: Structure and Anti-Structure*. Chicago: Aldine.

Turner, Victor. 1974. *Dramas, Fields, and Metaphors: Symbolic Action in Human Society*. Ithaca, N.Y.: Cornell University Press.

Valcarce, Carla. 2008. "Otra mirada a la Asamblea Constituyente." *T'inkazos: Revista Boliviana de ciencias sociales* 11, no. 23–24:41–48.

Van Cott, Donna Lee. 2003. "From Exclusion to Inclusion: Bolivia's 2002 Elections." *Journal of Latin American Studies* 35, no. 4:751–75.

Van Velsen, Jaap. 1967. "Extended-Case Method and Situational Analysis." In *The Craft of Social Anthropology*, edited by A. L. Epstein, 129–49. London: Tavistock.

Villegas Quiroga, Carlos. 2004. *Privatización de la industria petrolera en Bolivia: Trayectoria y efectos tributarios*. La Paz, Bol.: CIDES-UMSA, Cedla, Fobomade, Diakonia.

Virilio, Paul, and Sylvère Lotringer. 1983. *Pure War*. Translated by M. Polizotti. New York: Semiotext(e).

Virno, Paolo. 2004. *A Grammar of the Multitude: For an Analysis of Contemporary Forms of Life*. Los Angeles: Semiotext(e).

Vitale, Alex S. 2007. "The Command and Control and Miami Models at the 2004 Republican National Convention: New Forms of Policing Protests." *Mobilization: An International Quarterly* 12, no. 4:403–15.

Vos, Rob, Haeduck Lee, and José Antonio Mejía-Guerra. 1996. "Structural Adjustment and Poverty in Bolivia." IDB Publications (Working Paper) 6198. Inter-American Development Bank. http://publications.iadb.org/handle/11319/6198.

Wanderley, Fernanda. 2009. *¿Crecimiento, empleo y bienestar social: ¿Por qué Bolivia es tan desigual?* La Paz: Plural.

Webber, Jeffery R. 2016. "Evo Morales and the Political Economy of Passive Revolution in Bolivia, 2006–15." *Third World Quarterly* 37, no. 10:1855–76.

Wood, Lesley J. 2012. *Direct Action, Deliberation, and Diffusion: Collective Action After the WTO Protests in Seattle*. New York: Cambridge University Press.

Woodroffe, Jessica, and Mark Ellis-Jones. 2000. *States of Unrest: Resistance to IMF Policies in Poor Countries*. London: World Development Movement.

Yuen, Eddie. 2005. "The Uses of Chaos: Disaster, Accumulation, and Popular Anarchism." Paper presented at the Anarchism Now conference, May 7, Santa Cruz, Calif. https://bradleyallen.net/2005/05/anarchism-now-conference-ucsc/.

Zacu Mborobainchi, Bienvenido, and Ricardo Ontiveros. 2006. *Bienvenido Zacu Mborobainchi: Líder de la marcha por la Asamblea Constituyente*. La Paz, Bol.: CIPCA.

Zavaleta Mercado, René. 2011. Ensayos 1957–1974. La Paz, Bol.: Plural.

Zegada, María Teresa, Yuri Tórrez, and Gloria Cámara. 2008. *Movimientos sociales en tiempos de poder: Articulaciones y campos de conflicto en el gobierno del MAS*. Cochabamba, Bol.: Centro Cuarto Intermedio.

Zibechi, Raúl. 2006. *Dispersar el poder: Los movimientos como poderes antiestatales*. Buenos Aires: Tinta Limón Ediciones.

Zibechi, Raúl. 2008. *Territorios en resistencia: Cartografía política de las periferias urbanas Latinoamericanas*. Buenos Aires: Lavaca.

Zibechi, Raúl. 2010. *Dispersing Power: Social Movements as Anti-State Forces*. Oakland, Calif.: AK Press.

Zolberg, Aristide R. 1972. "Moments of Madness." *Politics & Society* 2, no. 2:183–207.

# INDEX

Note: Page references in italics refer to illustrative matter.

# ABOUT THE AUTHOR

**Carwil Bjork-James** is an assistant professor of anthropology at Vanderbilt University. His research, both ethnographic and historical, concerns disruptive protest, grassroots autonomy, state violence, and indigenous collective rights in Bolivia.